GREAT BRITAIN

TOP SIGHTS, AUTHENTIC EXPERIENCES

Damian Harper,
Oliver Berry, Fionn Davenport, Marc Di Duca,
Belinda Dixon, Catherine Le Nevez, Sophie McGrath,
Hugh McNaughtan, Lorna Parkes, Andy Symington,
Greg Ward, Neil Wilson

Contents

Houses of Parliament (p65)
BILL45 / SHUTTERSTOCK ©

Plan Your Trip
Great Britain's Top 12

R CLASSEN / SHUTTERSTOCK ©

London

Truly one of the world's greatest cities

London is mercurial and endlessly fascinating; you could spend a lifetime getting to know it, then realise it's gone and changed again. Stretching back from the mighty River Thames, its lush parks and historic districts are crammed with extraordinary sights: royal palaces, towering cathedrals, and remarkable museums and galleries. Add the pick of the world's theatres, restaurants, sports venues and shops, and you'll be very reluctant to leave. Left: Tower Bridge (p73); Right: Covent Garden Piazza

Edinburgh

Ancient, atmospheric and brimming with lively pubs

Edinburgh is a city of many moods – famous for its festivals and particularly vibrant in the summer. But spring sees the castle silhouetted against a vivid blue sky, while chill winter mornings create mystery as fog blurs the spires of the Old Town. Explore the ancient alleyways to find rain shining on cobbles and the warm glow emanating from countless pubs. Top: Edinburgh Castle (p218) as seen from Princes St Gardens; Bottom: A pub in Edinburgh

MAGDANATKA / SHUTTERSTOCK ©

Bath

Sublime architecture and chic city streets

Britain boasts many great cities, but Bath is the belle of the ball. The Romans built a health resort here, thanks to the area's natural hot springs. The waters were rediscovered in the 18th century, and Bath became the place to be seen. Today the stunning Georgian architecture of grand town houses and sweeping crescents means Bath would demand your undivided attention, even without its Roman remains and swish 21st-century spa. Roman Baths (p114)

3

The Scottish Highlands

Scenic grandeur and echoes of the past

The Highlands abound in breathtaking views. From the regal charm of Royal Deeside, via the brooding majesty of Glen Coe (pictured), to the mysterious waters of sweeping Loch Ness – these are landscapes that inspire awe. The region is scattered with fairy-tale castles and the hiking is suitably glorious. Add the nooks of warm Highland hospitality found in classic rural pubs and romantic hotels, and you have an unforgettable corner of the country.

Stonehenge

Massive and mysterious, and utterly compelling

Stonehenge is Britain's most iconic ancient site. People have been drawn to this myth-laden ring of bluestones for 5000 years, and we still don't know why it was built. Most visitors gaze at the megaliths from the path, but with enough planning you can book an early-morning or evening tour and walk around the inner ring. Experiencing this ethereal place, in the slanting sunlight and away from the crowds, is unforgettable.

MARTIN M303 / SHUTTERSTOCK ©

Skye

The Scottish island of your imagination

Of all Scotland's many islands, Skye is the most famous and best loved, thanks to a mix of history (Bonnie Prince Charlie and the 'Skye Boat Song'), accessibility (a bridge links to the mainland) and sheer, uninterrupted beauty. With jagged mountains, velvet moors and towering sea cliffs, Skye's scenery never fails to impress. And for those days when the mist comes in, there are plenty of castles, local museums and cosy pubs. Neist Point lighthouse (p270)

6

Oxford & the Cotswolds

World-famous university town meets rural idyll

For centuries, the brilliant minds and august institutions of Oxford University have made the city famous. It's a revered world you'll encounter as you stroll hushed college quads and cobbled lanes, discovering beautiful buildings, archaic traditions and stunning architecture. A short drive away lie the Cotswolds, where impossibly picturesque villages feature rose-clad cottages, honey-coloured churches, and pubs with fine ales and views of the lush green hills. Naunton, the Cotswolds (p125)

7

Stratford-upon-Avon

Literature and history in Shakespeare's home town

The pretty town of Stratford-upon-Avon is the birthplace of the nation's best-known dramatist, William Shakespeare. Today the town's tight knot of Tudor streets form a living map of Shakespeare's life and times. Crowds of fans and would-be thespians come to enjoy a play at the Royal Shakespeare Company (RSC) or visit the historic houses owned by Shakespeare and his relatives, with a respectful detour to the old stone church where the Bard was laid to rest.

9

The Lake District

Lyrical landscapes with literary links

William Wordsworth and his Romantic friends were the first to champion the charms of the Lake District, and it's not hard to see why. The soaring mountains, whaleback fells, razor-edge valleys and – of course – glistening lakes make this craggy corner of the country the spiritual home of English hiking. Strap on the boots, stock up on mint cake and drink in the views: inspiration is sure to follow.

DAVID IGNUT / SHUTTERSTOCK ©

RICHARD PINDE / SHUTTERSTOCK ©

ANTON_IVANOV / SHUTTERSTOCK ©

York

Roman and Viking history; dramatic moorland views

Yorkshire's capital, York, is rich in Roman remains and Viking heritage. It's also home to York Minster – the biggest medieval cathedral in all of northern Europe. With ancient city walls and a maze of medieval streets, the city is a living showcase for the highlights of English history. Yorkshire can also claim some of Britain's finest scenery, with brooding moors and green dales rolling down to a dramatic shore. Top: York cityscape with York Minster (p176); Bottom left: North York Moors (p189); Bottom right: York Minster nave (p178)

10

JUSTIN FOULKES / LONELY PLANET ©

Snowdonia

An adrenaline junkie's outdoor delight

The rugged northwest corner of Wales has rocky mountain peaks, glacier-hewn valleys, sparkling lakes and rivers, and charm-infused villages. The busiest part is around Snowdon itself, where many people hike to the summit, and many more take the jolly rack-and-pinion railway to the top. And all around, activity providers are just itching to set up adrenaline thrills ranging from zip-lining and inland surfing to learning snow-craft skills.

JOEYCHEUNG / SHUTTERSTOCK ©

Cambridge

Extraordinary architecture and rich traditions

University-town extraordinaire, Cambridge – with its tightly packed core of ancient colleges, picturesque riverside 'Backs' (college gardens) and surrounding green meadows – boasts a more tranquil appeal than its historic rival Oxford. Highlights include the intricate vaulting of King's College Chapel (pictured), while no visit is complete without an attempt to steer a punt along the river, or even better, find someone else to do it for you.

Plan Your Trip
Need to Know

When to Go

Warm to hot summers, mild winters
Cool to mild summers, cold winters

Fort William
GO May or Sep

Aberdeen
GO May–Sep

Edinburgh
GO Any time

Norwich
GO May–Sep

Brecon
GO May–Sep

London
GO Any time

Exeter
GO Apr–Oct

High Season (Jun–Aug)

○ The best weather. Accommodation rates peak around August school holidays.

○ Busy roads, especially in coastal areas, national parks and big-draw cities.

Shoulder (Mar–May, Sep & Oct)

○ Crowds reduce. Prices fall.

○ Weather often good. March to May: sunny spells and sudden showers. September to October: chance of warm, late-summer. For many Scottish outdoor activities, May and September are the best months.

Low Season (Nov–Feb)

○ Wet and cold. Expect snow falls, especially in mountain areas and the north.

Currency
Pound; also called 'pound sterling' (£)

Language
English; also Scottish Gaelic and Welsh

Visas
Generally not needed for stays of up to six months. Not a member of the Schengen Zone.

Money
Change bureaux and ATMs widely available, especially in cities and major towns.

Mobile Phones
The UK uses the GSM 900/1800 network, which covers the rest of Europe, Australia and New Zealand, but isn't compatible with the North American GSM 1900.

Time
Britain is on GMT. The clocks go forward for 'summer time' one hour at the end of March, and go back at the end of October. The 24-hour clock is used for transport timetables.

Daily Costs

Budget: **Less than £55**

- Dorm beds: £15–30
- Cheap meals in cafes and pubs: £7–11
- Long-distance coach: £15–40 (200 miles)

Midrange: **£55–120**

- Double room in a midrange hotel or B&B: £65–130 (London £100–200)
- Main course in a midrange restaurant: £10–20
- Long-distance train: £20–80 (200 miles)

Top End: **More than £120**

- Four-star hotel room: from £130 (London from £200)
- Three-course meal in a good restaurant: around £40
- Car rental per day: from £35

Useful Websites

BBC (www.bbc.co.uk) News and entertainment from the national broadcaster.

Visit Britain (www.visitbritain.com) Comprehensive official tourism website.

Lonely Planet (www.lonelyplanet.com/great-britain) Destination information, hotel bookings, traveller forum and more.

Traveline (www.traveline.info) Great portal site for public transport in all parts of Britain.

British Arts Festivals (www.artsfestivals.co.uk) Lists hundreds of festivals – art, literature, dance, folk and more.

Opening Hours

Expect shorter winter hours in rural areas; some places close completely from October to April.

Banks 9.30am to 4pm or 5pm Monday to Friday; some open 9.30am to 1pm Saturday.

Pubs & Bars 11am to 11pm Monday to Thursday, 11am to 1am Friday and Saturday, 12.30pm to 11pm Sunday.

Shops 9am to 5.30pm (or 6pm in cities) Monday to Saturday, and often 11am to 5pm Sunday. Big-city convenience stores open 24/7.

Restaurants Lunch is noon to 3pm, dinner 6pm to 9pm (later in cities).

Arriving in Great Britain

Heathrow Airport (London) Trains, the London Underground (tube) and buses to central London run from just after 5am to before midnight (night buses run later); fares from £6 to £22.

Gatwick Airport (London) Trains to central London run from 4.30am to 1.35am (£10 to £20); hourly buses to central London around the clock from £8.

St Pancras International (central London) Receives Eurostar trains from Paris or Brussels; linked by London-wide underground lines.

Victoria Coach Station (central London) Buses from Europe arrive here; frequent underground links.

Edinburgh Airport (Edinburgh) Frequent trams (£6) and buses (£4.50) to Edinburgh city centre. Night buses every 30 minutes from 12.30am to 4am (£4).

Getting Around

Transport can be expensive compared to Continental Europe. Bus and rail services are sparse in remote regions. For timetables, see www.traveline.info.

Car Set your own pace, especially in far-flung parts. Widespread car hire.

Train Relatively expensive. Extensive, frequent coverage, country-wide.

Bus Cheaper and slower than trains; useful in more remote regions.

For more on **getting around**, see p311

Plan Your Trip
Hot Spots for...

History

In Great Britain the past is ever-present, with countless headline sights bringing it vividly to life. Prepare for a magical history tour.

ATTILA JANDI / SHUTTERSTOCK ©

London (p35)
Home to (arguably) the world's best parks, unique royal palaces and remarkably diverse museums.

Tower of London (p42)
Executions, royal intrigue and the spectacular Crown Jewels.

Edinburgh (p215)
From crag-top castles to a maze of medieval alleys – Edinburgh's history is written in its streets.

Rosslyn Chapel (p224)
The dim, densely decorated chapel in *The Da Vinci Code*.

Stonehenge (p101)
This mysterious, mighty monument exerts an almost hypnotic draw, amid a landscape rich in history.

Stone Circle Access (p106)
Book months in advance to walk between the stones.

The Great Outdoors

From Scotland's epic isles, via adventure-packed Wales to the sublime Lake District, Britain offers an extraordinary diversity of terrain that begs to be explored.

MATTIA QUERCI / SHUTTERSTOCK ©

Skye (p265)
Scotland's wild isle has a 50-mile-long patchwork of moors, mountains, lochs and towering sea cliffs.

Skye Wilderness Safaris (p271)
Hike into the Quiraing or through the Cuillin Hills.

Snowdonia (p205)
An extraordinary array of adrenaline activities includes hiking, caving and white-water sports.

Surf Snowdonia (p209)
An adventure park centred on a vast artificial wave pool.

Lake District (p191)
Painters and poets know it: the best place in England for natural splendour.

Windermere Lake (p203)
Cruise the lake aboard a modern or period vessel.

Arts & Architecture

Thriving theatres, galleries packed with world-class art, jagged castles, Georgian cityscapes, ornate stately homes — Britain will excite and delight you to your cultural core.

VICTOR MASCHEK / SHUTTERSTOCK ©

London (p35)
Blockbuster theatre shows, exquisite ballet and opera, iconic architecture and extraordinary art.

Tate Modern (p46)
Tag along on a free tour of the modern art powerhouse.

Bath (p111)
One of Britain's most beautiful cities — Georgian architecture, a Roman bathhouse and a sophisticated air.

No 1 Royal Crescent (p117)
A glimpse into the refined splendour of Georgian life.

Stratford-upon-Avon (p147)
Few places are as steeped in Shakespeare as the birthplace of the Bard.

RSC Guided Tours (p157)
Go behind the scenes of one of the world's grand stages.

Food

Britain's culinary renaissance surges on. All over the country, stylish eateries and gourmet gastropubs are delighting in a new-found passion for quality local produce.

EUNICE YEUNG / SHUTTERSTOCK ©

Oxford & the Cotswolds (p125)
From tapas to modern-British degustations, discover globetrotting restaurants and seasonal produce.

Edamamé (p141)
Join the line for some divine Japanese treats.

London (p35)
A dining destination of head-spinning culinary diversity, from Michelin-starred restaurants to street food.

Claridge's Foyer & Reading Room (p88)
Afternoon tea? Do it in style.

Skye (p265)
A small island delivering a big culinary lesson: superb restaurants can be found in surprising places.

Scorrybreac (p273)
An intimate eatery serving Skye's local produce.

Plan Your Trip
Essential Great Britain

STEPHEN FINN / SHUTTERSTOCK ©

Activities

The British love the great outdoors, and every weekend sees a mass exodus from the towns and cities to the mountains, hills, moors and shores. Hiking and biking are the most popular pursuits, but there's a huge range of activities available – from fishing and horse riding to skiing, climbing, kayaking and sailing. The Scottish Highlands, North Wales, Yorkshire and the Lake District are focal points for many activities. Stop off there and you might find getting wet and muddy is the highlight of your trip.

Shopping

From charity-shop finds to bespoke suits, Great Britain offers thousands of ways to spend your hard-earned cash. London boasts many big-name shopping attractions, including Harrods, Hamleys and Camden Market. In Edinburgh, Princes St's department stores are augmented by shops selling everything from designer threads and handmade jewellery to tartan goods. Oxford, Cambridge and York are dotted with antiques and secondhand bookshops. And everywhere there's a resurgence in farmers markets championing local produce. Get ready to spend.

Entertainment

As you'd expect, London offers theatre, dance and classical-music scenes that are among the best in the world. However you budget your time and money in the capital, make sure you take in a show. Edinburgh also has a thriving cultural scene, typified by its annual feast of performance: the Edinburgh Festival Fringe. The university cities of Cambridge and Oxford – and to a lesser extent Bath – are cultural hot spots, too, with a wealth of new theatre works and classical concerts.

PEDRO RUFO / SHUTTERSTOCK ©

Eating

Britain has enjoyed a culinary revolution over the past two decades. London is recognised as having one of the best restaurant scenes in the world, but the rest of Britain is also scattered with fine eateries making the most of superb local produce – you'll find happy feeding grounds in Edinburgh, the Highlands, the Cotswolds, Oxford, Cambridge, York and Bath, to name just a few. And everywhere in between all kinds of eateries – from swish restaurants to rural inns – are championing the culinary mantra: local, seasonal, organic.

Drinking & Nightlife

Despite the growth of stylish clubs and designer bars, the traditional neighbourhood or village pub is still the centre of social life, and a visit can lead you right under the nation's skin. In these 'locals'

★ Best Restaurants

Gordon Ramsay (p90)

Edamamé (p141)

The Circus (p121)

Cochon Aveugle (p187)

Timberyard (p241)

the welcome is genuine, the fire is real and that tankard has hung on that hook for centuries. So now is the time to try the alcoholic beverages most associated with England (beer) and Scotland (whisky). Sampling them and appreciating their complexities – as well as visiting breweries and distilleries – could keep you occupied the whole trip.

From left: Theatre group promoting their show at the Edinburgh Festival Fringe (p222); a London market (p52)

Plan Your Trip
Month by Month

January
🎊 London Parade
A ray of light in the gloom, the New Year's Day Parade in London (to use its official title; www.londonparade.co.uk) is one of the biggest events of its kind in the world, featuring marching bands, street performers, classic cars, floats and displays winding their way through the streets.

February
🎊 Jorvik Viking Festival
The ancient Viking capital of York becomes home once again to invaders and horned helmets galore, with the intriguing addition of longship races (www.jorvik-viking-festival.co.uk).

🕴 Fort William Mountain Festival
Britain's capital of the outdoors, near Ben Nevis in Scotland, celebrates the peak of the winter season with ski workshops, mountaineering films and talks by famous climbers (www.mountainfestival.co.uk).

March
☆ University Boat Race
Annual race down the River Thames in London between the rowing teams from Cambridge and Oxford universities; an institution since 1829 that still enthrals the country (www.theboatrace.org).

☆ Six Nations Rugby Championship
The highlight of the rugby calendar (www.rbs6nations.com) runs from late January to March, with the home nations playing at London's Twickenham, Edinburgh's Murrayfield and Cardiff's Principality stadiums.

April
🏃 London Marathon
More than 35,000 runners take to the streets; superfit athletes cover the 26.22 miles in just over two hours, while others dress up in daft costumes and take considerably longer (www.virginmoneylondonmarathon.com).

BENNY HAWES / SHUTTERSTOCK ©

✿ Beltane
Thousands of revellers climb Edinburgh's Calton Hill for this modern revival of a pagan fire festival (www.beltane.org) marking the end of winter.

✿ Spirit of Speyside
Based in Dufftown, a Scottish festival of whisky, food and music, with five days of art, cooking, distillery tours and outdoor activities (www.spiritofspeyside.com).

May
☆ FA Cup Final
Grand finale of the football (soccer) season for over a century. Teams from across England battle it out over the winter months, culminating in this heady spectacle at Wembley Stadium – the home of English football.

✿ Chelsea Flower Show
The Royal Horticultural Society flower show at Chelsea is the highlight of the gardener's year (www.rhs.org.uk/chelsea).

★ Best Festivals
Glastonbury Festival, June

Edinburgh International Festival and Festival Fringe, August

Trooping the Colour, June

Braemar Gathering, September

Guy Fawkes Night, November

June
☆ Cotswolds Olimpicks
Welly-wanging, pole-climbing and shin-kicking are the key disciplines at this traditional Gloucestershire sports day, held every year since 1612 (www.olimpickgames.co.uk).

☆ Trooping the Colour
Military bands and bear-skinned grenadiers march down London's Whitehall in this martial pageant to mark the monarch's birthday (www.trooping-the-colour.co.uk).

From left: London Marathon; Glastonbury Festival (p24)

☆ Wimbledon Tennis

The world's best-known tennis tournament, attracting all the big names, while crowds cheer and eat tons of strawberries and cream (www.wimbledon.com).

☆ Glastonbury Festival

One of Britain's favourite pop and rock gatherings is invariably muddy, and still a rite of passage for every self-respecting British music fan (www.glastonbury festivals.co.uk).

July

☆ Great Yorkshire Show

Harrogate plays host to one of Britain's largest county shows (www.greatyorkshire show.co.uk). This is the place for Yorkshire grit, Yorkshire tykes, Yorkshire puddings, Yorkshire beef...

☆ International Musical Eisteddfod

Festival of international folk music at Llangollen, with eclectic fringe and big-name evening concerts.

☆ Cowes Week

Britain's biggest yachting spectacular on the choppy seas around the Isle of Wight (www.aamcowesweek.co.uk).

☆ Womad

Roots and world music take centre stage at this festival (www.womad.org) in a country park in the south Cotswolds.

August

☆ Edinburgh's Festivals

Edinburgh's most famous August happenings are the International Festival and Festival Fringe, but this month the city also has an event for anything you care to name – books, art, theatre, music, comedy, marching bands... (www.edinburghfestivals. co.uk).

☆ Notting Hill Carnival

London's famous multicultural Caribbean-style street carnival in the district of Notting Hill. Steel drums, dancers, outrageous costumes (www.thelondonnottinghill carnival.com).

September

☆ Braemar Gathering

The biggest and most famous Highland Games in the Scottish calendar, traditionally attended by members of the Royal Family. Highland dancing, caber tossing and bagpipe playing (www.braemar gathering.org).

October

✕ Falmouth Oyster Festival

The West Country port of Falmouth marks the start of the traditional oyster-catching season (www.falmouthoysterfestival.co.uk) with a celebration of local food from the sea and fields of Cornwall.

November

☆ Guy Fawkes Night

Also called Bonfire Night (www.bonfire night.net); on 5 November fireworks fill Britain's skies in commemoration of a failed attempt to blow up parliament, way back in 1605.

☆ Remembrance Day

Red poppies are worn and wreaths are laid in towns and cities around the country on 11 November in commemoration of fallen military personnel (www.poppy.org.uk).

December

☆ New Year Celebrations

The last night of December sees fireworks and street parties in town squares across the country. London's Trafalgar Sq is where the city's largest crowds gather to welcome the New Year.

Plan Your Trip
Get Inspired

Read

Notes from a Small Island (Bill Bryson; 1995) An American's fond and astute take on Britain.

Raw Spirit (Iain Banks; 2003) An enjoyable jaunt around Scotland in search of the perfect whisky.

Slow Coast Home (Josie Drew; 2003) The chatty tale of a 5000-mile cycle tour through England and Wales.

On the Black Hill (Bruce Chatwin; 1982) Traces 20th-century Welsh rural life through the lens of an oddball pair of twins.

On the Slow Train (Michael Williams; 2011) A paean to the pleasure of British rail travel.

Watch

Brief Encounter (1945) Classic tale of a buttoned-up English love affair.

Whisky Galore! (1949) Classic Ealing comedy about Scots outfoxing the government when a cargo of whisky gets ship-wrecked; remade in 2016.

Trainspotting (1996) The gritty underbelly of life among Edinburgh drug addicts.

Withnail & I (1987) Cult comedy about two out-of-work actors on a disastrous Lake District holiday.

Submarine (2010) Scabrous coming-of-age tale set in 1980s-era Swansea.

Listen

Waterloo Sunset (The Kinks; 1967) Ray Davies' love letter to a London sunset.

A Day in the Life (The Beatles; 1967) The stand-out from Sgt Pepper's.

God Save The Queen (The Sex Pistols; 1977) The Pistols do the national anthem.

Ghost Town (The Specials; 1981) Classic track from the maestros of two-tone.

Parklife (Blur; 1994) Britpop-meets-Barnet courtesy of Damon Albarn and co.

Common People (Pulp; 1994) Jarvis Cocker's wry commentary on British class.

Above: Jacobite Steam Train (p260)

Plan Your Trip
Five-Day Itineraries

Capitals & Colleges

On this trip you'll experience Britain's best cities and oldest universities. Start with a day in Oxford for a taste of prestigious college life, then it's two days in London and Edinburgh discovering your favourite parts of these two irresistible cities.

Edinburgh (p215) Meander down the Royal Mile, puzzle over Rosslyn Chapel's symbols, explore Edinburgh Castle, sip a whisky (or two); the two days will fly by.

London (p35) Go royal (Buckingham Palace, Windsor Castle), go cultural (West End theatres, V&A), go shopping (Harrods, Borough Market); just make sure you go. ✈ 1 hr to Edinburgh

Oxford (p125) Christ Church College, the Bodleian Library, punting and Tolkien's favourite pub does for starters in this extraordinarily atmospheric city. 🚆 1¼ hrs to London

Glorious Scotland

Scotland, they say, stays with you. This trip ensures it does, leading from Edinburgh's blockbuster sights and cultural venues into the Highlands, to find scenery, wildlife and distilleries. It ends with a jaunt to the hauntingly beautiful Isle of Skye.

Isle of Skye (p265) Hike the slopes of the Cuillin Hills beneath knife-edge ridges, sea-kayak around sheltered coves and fall in love with pretty harbour-town Portree.

The Highlands (p247) Time for a Highland fling; towering Ben Nevis, glowering Glen Coe and glittering Loch Ness. Prepare for spectacular views. 🚗 2½ hrs to Portree

Edinburgh (p215) Historic Holyroodhouse, Edinburgh's winding medieval alleyways and (some of) the city's 700 pubs and bars can be squeezed into a day. 🚗 3 hrs to Fort William

Plan Your Trip
10-Day Itinerary

Mountains & Moors

Pack your hiking boots and your water-proofs: this outdoor extravaganza winds through some of Wales' and England's best wild spaces. Start by increasing your heart rate in activity-central Snowdonia, then peel off north to hike the Lake District and Yorkshire's dales and moors.

Yorkshire Dales (p189) Hit the trails again, through high heather moorland, stopping at quaint village inns.

The Lake District (p191) Spend three days exploring towering hills and glinting lakes. Travel on foot, by car, boat, bike or horse – it's up to you.
🚗 2¼ hrs to York

York (p173) Soak up city life for a few days: Viking heritage, Roman walls, mazy lanes, and plenty of excellent restaurants and bars.
🚗 1¼ hrs to Grassington

Snowdonia (p205) Climb Snowdon (the mountain), then zip down a zip line, try inland surfing and go trampolining underground. Yes, really.
🚗 3 hrs to Kendal

Plan Your Trip
Two-Week Itinerary

Historic South

Energising cities, must-see ancient sites and two world-class universities – this is a tour of Britain's big heritage draw-cards. After three leisurely London days, meander west to take in Stonehenge, Georgian-era Bath and the bucolic Cotswolds before heading off to prestigious seats of literature and learning.

Stratford-upon-Avon (p147) Strolling from sight to sight in Shakespeare's home town means you'll walk a veritable map of his life. Finish with a show at the RSC. 🚗 1 hr to Oxford

The Cotswolds (p125) Cruise rolling hills, stopping at honey-coloured villages for afternoon tea. Burford, the Slaughters and Chipping Campden are highlights. 🚗 ¼ hr to Stratford-upon-Avon

Bath (p111) Take two days to drink in Bath's Roman and Georgian beauty. Don't miss an alfresco, roof-top dip in the swish spa. 🚗 1 hr to Bibury

MICHELE PRISCO / 500PX

Cambridge (p158) King's College Chapel and Trinity College are must-dos, as is a chauffeur-driven punt. The Fitzwilliam and Polar museums are tempting, too.

Oxford (p125) Two days sees you touring college quads, atmospheric libraries and eclectic museums; plus stopping by ancient pubs and Harry Potter sights. 🚗 2 hrs to Cambridge

London (p35) Explore the Tower of London, the Tate Modern and the British Museum, plus hip eateries and pubs. 🚌 1½ hr to Salisbury, then 🚌 ½ hr to Stonehenge

Stonehenge (p101) Learn about Stonehenge's construction at the high-tech, on-site museum, then visit the vast stones themselves. 🚌 ½ hr to Salisbury, then 🚌 1hr to Bath

Plan Your Trip
Family Travel

TUPUNGATO / SHUTTERSTOCK ©

Britain is ideal for travelling with children because of its compact size, packing a lot of attractions into a small area. So when the kids in the back seat ask 'Are we there yet?', your answer can often be 'Yes, we are'.

Many places of interest cater for kids as much as adults. At historic castles, for example, mum and dad can admire the medieval architecture, while the kids will have great fun striding around the battlements. In the same way, many national parks and holiday resorts organise specific activities for children. It goes without saying that everything ramps up in the school holidays.

When to Go

The best time for families to visit Britain is pretty much the best time for everyone else: from April/May to the end of September. It's worth avoiding August – the heart of school summer holidays – when prices go up and roads are busy, especially near the coast. Other school holidays are the two weeks around Easter Sunday, and mid-December to early January, plus three week-long 'half-term' breaks – usually late February (or early March), late May and late October.

Accommodation

Some hotels welcome kids (with their parents) and provide cots, toys and babysitting services, while others maintain an adult atmosphere. Many B&Bs offer 'family suites' of two adjoining bedrooms with one bathroom, and an increasing number of hostels (YHA, SYHA and independent) have family rooms with four or six beds – some even with private bathroom attached. If you want to stay in one place for a while, renting a holiday cottage is ideal. Camping is very popular with British families, and there are lots of fantastic campsites, but you'll usually need all your own gear.

Best Regions for Kids

London Children's attractions galore, with many free. Ample green space.

PIG3 / SHUTTERSTOCK ©

Lake District Kayaks for teenagers; boat rides and Beatrix Potter for youngsters.

Oxford & the Cotswolds Oxford has Harry Potter connections; the Cotswolds is ideal for little-leg strolls.

Snowdonia Zip wires, artificial surf lagoons and vast, subterranean trampolines.

Edinburgh Tons of kid-friendly museums and castles.

Scottish Highlands Hardy teenagers plunge into outdoor activities; Nessie-spotting at Loch Ness is fun for all the family.

Baby-Changing Facilities

Most museums and other attractions in Britain usually have good baby-changing facilities (cue old joke: I swapped mine for a nice souvenir). Elsewhere, some city-centre public toilets have baby-changing areas, although these can be a bit grimy; your best bet for clean facilities is an up-market department store. On the road, baby-changing facilities are generally

> ★ **Best Experiences for the Family**
>
> Science Museum (p79), London
> Ghost Hunt of York (p185), York
> Roman Baths (p115), Bath
> Natural History Museum (p77), London
> National Railway Museum (p182), York

bearable at motorway service stations and OK at out-of-town supermarkets.

Useful Websites

Baby Goes 2 (www.babygoes2.com) Advice, tips and encouragement (and a stack of adverts) for families on holiday.

MumsNet (www.mumsnet.com) No-nonsense advice on travel and more from a vast network of UK mothers.

From left: Science Museum (p79); Natural History Museum (p77)

The Shard (p77) offers views of the whole city

30 St Mary Axe (p61), aka 'the Gherkin'

North London
An eclectic off
from the Britis
to Camden Ma
London Zoo.

Camden
Market ⊙

⊙ St Pancras
International
(Eurostar)

🚇 Euston ⊖

**Clerkenwell, Shore-
ditch & Spitalfields**
A regenerated, crea-
tive area of excellent
markets and a lively
nightlife.

🚇 Paddington
⊖

The West End
Bursting with life and
packed with blockbuster
sights, shops, theatres
and bars.

Nationa
Gallery
🏛
⊙

Trafalgar
Square

Buckingham
Palace
🏛

Ho
Par

⊙ Victoria
Westminster
Abbey

⊖ Victoria
🚇

←
(18mi)

**Windsor
Castle**

Natural
History 🏛
Museum

Victoria &
🏛 Albert
Museum

Tate 🏛
Britain

Kensington & Hyde Park
London's museum cen-
tral: the extraordinary
V&A, Natural History
and Science Museums.

Sky Garden (p88) is a public garden in a skyscraper

of London
ll of history

ering,
h Library
rket and

East London
In the multicultural east, expect standout Asian cuisine, canal-side pubs and the remarkable Queen Elizabeth Olympic Park.

King's Cross

The City
London's business district is home to big-name attractions including the Tower of London and St Paul's.

British Museum

St Paul's Cathedral

Shakespeare's Globe

Tower of London

River Thames

Charing Cross

National Theatre

Tower Bridge

London Bridge

Waterloo

uses of liament

Tate Modern

Greenwich & South London
Regal riverside Greenwich is awash with grand architecture and maritime sights.

Greenwich (2mi)

The South Bank
Superb galleries, museums and theatre options, plus a prime foodie market.

Westminster & the West End Map (p64)
The City, the South Bank & East London Map (p74)
Kensington, Camden & North London Map (p78)

0
0
2 km
1 mile

St Paul's
Cathedral (p71)

Tower Bridge
(p73)

The Tow
(p42) is f

LONDON

In This Chapter

London at a Glance...

Everyone comes to London with preconceptions shaped by books, movies and songs. Whatever yours are, prepare to have them exploded by this amorphous city. Beyond the instantly recognisable architecture, London is a city of the imagination, whether in theatrical innovation, contemporary art, pioneering music, food or design. And it's a city with both wide-open vistas and sight-packed, high-density streets. From major museums, galleries and iconic attractions to sweeping parks and riverside panoramas – there's plenty to fall in love with.

Two Days in London

Make your first stop London's beating heart, **Trafalgar Square** (p67), then spend a good couple of hours discovering the **National Gallery** (p67). Next, tour the **Houses of Parliament** (p65) before dining at **Palomar** (p87). On day two stroll to the **Tate Modern** (p47), then over the **Millennium Bridge** (p47) to **St Paul's Cathedral** (p71). Evening brings supper at **Brasserie Zedel** (p87) and drinks at **Dukes London** (p93).

Four Days in London

Roam the **Tower of London** (p43), then ride a London bus to the **British Museum** (p39), before drinks at the **American Bar** (p93) with dinner at **Gymkhana** (p87). On day four hop on a boat to cruise to Greenwich for the **Royal Observatory** (p83) and the **Cutty Sark** (p83). Relax with a modern-British meal at **St John** (p91) followed by a **Zetter Townhouse** (p94) cocktail (or two).

GAGLIARDIMAGES / SHUTTERSTOCK ©

Millennium Bridge (p47) leading to St Paul's Cathedral (p71)

Arriving in London

Heathrow Airport Trains, the tube and buses to the centre (£5.70 to £21.50). Taxi £46 to £87.

Gatwick Airport Train (£10 to £20), bus (from £5) or taxi (£100) to the centre.

Stansted Airport Train (£23.40), bus (from £12) or taxi (from £130) to the centre.

St Pancras International Train Station In Central London (for Eurostar train arrivals, p98); connected to the tube.

Where to Stay

Hanging your hat (or anything else you care to remove) in London can be painfully expensive, and you'll almost always need to book well in advance. Decent hostels are easy to find but aren't as cheap as you might hope for. Hotels range from no-frills chains through to the world's most ritzy establishments, such as the Ritz itself. B&Bs are often better value and more atmospheric than hotels.

British Museum

One of the oldest and finest in the world, this famous museum boasts vast Egyptian, Etruscan, Greek, Roman, European and Middle Eastern galleries, among others. It is frequently London's most-visited attraction, drawing 6.5 million visitors annually.

Great For...

☑ Don't Miss

The Rosetta Stone. This sizeable jagged fragment was the key to deciphering Egyptian hieroglyphics.

Great Court

Covered with a spectacular glass-and-steel roof designed by Norman Foster in 2000, the Great Court is the largest covered public square in Europe. In its centre is the world-famous Reading Room.

Ancient Egypt, Middle East & Greece

The Ancient Egypt collection is the star of the show. It comprises sculptures, fine jewellery, papyrus texts, coffins and mummies, including the beautiful and intriguing Mummy of Katebet (room 63). The most prized item in the collection is the Rosetta Stone (room 4), discovered in 1799. In the same room, look out for the enormous bust of the pharaoh Ramesses the Great.

Great Court

❶ Need to Know

Map p64; ☎020-7323 8299; www.british
museum.org; Great Russell St & Montague Pl,
WC1; ⊙10am-5.30pm Sat-Thu, to 8.30pm Fri;
⊜Russell Sq, Tottenham Court Rd FREE

✕ Take a Break

Enjoy a traditional cream tea at **Tea &
Tattle** (Map p64; ☎07722 192703; www.
teaandtattle.com; 41 Great Russell St,
WC1; afternoon tea for one/two £17/33.50;
⊙9am-6.30pm Mon-Fri, noon-4pm Sat; ☜;
⊜Tottenham Court Rd), across the road.

★ Top Tip

Audio and family guides (adult/child
£7/6) are available from the audio-guide
desk in the Great Court.

Assyrian treasures from ancient Mesopotamia include the 16-tonne Winged Bulls
from Khorsabad (room 10).

Another major highlight is the controversial Parthenon sculptures (Elgin Marbles;
room 18), which were taken from the Parthenon in Athens by Lord Elgin (the British
ambassador to the Ottoman Empire).

Roman & Medieval Britain

The Mildenhall Treasure (room 49) is a collection of pieces of AD 4th-century Roman
silverware from Suffolk with both pagan
and early-Christian motifs.

Don't miss Lindow Man in room 50 – the
well-preserved remains of a 1st-century
man, he was discovered in a bog in northern England in 1984. Equally fascinating are
artefacts from the Sutton Hoo Ship-Burial,
an elaborate 7th-century Anglo-Saxon
burial site from Suffolk.

Perennial favourites are the Lewis
Chessmen (room 40), 12th-century game
pieces carved from walrus tusk and whale
teeth that were found on a remote Scottish
island.

Enlightenment Galleries

Formerly known as the King's Library,
this neoclassical space (room 1) contains
collections tracing how modern biology,
archaeology, linguistics and geography
emerged during the 18th-century
Enlightenment.

Tours

There are up to 15 free 30- to 40-minute
Eye-opener tours of individual galleries daily. There are also free 45-minute lunchtime
gallery talks (1.15pm Tuesday to Friday), a
1½-hour highlights tour (£14; 11.30am and
2pm Friday, Saturday and Sunday) and free
Friday-evening 20-minute spotlight tours.

The British Museum

A HALF-DAY TOUR

The British Museum, with almost eight million items in its permanent collection, is so vast and comprehensive that it can be daunting for the first-time visitor. To avoid a frustrating trip – and getting lost on the way to the Egyptian mummies – set out on this half-day exploration, which takes in some of the museum's most important sights. If you want to see and learn more, join a tour or grab an audioguide (£7).

A good starting point is the **❶Rosetta Stone**, the key that cracked the code to ancient Egypt's writing system. Nearby treasures from Assyria – an ancient civilisation centred in Mesopotamia between the Tigris and Euphrates Rivers – including the colossal **❷Winged Bulls from Khorsabad**, give way to the **❸Parthenon Sculptures**, highpoints of classical Greek art that continue to influence us today. Be sure to see both the sculptures and the monumental frieze celebrating the

Winged Bulls from Khorsabad
This awesome pair of alabaster winged bulls with human heads once guarded the entrance to the palace of Assyrian King Sargon II at Khorsabad in Mesopotamia, a cradle of civilisation in present-day Iraq.

Parthenon Sculptures
The Parthenon, a white marble temple dedicated to Athena, was part of a fortified citadel on the Acropolis in Athens. There are dozens of sculptures and friezes with models and interactive displays explaining how they all once fitted together.

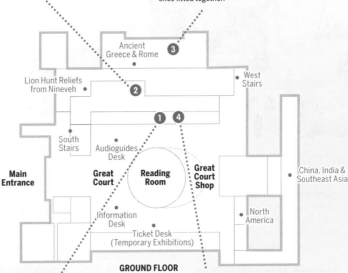

Ancient Greece & Rome ❸

Lion Hunt Reliefs from Nineveh ❷

West Stairs

South Stairs

Audioguides Desk

❶ ❹

Main Entrance

Great Court

Reading Room

Great Court Shop

China, India & Southeast Asia

Information Desk

North America

Ticket Desk (Temporary Exhibitions)

GROUND FLOOR

Rosetta Stone
Written in hieroglyphic, demotic (cursive ancient Egyptian script used for everyday use) and Greek, the 762kg stone contains a decree exempting priests from tax on the first anniversary of young Ptolemy V's coronation.

Bust of Pharaoh Ramesses II
The most impressive sculpture in the Egyptian galleries, this 725kg bust portrays Ramesses the Great, scourge of the Israelites in the Book of Exodus, as great benefactor.

birth of Athena. En route to the West Stairs is a huge ❹ **Bust of Pharaoh Ramesses II**, just a hint of the large collection of ❺ **Egyptian mummies** upstairs. (The earliest, affectionately called Ginger because of wispy reddish hair, was preserved simply by hot sand.) The Romans introduce visitors to the early Britain galleries via the rich ❻ **Mildenhall Treasure**. The Anglo-Saxon ❼ **Sutton Hoo Ship Burial** and the medieval ❽ **Lewis Chessmen** follow.

EATING OPTIONS

Court Cafe At the northern end of the Great Court; takeaway counters with salads and sandwiches; communal tables.

Gallery Cafe Slightly out of the way off Room 12; quieter; offers hot dishes.

Great Court Restaurant Upstairs overlooking the former Reading Room; sit-down meals.

Lewis Chessmen
The much-loved 78 chess pieces portray faceless pawns, worried-looking queens, bishops with their mitres turned sideways and rooks (or castles) as 'warders', gnawing away at their shields.

ILEANA_BT / SHUTTERSTOCK ©

Egyptian Mummies
Among the rich collection of mummies and funerary objects is 'Ginger', who was buried at the site of Gebelein, in Upper Egypt, almost 5500 years ago, and Katebet, a one-time chantress (ritual performer) at the Amun temple in Karnak.

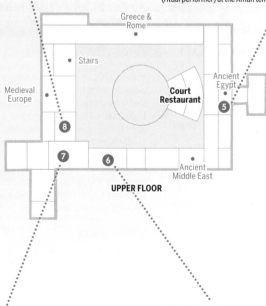

Greece & Rome

Stairs

Medieval Europe

Ancient Egypt

Court Restaurant

❺

❽

❼

❻

Ancient Middle East

UPPER FLOOR

Sutton Hoo Ship Burial
This unique grave of an important (but unidentified) Anglo-Saxon royal has yielded drinking horns, gold buckles and a stunning helmet with face mask.

Mildenhall Treasure
Roman gods such as Neptune and Bacchus share space with early Christian symbols like the *chi-rho* (short for 'Christ') on the find's almost three dozen silver bowls, plates and spoons.

ENTRY TO THE TRAITORS GATE

Tower of London

The unmissable Tower of London offers a window into a gruesome and compelling history. This was where two kings and three queens met their deaths and countless others were imprisoned.

Great For...

☑ Don't Miss

The spectacular Crown Jewels, including the Imperial State Crown, set with 2868 diamonds.

In the 1070s, William the Conqueror started work on the White Tower to replace the castle he'd previously had built here. By 1285, two walls with towers and a moat were built around it and the defences have barely been altered since. A former royal residence, treasury, mint and armoury, it became most famous as a prison when Henry VIII moved to Whitehall Palace in 1529 and started meting out his preferred brand of punishment.

White Tower

The most striking building is the central White Tower, with its solid Norman architecture and four turrets. Today on the entrance floor it houses a collection from the Royal Armouries, including Henry VIII's commodious suit of armour. On the middle floor is St John's Chapel, dating from 1080

❶ Need to Know

Map p74; ☎0844 482 7777; www.hrp.org.uk/tower-of-london; Petty Wales, EC3; adult/child £24.80/11.50, audio guide £4/3; ☺9am-4.30pm Tue-Sat, from 10am Sun & Mon; ⊖Tower Hill

✕ Take a Break

The New Armouries Cafe in the south-eastern corner of the inner courtyard offers hot meals and sandwiches.

★ Top Tip

Book online for cheaper rates for the Tower.

and therefore the oldest place of Christian worship in London.

Crown Jewels

Waterloo Barracks now contains the glittering Crown Jewels, including the platinum crown of the late Queen Mother, set with the 106-carat Koh-i-Noor (Mountain of Light) diamond and the Imperial State Crown, worn by the Queen at the State Opening of Parliament. Slow-moving travelators shunt wide-eyed visitors past the collection.

The Bloody Tower

On the far side of the White Tower is the Bloody Tower, where the 12-year-old Edward V and his little brother Richard were held 'for their own safety' and later murdered, perhaps by their uncle, the future Richard III. Sir Walter Raleigh did a 13-year stretch here, too, under James I, when he wrote his *Historie of the World*.

Executions & Ravens

In front of the Chapel Royal of St Peter ad Vincula stood Henry VIII's scaffold, where nobles such as Anne Boleyn and Catherine Howard (Henry's second and fifth wives) were beheaded. Look out for the latest in the Tower's long line of famous ravens, which legend says could cause the White Tower to collapse should they leave (their wing feathers are clipped in case they get any ideas).

Guided Tours

To get your bearings, take the entertaining (and free) guided tour with any of the Beefeaters. Hour-long tours leave every 30 minutes from the bridge near the main entrance; the last tour is an hour before closing.

Tower of London

TACKLING THE TOWER

Although it's usually less busy in the late afternoon, don't leave your assault on the Tower until too late in the day. You could easily spend hours here and not see it all. Start by getting your bearings on one of the Yeoman Warder (Beefeater) tours; they are included in the cost of admission, entertaining and the easiest way to access the ❶ Chapel Royal of St Peter ad Vincula, which is where they finish up.

When you leave the chapel, the ❷ Scaffold Site is directly in front. The building immediately to your left is Waterloo Barracks, where the ❸ Crown Jewels are housed. These are the absolute highlight of a Tower visit, so keep an eye on the entrance and pick a time to visit when it looks relatively quiet. Once inside, take things at your own pace. Slow-moving travelators shunt you past the dozen or so crowns that are the treasury's centrepieces, but feel free to double-back for a second or even third pass.

Allow plenty of time for the ❹ White Tower, the core of the whole complex, starting with the exhibition of royal armour. As you continue onto the 1st floor, keep an eye out for ❺ St John's Chapel.

The famous ❻ ravens can be seen in the courtyard south of the White Tower. Next, visit the ❼ Bloody Tower and the torture displays in the dungeon of the Wakefield Tower. Head next through the towers that formed the ❽ Medieval Palace, then take the ❾ East Wall Walk to get a feel for the castle's mighty battlements. Spend the rest of your time poking around the many other fascinating nooks and crannies of the Tower complex.

BEAT THE QUEUES

➡ Buy tickets online, avoid weekends and aim to be at the Tower first thing in the morning, when queues are shortest.

➡ An annual Historic Royal Palaces membership allows you to jump the queues and visit the Tower (and four other London palaces) as often as you like.

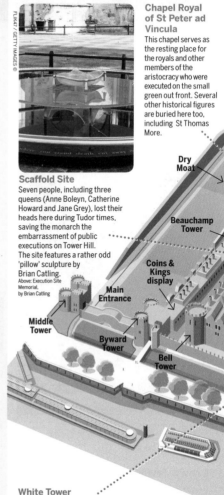

FLIKA7 / GETTY IMAGES ©

Chapel Royal of St Peter ad Vincula
This chapel serves as the resting place for the royals and other members of the aristocracy who were executed on the small green out front. Several other historical figures are buried here too, including St Thomas More.

Dry Moat

Scaffold Site
Seven people, including three queens (Anne Boleyn, Catherine Howard and Jane Grey), lost their heads here during Tudor times, saving the monarch the embarrassment of public executions on Tower Hill. The site features a rather odd 'pillow' sculpture by Brian Catling.
Above: Execution Site Memorial, by Brian Catling

Beauchamp Tower

Coins & Kings display

Main Entrance

Middle Tower

Byward Tower

Bell Tower

White Tower
Much of the White Tower is taken up with an exhibition on 500 years of royal armour. Look for the virtually cuboid suit made to match Henry VIII's bloated 49-year-old body, complete with an oversized armoured codpiece to protect, ahem, the crown jewels.

CHRISDORNEY / SHUTTERSTOCK ©

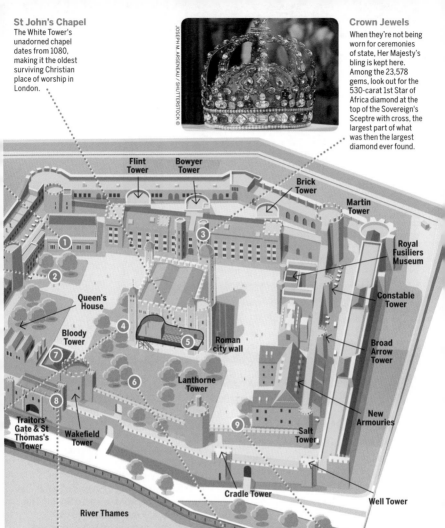

St John's Chapel
The White Tower's unadorned chapel dates from 1080, making it the oldest surviving Christian place of worship in London.

Crown Jewels
When they're not being worn for ceremonies of state, Her Majesty's bling is kept here. Among the 23,578 gems, look out for the 530-carat 1st Star of Africa diamond at the top of the Sovereign's Sceptre with cross, the largest part of what was then the largest diamond ever found.

JOSEPH M. ARSENEAU / SHUTTERSTOCK ©

Flint Tower

Bowyer Tower

Brick Tower

Martin Tower

Royal Fusiliers Museum

Constable Tower

Broad Arrow Tower

Queen's House

Bloody Tower

Roman city wall

New Armouries

Lanthorne Tower

Wakefield Tower

Salt Tower

Traitors' Gate & St Thomas's Tower

Cradle Tower

Well Tower

River Thames

Medieval Palace
This part of the Tower complex was begun around 1220 and was home to England's medieval monarchs. Look for the recreations of the bedchamber of Edward I (1272–1307) in St Thomas's Tower and the throne room of his father, Henry III (1216–72) in the Wakefield Tower.

CRISTIAN SANTINON / SHUTTERSTOCK ©

Ravens
This stretch of green is where the Tower's half-dozen ravens are kept, fed on raw meat and blood-soaked biscuits. According to legend, if the ravens depart the fortress, the Tower will fall.

Wall Walk
Follow the inner ramparts along the Tower's eastern and northern fortifications. Each of the seven towers along the way has themed displays, covering everything from the royal menagerie to the Tower during WWI.

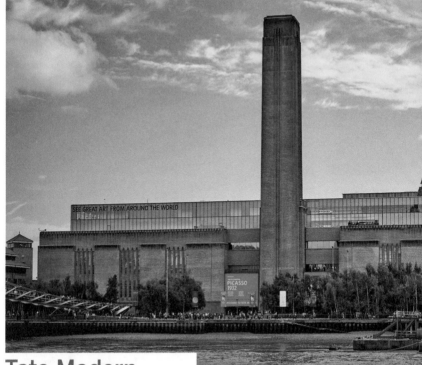

Tate Modern

A spellbinding synthesis of modern art and capacious industrial brick design, Tate Modern has been extraordinarily successful in taking challenging works and making us love them.

One of London's most amazing attractions, this outstanding modern- and contemporary-art gallery is housed in the creatively revamped Bankside Power Station south of the Millennium Bridge. The secret of its success has been to combine both free permanent collections and fee-paying, big-name temporary exhibitions. The stunning Switch House extension opened in 2016, increasing available exhibition space by 60%.

The Building

The 4.2 million bricks of the 200m-long Tate Modern is an imposing sight, designed by Swiss starchitects Herzog and de Meuron, who scooped the prestigious Pritzker Prize for their transformation of the empty power station. Leaving the building's central 99m-high chimney, adding

Great For...

☑ **Don't Miss**

Works by big-name, must-see artists, including Matisse, Warhol and Hirst.

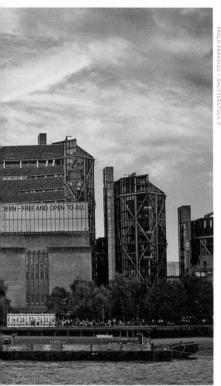

PAOLO PARADISO / SHUTTERSTOCK ©

❶ Need to Know

Map p74; ☏020-7887 8888; www.tate.org.
uk; Bankside, SE1; ◷10am-6pm Sun-Thu, to
10pm Fri & Sat; 🚻; ⊖Blackfriars, Southwark,
London Bridge `FREE`

✕ Take a Break

The Tate Modern Cafe dishes up sandwiches, drinks and light meals to hungry
art fans.

★ Top Tip

Free guided highlights tours depart at
11am, noon, 2pm and 3pm daily. Audio
guides (£4) are also available.

a two-storey glass box onto the roof and
employing the cavernous Turbine Hall as a
dramatic entrance space were three huge
achievements. Herzog and de Meuron also
designed the new 10-storey Tate extension.

The Collections

As a supreme collection of modern art, the
contents of the museum are, however, the
main draw. At their disposal, the curators
have paintings by Georges Braque, Henri
Matisse, Piet Mondrian, Andy Warhol, Mark
Rothko and Jackson Pollock as well as
pieces by Joseph Beuys, Damien Hirst,
Louise Bourgeois, Claes Oldenburg and
Auguste Rodin.

Tate Modern's permanent collection is
arranged by both theme and chronology on
levels 2 and 4 of Boiler House and levels 0,
2, 3 and 4 of Switch House. With more than

60,000 works on constant rotation, if there's
a particular piece you want to see, check the
website to see if (and where) it's hanging.

The location is also supreme, as the
balconies on level 3 with their magnificent
views will attest. The Millennium Bridge
elegantly conveys views direct from the
Tate Modern to St Paul's Cathedral on the
far bank of the river.

To visit the sister-museum Tate Britain
(p69), hop on the **Tate Boat** (Map p74; www.
tate.org.uk/visit/tate-boat; one-way adult/child
£8.30/4.15) from Bankside Pier.

What's Nearby

The elegant steel, aluminium and concrete
Millennium Bridge (Map p74; ⊖St Paul's,
Blackfriars) staples the south bank of the
Thames, in front of Tate Modern, to the
north. The low-slung frame designed by
Lord Norman Foster and Anthony Caro
looks spectacular, particularly when lit up
at night, and the view along it to St Paul's
has become an iconic image.

The Proms at Royal Albert Hall (p51)

Entertainment Capital

The West End is synonymous with musicals, and no trip to London would be complete without an evening of Mamma Mia!, Les Misérables or Phantom of the Opera. If musicals don't float your boat, there are more alternatives than you'll have evenings to fill: fringe theatre, dance, opera and classical concerts.

Great For...

ℹ Need to Know

Buy cheap tickets on the day at the venue or from **Tkts Leicester Sq** (www. tkts.co.uk/leicester-square; The Lodge, Leicester Sq, WC2; ⊘10am-7pm Mon-Sat, 11am-4.30pm Sun; ⊖Leicester Sq) booths.

★ **Top Tip**

At the Royal Opera House, discounted tickets for each day of the week (for the first 49 people; £4 to £68) go on sale on Friday at 1pm.

Theatre

A night out at the theatre is as much a must-do London experience as a ride on the top deck of a double-decker bus. London's Theatreland in the dazzling West End – from Aldwych in the east, past Shaftesbury Ave to Regent St in the west – has a concentration of theatres only rivalled by New York's Broadway. It's a thrillingly diverse scene, encompassing Shakespeare's classics performed with old-school precision, edgy new works, raise-the-roof musicals and some of the world's longest-running shows.

There are around 40 theatres in the West End alone, but Theatreland is just the brightest facet of London's sparkling theatre world, where venues range from highbrow theatrical institutions to tiny fringe stages tucked away above pubs.

If you love Shakespeare and the theatre, **Shakespeare's Globe** (Map p74; ☑020-7401 9919; www.shakespearesglobe.com; 21 New Globe Walk, SE1; seats £20-45, standing £5; ⊖Blackfriars, London Bridge) will knock your theatrical socks off. This authentic Shakespearean theatre is a wooden 'O' without a roof over the central stage area, and although there are covered wooden bench seats in tiers around the stage, many people (there's room for 700) do as 17th-century 'groundlings' did, standing in front of the stage.

The **National Theatre** (Map p74; ☑020-7452 3000; www.nationaltheatre.org.uk; South Bank, SE1; 👹; ⊖Waterloo), England's flagship theatre (its full name is the Royal National Theatre), showcases a mix of classic and contemporary plays performed by excellent casts in three theatres (Olivier, Lyttelton and Dorfman).

The cosy **Donmar Warehouse** (Map p64; ☑020-3282 3808; www.donmarwarehouse.com; 41 Earlham St, WC2; ⊖Covent Garden) is London's

A theatre ticket booth in London

'thinking person's theatre'. Current artistic director Josie Rourke has staged some intriguing and successful productions, including the well-received comedy *My Night with Reg*.

Opera, Ballet & Classical Music

With multiple world-class orchestras and ensembles, quality venues, reasonable ticket prices and performances covering the whole musical gamut from traditional crowd-pleasers to innovative compositions, London will satisfy even the fussiest classical music, opera or ballet buff.

The **Royal Albert Hall** (Map p78; ✆0845 401 5034; www.royalalberthall.com; Kensington Gore, SW7; ◉South Kensington) hosts classical music, rock and other performances, but is famously the venue for the BBC-sponsored Proms. Booking is possible, but from mid-July to mid-September Proms punters queue for £5 standing (or 'promenading') tickets that go on sale one hour before curtain-up. Otherwise, the box office and prepaid-ticket collection counter are through door 12 (south side of the hall).

The £210 million redevelopment for the millennium gave classic opera a fantastic setting in the **Royal Opera House** (Map p64; ✆020-7304 4000; www.roh.org.uk; Bow St, WC2; tickets £4-270; ◉Covent Garden), and coming here for a night is a sumptuous affair. Although the program has been fluffed up by modern influences, the main attractions are still the opera and classical ballet – all are wonderful productions and feature world-class performers.

☑ Don't Miss

Book an informative one-hour front-of-house grand tour, operating most days at the Royal Albert Hall.

Tickets

○ Book well ahead for live performances and if you can, buy directly from the venue.

○ Enquire at the theatre's own box office about cut-price standby tickets or limited late releases for otherwise sold-out shows.

○ Student standby tickets are sometimes available one hour or so before performances start. Some theatres have cheap tickets or cheap student/youth tickets on certain days.

○ Shakespeare's Globe offers 700 standing tickets (£5) for each performance. A handful of 10p standing tickets are available for performances at the Jerwood Theatre Downstairs at the Royal Court Theatre.

○ Midweek matinees at such venues as the Royal Opera House are usually much cheaper than evening performances; restricted-view seats can be cheap.

○ At gigs, be wary of touts outside the venue on the night. Tickets may be counterfeit or stolen.

PCRUCIATTI / GETTY IMAGES ©

✕ Take a Break

Stop at Lamb & Flag (p93) for a pre-theatre drink.

A stall at Camden Market (p54)

London's Markets

The capital's famed markets are a treasure trove of foodie treats, small designers, unique jewellery pieces, colourful vintage items and bric-a-brac. They're a joyful antidote to impersonal, carbon-copy shopping centres.

Great For...

ⓘ Need to Know

Take an umbrella: Camden and Old Spitalfields markets are both mainly covered, but many aren't.

★ **Top Tip**

Camden Market comprises four distinct market areas. They tend to sell similar kinds of things, but each has its own specialities and quirks.

IVAN / GETTY IMAGES ©

Borough Market

Located here in some form or another since the 13th century (and possibly since 1014), **'London's Larder'** (Map p74; www.boroughmarket.org.uk; 8 Southwark St, SE1; ⏱10am-5pm Wed & Thu, 10am-6pm Fri, 8am-5pm Sat; ⊖London Bridge) has enjoyed an astonishing renaissance in the past 15 years. Always overflowing with food lovers, inveterate gastronomes, wide-eyed visitors and Londoners in search of inspiration for their dinner party, this fantastic market has become firmly established as a sight in its own right. The market specialises in high-end fresh products; there are also plenty of takeaway stalls and an unreasonable number of cake stalls!

Portobello Road Markets

Lovely on a warm summer's day, **Portobello Road Market** (Map p78; www.portobellomarket.org; Portobello Rd, W10; ⏱8am-6.30pm Mon-Wed, Fri & Sat, to 1pm Thu; ⊖Notting Hill Gate, Ladbroke Grove) is an iconic London attraction with an eclectic mix of street food, fruit and veg, antiques, curios, collectables, vibrant fashion and trinkets. Although the shops along Portobello Rd open daily and the fruit and veg stalls (from Elgin Cres to Talbot Rd) only close on Sunday, the busiest day by far is Saturday, when antique dealers set up shop (from Chepstow Villas to Elgin Cres).

Camden Market

Although – or perhaps because – it stopped being cutting-edge several thousand cheap leather jackets ago, **Camden**

Leadenhall Market

Market (Map p78; www.camdenmarket.com; Camden High St, NW1; ⏰10am-6pm; ⊖Camden Town, Chalk Farm) attracts millions of visitors each year and is one of London's most popular attractions. What started out as a collection of attractive craft stalls by Camden Lock on the Regent's Canal now extends most of the way from Camden Town tube station to Chalk Farm tube station.

Old Spitalfields Markets

Traders have been hawking their wares here since 1638 and it's still one of London's best markets. Today's covered **market** (Map p74; www.oldspitalfieldsmarket.com; Commercial St, E1; ⏰10am-5pm Mon-Fri & Sun, 10am-6pm Sat;

> ☑ **Don't Miss**
>
> The Sunday Upmarket, at Brick Lane, which only pops up at the weekend.

⊖Liverpool St) was built in the late 19th century, with the more modern development added in 2006. Sundays are the biggest and best days, but Thursdays are good for antiques and Fridays for independent fashion. There are plenty of food stalls, too.

Sunday UpMarket

The **Sunday UpMarket** (Map p74; www.sundayupmarket.co.uk; Old Truman Brewery, 91 Brick Lane, E1; ⏰11am-6pm Sat, 10am-5pm Sun; ⊠Shoreditch High St) within the beautiful red-brick buildings of the Old Truman Brewery is the best of all the Sunday markets, with young designers selling their wares, quirky crafts and a drool-inducing array of food stalls.

Leadenhall Market

A visit to this covered mall off Gracechurch St is a step back in time. There's been a market on this site since the Roman era, but the architecture that survives is all cobblestones and late-19th-century Victorian ironwork. **Leadenhall Market** (Map p74; www.leadenhallmarket.co.uk; Whittington Ave, EC3; ⏰public areas 24hr; ⊖Bank) appears as Diagon Alley in *Harry Potter and the Philosopher's Stone* and an optician's shop was used for the entrance to the Leaky Cauldron wizarding pub in *Harry Potter and the Goblet of Fire*.

Broadway Market

There's been a **market** (www.broadwaymarket.co.uk; Broadway Market, E8; ⏰9am-5pm Sat; ⊠394) down this pretty street since the late 19th century. The focus these days is artisan food, arty knick-knacks, books, records and vintage clothing. Stock up on edible treats then head to **London Fields** (Richmond Rd, E8; ⊠London Fields) for a picnic.

> ✕ **Take a Break**
>
> The **Ten Bells** (Map p74; www.tenbells.com; 84 Commercial St, E1; ⏰noon-midnight Sun-Wed, to 1am Thu-Sat; 🔊; ⊖Shoreditch High St) pub, perfectly positioned for a pint after a wander around Spitalfields Market.

Windsor Castle

The world's largest and oldest continuously occupied fortress, Windsor Castle is a majestic vision of battlements and towers. It's used for state occasions and is one of the Queen's principal residences; if she's home, the Royal Standard flies from the Round Tower. Known for its lavish state rooms and beautiful chapels, it's hugely popular; book online to avoid queues.

Great For...

ℹ Need to Know

📞03031-237304; www.royalcollection.org.uk; Castle Hill; adult/child £21.20/12.30; ⊗9.30am-5.15pm Mar-Oct, 9.45am-4.15pm Nov-Feb, last admission 1hr 15min before closing, all or part of castle subject to occasional closures; 🚶; 🚌702 from London Victoria, 🚆London Waterloo to Windsor & Eton Riverside, 🚆London Paddington to Windsor & Eton Central via Slough

★ **Top Tip**

Join a free guided tour (frequent) or grab a free audio tour.

William the Conqueror first established a royal residence in Windsor in 1080. Since then successive monarchs have rebuilt, remodelled and refurbished the castle complex to create the massive, sumptuous palace that stands here today. Henry II replaced the original wooden stockade in 1170 with a stone round tower and built the outer walls to the north, east and south; Edward III turned Windsor into a Gothic palace; Charles II gave the State Apartments a glorious baroque makeover; George IV swept in with his team of artisans; and Queen Victoria refurbished an ornate chapel in memory of her beloved Albert.

Queen Mary's Dolls' House

Your first stop is likely to be the incredible dolls' house designed by Sir Edwin Lutyens for Queen Mary between 1921 and 1924.

A fine Edwardian mansion built on a scale of 1:12, the attention to detail is spellbinding: there's running water, electricity and lighting, tiny Crown Jewels, a silver service and wine cellar, and even a fleet of six cars in the garage. You may have to queue.

State Apartments

Flanked by armour and weapons, the Grand Staircase sets the tone for the spectacular State Apartments above, dripping in gilt and screaming 'royal' from every painted surface and sparkling chandelier. Presided over by a statue of Queen Victoria, the Grand Vestibule displays artefacts and treasures donated by or captured from the countries of the British Empire, while the Waterloo Chamber celebrates the 1815 victory over Napoleon. St George's Hall beyond still hosts state

Changing of the Guard

banquets; its soaring ceiling is covered in the painted shields of the Knights of the Garter.

St George's Chapel

This elegant chapel, commissioned for the Order of the Garter by Edward IV in 1475, is one of England's finest examples of Perpendicular Gothic architecture. The nave and beautiful fan-vaulted roof were completed under Henry VII, but the final nail was driven under Henry VIII in 1528.

Along with Westminster Abbey, it serves as a royal mausoleum. Both Henry VIII and

Charles I lie beneath the beautifully carved 15th-century Quire, while the Queen's father (George VI) and mother (Queen Elizabeth) rest in a side chapel. Prince Harry married Meghan Markle here in May 2018.

St George's Chapel closes on Sunday, but you can attend a morning service or evensong (at 5.15pm).

Albert Memorial Chapel

Built in 1240 and dedicated to St Edward the Confessor, the small Albert Memorial Chapel was the place of worship for the Order of the Garter until St George's Chapel snatched away that honour. After Prince Albert died at Windsor Castle in 1861, Queen Victoria ordered its elaborate redecoration as a tribute to her husband and consort. A major feature of the restoration is the magnificent vaulted roof, whose gold mosaic pieces were crafted in Venice.

There's a monument to the prince, although he's actually buried with Queen Victoria in the Royal Mausoleum at Frogmore House in Windsor Great Park. Their youngest son, Prince Leopold (Duke of Albany), is, however, buried in the Albert Memorial Chapel.

Changing of the Guard

A fabulous spectacle, with triumphant tunes from a military band and plenty of foot stamping from smartly attired soldiers in red uniforms and bear-skin caps, the changing of the guard draws crowds to Windsor Castle each day. Weather permitting, it usually takes place at 11am on Tuesdays, Thursdays and Saturdays.

> **☑ Don't Miss**
> As well as the sumptuous decor in the State Apartments, zoom in on the art works, including pieces by Rubens, Canaletto and Anthony van Dyck.

KIEVVICTOR / SHUTTERSTOCK ©

> **✗ Take a Break**
> Duck into the **Two Brewers** (☎01753-855426; www.twobrewerswindsor.co.uk; 34 Park St, Windsor; mains £14-26; ⊘11.30am-11pm Mon-Thu, to 11.30pm Fri & Sat, noon-10.30pm Sun), an atmospheric inn on the edge of Windsor Great Park.

City Walking Tour

The City of London has as much history in its single square mile as the rest of London put together. From churches and finance houses to markets and museums, this walk picks out just a few of its many highlights.

Start Farringdon
Distance 1.5 miles
Duration Three hours

2 Head through the Tudor gatehouse toward the colourful Victorian arches of **Smithfield Market** (☎020-7248 3151; www.smithfield market.com; ⊙2-10am Mon-Fri), London's last surviving meat market.

1 Explore the wonderful 12th-century **St Bartholomew-the-Great** (p74), one of London's oldest churches.

3 Follow the roundabout and nip up the stairs to explore the excellent galleries of the **Museum of London** (p76).

4 Head to Aldermanbury and the impressive 15th-century **Guildhall** (☎020-7332 1313; www.cityoflondon. gov.uk/guildhallgalleries; ⊙10am-4.30pm daily May-Sep, Mon-Sat Oct-Apr). In its courtyard note the black outline of the Roman amphitheatre.

Take a Break Stop for a bite to eat in the restaurant at **Fortnum & Mason** in the impressive courtyard of the Royal Exchange.

5 At the imposing, colonnaded **Royal Exchange** (☎020-7283 8935; www.theroyalexchange.co.uk), head inside to to explore the very smart retail environment of Fortnum & Mason.

Classic Photo The sweeping, bullet-shaped lines of 30 St Mary Axe make a great pic.

8 Once on Lime St, **30 St Mary Axe** (www.thegherkinlondon.com), aka 'the Gherkin', looms up – tangible testimony to the city's ability to constantly reinvent itself.

6 Next, it's into wonderful **Leadenhall Market** (p55), trying to spot Harry Potter similarities – it appears in one film as Diagon Alley.

7 Leaving the market by the far end, marvel at the external vents, ducting and stairs of the insurance brokers **Lloyd's** (www.lloyds.com/lloyds/about-us/the-lloyds-building) of London.

◉ SIGHTS

London has more than a few sights that are instantly recognisable all around the world. The most famous of these are in the historic City of London (the Tower of London, Tower Bridge, St Paul's Cathedral) and the West End (British Museum, Trafalgar Square, the Houses of Parliament, Westminster Abbey, Buckingham Palace). Further west, South Kensington is known for its grand Victorian museums, while the South Bank of the Thames has such landmarks as the London Eye, Shakespeare's Globe and the Tate Modern. Other less famous but equally fascinating sights are scattered all around the capital.

◉ The West End

Encompassing many of London's poshest neighbourhoods as well as superlative restaurants, hotels and shops, the West End should be your first port of call.

Westminster Abbey   Church

(Map p64; ☎020-7222 5152; www.westminster-abbey.org; 20 Dean's Yard, SW1; adult/child £22/9, cloister & gardens free; ⊘9.30am-3.30pm Mon, Tue, Thu & Fri, to 6pm Wed, to 1.30pm Sat; ⊖Westminster) A splendid mixture of architectural styles, Westminster Abbey is considered the finest example of Early English Gothic (1190–1300). It's not merely a beautiful place of worship – the Abbey also serves up the country's history cold on slabs of stone. For centuries, the country's greatest have been interred here, including 17 monarchs from Henry III (died 1272) to George II (1760). Never a cathedral (the seat of a bishop), Westminster Abbey is what is called a 'royal peculiar', administered by the Crown.

Every monarch since William the Conqueror has been crowned here, with the exception of a couple of unlucky Eds who were either murdered (Edward V) or abdicated (Edward VIII) before the magic moment.

At the heart of the Abbey is the beautifully tiled **sanctuary** (sacrarium), a stage for coronations, royal weddings and funerals. George Gilbert Scott designed the ornate high altar in 1873. In front of the altar is the **Cosmati marble pavement** dating to 1268. It has intricate designs of

Westminster Abbey

small pieces of marble inlaid into plain marble, which predict the end of the world (in AD 19,693!). At the entrance to the lovely **Chapel of St John the Baptist** is a sublime alabaster Virgin and Child bathed in candlelight.

The most sacred spot in the Abbey, the **shrine of St Edward the Confessor**, lies behind the main altar; access is restricted to several prayer meetings daily to protect the 13th-century flooring. St Edward was the founder of the Abbey and the original building was consecrated a few weeks be-fore his death. His tomb was slightly altered after the original was destroyed during the Reformation but still contains Edward's remains – the only complete saint's body in Britain. Ninety-minute **verger-led tours** (£5 plus admission) of the Abbey include a visit to the shrine.

The **quire** (choir), a space of gold, blue and red Victorian Gothic by Edward Blore, dates back to the mid-19th century. It sits where the original choir for the monks' worship would have been but bears little resemblance to the original. Nowadays, the quire is still used for singing, but its regular occupants are the Westminster Choir – 22 boys and 12 'lay vicars' (men) who sing the daily services and evensong (5pm week-days, 3pm weekends).

Henry III began work on the new building in 1245 but didn't complete it; the Gothic nave was finished under Richard II in 1388. Henry VII's magnificent Perpendicular Gothic-style **Lady Chapel** was consecrated in 1519 after 16 years of construction.

At the west end of the nave is the **Tomb of the Unknown Warrior**, killed in WWI in northern France and laid to rest here in 1920. Nearby is St George's Chapel, which contains the rather ordinary-looking **Coronation Chair**, used in every corona-tion since the early 14th century (apart from that of joint-monarchs Mary II and William III, who had their own chairs fash-ioned for the event).

Apart from the royal graves, keep an eye out for the many famous common-ers interred here, especially in **Poets' Corner**, where you'll find the resting places

 **No 10
Downing Street**

The official office of British leaders since 1732, when George II presented No 10 to 'First Lord of the Treasury' Robert Walpole, this has also been the prime minister's London residence since re-furbishment in 1902. For such a famous address, **No 10** (Map p64; www.number10. gov.uk; 10 Downing St, SW1; ⊖Westminster) is a small-looking Georgian building on a plain-looking street, hardly warranting comparison with the White House, for example. Yet it is actually three houses joined into one and boasts roughly 100 rooms plus a 2000-sq-metre garden.

DZARZYCKA / GETTY IMAGES ©

of Chaucer, Dickens, Hardy, Tennyson, Dr Johnson and Kipling, as well as memo-rials to other greats (Shakespeare, Jane Austen, the Brontës etc). Nearby you'll find the graves of Handel and Sir Isaac Newton.

The octagonal **Chapter House** dates from the 1250s and was where the monks would meet for daily prayer and their job assignments, up until Henry VIII's suppres-sion of the monasteries some three cen-turies later. To the right of the entrance to Chapter House is what is claimed to be the oldest door in Britain – it's been there since the 1050s. Used as a treasury and 'Royal Wardrobe', the cryptlike **Pyx Chamber** dates from about 1070, though the Altar of St Dunstan within it is even older.

Parts of the Abbey complex are free to visitors. This includes the **Cloister** and the 900-year-old **College Garden** (Map p64; ⊙10am-6pm Tue-Thu Apr-Sep, to 4pm

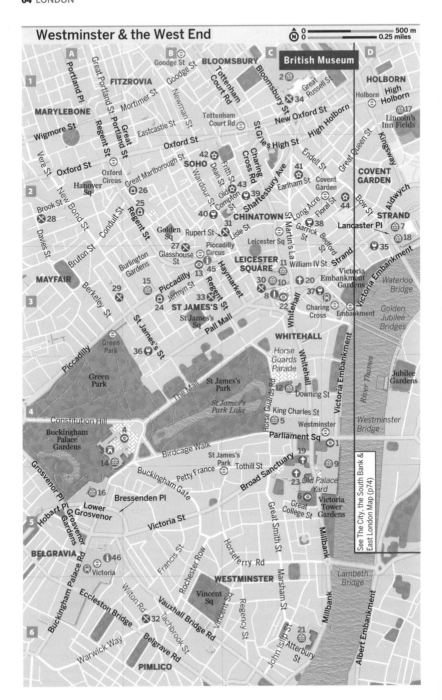

Westminster & the West End

N 0 500 m
0 0.25 miles

A | B | C | D

MARYLEBONE

FITZROVIA

BLOOMSBURY

British Museum

HOLBORN

SOHO

COVENT GARDEN

CHINATOWN

STRAND

MAYFAIR

LEICESTER SQUARE

ST JAMES'S

WHITEHALL

Green Park

Horse Guards Parade

St James's Park

St James's Park Lake

Buckingham Palace Gardens

Constitution Hill

The Mall

Birdcage Walk

Downing St

King Charles St

Parliament Sq

River Thames

Jubilee Gardens

Westminster Bridge

Golden Jubilee Bridges

Waterloo Bridge

Victoria Embankment Gardens

BELGRAVIA

WESTMINSTER

PIMLICO

Lambeth Bridge

See The City, the South Bank & East London Map (p74)

Westminster & the West End

◎ Sights

1	Big Ben	D4
2	British Museum	C1
3	Buckingham Palace	A4
4	Changing of the Guard	B4
5	Churchill War Rooms	C4
6	College Garden	C5
7	Courtauld Gallery	D2
8	Fourth Plinth Commission	C3
9	Houses of Parliament	D4
10	National Gallery	C3
11	National Portrait Gallery	C3
12	No 10 Downing Street	C4
13	Piccadilly Circus	B3
14	Queen's Gallery	A4
15	Royal Academy of Arts	B3
16	Royal Mews	A5
17	Sir John Soane's Museum	D1
18	Somerset House	D2
19	St Margaret's Church	C4
20	St Martin-in-the-Fields	C3
21	Tate Britain	C6
22	Trafalgar Square	C3
23	Westminster Abbey	C5

⊖ Shopping

24	Fortnum & Mason	B3
25	Hamleys	B2
26	Liberty	B2

⊗ Eating

27	Brasserie Zédel	B3
28	Claridge's Foyer & Reading Room	A2
29	Gymkhana	A3
	National Cafe	(see 11)
30	National Dining Rooms	C3
31	Palomar	C2
32	Pimlico Fresh	B6
	Portrait	(see 11)
33	Shoryu	B3
34	Tea & Tattle	C1

⊖ Drinking & Nightlife

35	American Bar	D3
36	Dukes London	B3
37	Heaven	C3
38	Lamb & Flag	C2
39	She Soho	C2
40	Village	B2

⊙ Entertainment

41	Donmar Warehouse	C2
42	Pizza Express Jazz Club	B2
43	Ronnie Scott's	C2
44	Royal Opera House	D2

⊙ Information

45	Piccadilly Circus Underground Station Tourist Information	B3
46	Victoria Station Tourist Information Centre	A5

Oct-Mar; ⊖Westminster). Adjacent to the abbey is **St Margaret's Church** (Map p64; ☏020-7654 4840; www.westminster-abbey. org/st-margarets-church; ⊙9.30am-3.30pm Mon-Fri, to 1.30pm Sat, 2-4.30pm Sun; ⊖Westminster), the House of Commons' place of worship since 1614, where windows commemorate churchgoers Caxton and Milton, and Sir Walter Raleigh is buried by the altar.

Completed in 2018, the **Queen's Diamond Jubilee Galleries** are a new museum and gallery space located in the medieval triforium, the arched gallery above the nave. Among its exhibits are the death masks of generations of royalty, wax effigies representing Charles II and William III (who is on a stool to make him as tall as his wife, Mary II), armour and stained glass. Highlights are the graffiti-inscribed Mary Chair (used for the coronation of Mary II)

and the Westminster Retable, England's oldest altarpiece, from the 13th century.

Houses of Parliament Historic Building
(Palace of Westminster; Map p64; www. parliament.uk; Parliament Sq, SW1; ⊖Westminster) **FREE** A visit here is a journey to the heart of UK democracy. Officially called the Palace of Westminster, the Houses of Parliament's oldest part is 11th-century **Westminster Hall**, one of only a few sections that survived a catastrophic fire in 1834. Its roof, added between 1394 and 1401, is the earliest known example of a hammerbeam roof. The rest is mostly a neo-Gothic confection built by Charles Barry and Augustus Pugin over 20 years from 1840. The palace's most famous feature is its clock tower, officially the Elizabeth Tower but better known as **Big Ben** (Map p64).

Changing of the Guard

A London 'must see', the **Changing of the Guard** (Map p64; http://changing-guard.com) is when the Old Guard (Foot Guards of the Household Regiment) comes off duty to be replaced by the New Guard on the forecourt of Buckingham Palace. Tourists gape – sometimes from behind as many as 10 people – at the bright-red uniforms, bearskin hats and full-on pageantry. The official name for the ceremony is Guard Mounting and it lasts for around 45 minutes.

The ceremony usually takes place daily at 11am in June and July and on Sunday, Monday, Wednesday and Friday, weather permitting, during the rest of the year, but be sure to check the website before setting out.

Buckingham Palace   Palace

(Map p64; ☏0303 123 7300; www.royal collection.org.uk/visit/the-state-rooms-buckingham-palace; Buckingham Palace Rd, SW1; adult/child/under 5yr £24/13.50/free; ⊗9.30am-7pm (to 6pm Sep) Jul-Sep only; ⊖Green Park, St James's Park) Built in 1703 for the Duke of Buckingham, Buckingham Palace replaced St James's Palace as the monarch's official London residence in 1837. Queen Elizabeth II divides her time between here, Windsor Castle and, in summer, Balmoral Castle in Scotland. If she's in residence, the square yellow, red and blue Royal Standard is flown; if not, it's the Union Flag. Some 19 lavishly furnished **State Rooms** are open

to visitors when Her Majesty takes her holidays from late July to September.

Hung with artworks by the likes of Rembrandt, Van Dyck, Canaletto, Poussin and Vermeer, the State Rooms are open for self-guided tours that include the **Throne Room**, with his-and-her pink chairs monogrammed 'ER' and 'P'. Access is by timed tickets with admission every 15 minutes (audio guide included) and visits take about two hours.

Admission includes entry to a themed special exhibition (eg royal couture during the Queen's reign, growing up at the palace) in the enormous Ballroom, which changes each summer. It also allows access to part of the palace gardens as you exit, although you must join the three-hour State Rooms & Garden Highlights Tour (adult/child/under five years £33/19.70/free) to see the wisteria-clad Summer House and other famous features, and to get an idea of the garden's full size (16 hectares).

Your ticket to Buckingham Palace is good for a return trip if bought direct from the palace ticket office (ask to have it stamped as you leave). You can even make your ticket purchase a donation and gain free access for a whole year (ask at the ticket office).

Originally designed by John Nash as a conservatory, the **Queen's Gallery** (Map p64; www.royalcollection.org.uk/visit/the-queens-gallery-buckingham-palace; South Wing; adult/child £10.30/5.30, incl Royal Mews £19/10; ⊗10am-5.30pm) showcases some of the palace's treasures on a rotating basis, through temporary exhibitions. Enter from Buckingham Gate.

Indulge your Cinderella fantasies while inspecting the exquisite state coaches in the **Royal Mews** (Map p64; www.royalcollection.org.uk/visit/royalmews; Buckingham Palace Rd, SW1; adult/child £11/6.40, with Queen's Gallery £19/10; ⊗10am-5pm Apr-Oct, to 4pm Mon-Sat Feb, Mar & Nov; ⊖Victoria), a working stable looking after the royals' immaculately groomed horses and the opulent vehicles they use for getting from A to B. Highlights include the magnificent Gold State Coach of 1762 and the 1911 Glass Coach.

A Royal Day Out (adult/child/under five years £42.30/23.30/free) is a combined ticket including entry to the State Rooms, Queen's Gallery and Royal Mews.

Trafalgar Square
Square

(Map p64; ⊖Charing Cross) Trafalgar Sq is the true centre of London, where rallies and marches take place, tens of thousands of revellers usher in the New Year and locals congregate for anything from communal open-air cinema and Christmas celebrations to political protests. It is dominated by the 52m-high **Nelson's Column** and ringed by many splendid buildings, including the National Gallery (p67) and the church of **St Martin-in-the-Fields** (Map p64; ☏020-7766 1100; www.stmartin-in-the-fields.org; ⊙8.30am-1pm & 2-6pm Mon, Tue, Thu & Fri, 8.30am-1pm & 2-5pm Wed, 9.30am-6pm Sat, 3.30-5pm Sun).

National Gallery
Gallery

(Map p64; ☏020-7747 2885; www.national gallery.org.uk; Trafalgar Sq, WC2; ⊙10am-6pm Sat-Thu, to 9pm Fri; ⊖Charing Cross) FREE With some 2300 European masterpieces on display, this is one of the world's great art collections, with seminal works from every important period in the history of art – from the mid-13th to the early 20th century, including masterpieces by Leonardo da Vinci, Michelangelo, Titian, Van Gogh and Renoir.

Many visitors flock to the East Wing (1700–1900), where works by 18th-century British artists such as Gainsborough, Constable and Turner, and seminal Impressionist and post-Impressionist masterpieces by Van Gogh, Renoir and Monet await.

The modern Sainsbury Wing on the gallery's western side houses paintings from 1250 to 1500. Here you will find largely religious works commissioned for private devotion (eg the *Wilton Diptych*) as well as more unusual masterpieces, such as Botticelli's *Venus and Mars* and Van Eyck's *Arnolfini Portrait*. Leonardo Da Vinci's *Virgin of the Rocks*, in room 20, is a stunning masterpiece.

Works from the High Renaissance (1500–1600) embellish the West Wing where Michelangelo, Titian, Raphael, Correggio, El Greco and Bronzino hold court; Rubens, Rembrandt and Caravaggio grace the North Wing (1600–1700). Notable are two self-portraits of Rembrandt

Trafalgar Square

National Portrait Gallery

(age 34 and 63) and the beautiful *Rokeby Venus* by Velázquez in room 30.

The comprehensive audio guides (£4) are highly recommended, as are the free one-hour taster tours that leave from the information desk in the Sainsbury Wing daily at 11.30am and 2.30pm, with late tours at 7pm Friday. There are also special trails and activity sheets for children.

Don't overlook the astonishing floor mosaics in the main vestibule inside the entrance to the National Gallery.

The **National Dining Rooms** (Map p64; ☑020-7747 2525; www.nationalgallery.org.uk/visiting/eat-and-drink; 1st fl, Sainsbury Wing; mains £14.50-21; ☺10am-5.30pm Sat-Thu, to 8.30pm Fri) offers à la carte meals and afternoon teas but perhaps a better choice is the **National Cafe** (Map p64; ☑020-7747 5942; www.nationalgallery.org.uk/visiting/eat-and-drink; ground fl; 2-/3-course set lunch £17/21; ☺8am-7pm Mon-Fri, to 10pm Tue-Thu, to 10.30pm Fri, 9am-7pm Sat, 9am-6pm Sun) with good set lunches and more generous opening times.

If you want to get sketching, bring your own stool and hand-held pad along and select your artwork. Occasional music performances are held in the National Gallery on Friday evenings; check the website for details.

National Portrait Gallery Gallery

(Map p64; ☑020-7321 0055; www.npg.org.uk; St Martin's Pl, WC2; ☺10am-6pm Sat-Wed, to 9pm Thu & Fri; ⊖Charing Cross, Leicester Sq) **FREE**
What makes the National Portrait Gallery so compelling is its familiarity; in many cases, you'll have heard of the subject (royals, scientists, politicians, celebrities) or the artist (Andy Warhol, Annie Leibovitz, Lucian Freud) but not necessarily recognise the face. Highlights include the famous 'Chandos portrait' of William Shakespeare, the first artwork the gallery acquired (in 1856) and believed to be the only likeness made during the playwright's lifetime, and a touching sketch of novelist Jane Austen by her sister.

A further highlight is the 'Ditchley portrait' of Queen Elizabeth I displaying her might by standing on a map of England, her feet on Oxfordshire. The collection is organised chronologically (starting with the early Tudors on the 2nd floor), and then by theme. The 1st-floor portraits illustrate the rise and fall of the British Empire through the Victorian era and the 20th century. Don't miss the high-kitsch statue of Victoria and Albert in Anglo-Saxon dress in room 21.

The ground floor is dedicated to modern figures, using a variety of media (sculpture, photography, video etc). Among the most popular have been the iconic Blur portraits by Julian Opie, Sam Taylor-Johnson's *David*, a (low-res by today's standards) video-portrait of David Beckham asleep after football training and Michael Craig-Martin's *Dame Zaha Hadid*. Don't miss *Self* by Mark Quinn, a frozen, refrigerated sculpture of the artist's head, made from 4.5L of his own blood and recast every five years. The excellent audio guide (£3) highlights more than 300 portraits and allows you to hear the voices of some of the subjects and artists.

The Portrait (p88) restaurant does wonderful food and has superb views towards Westminster.

Piccadilly Circus
Square

(Map p64; ⊖Piccadilly Circus) Architect John Nash had originally designed Regent St and Piccadilly in the 1820s to be the two most elegant streets in London but, restrained by city planners, he couldn't realise his dream to the full. He may be disappointed, but suitably astonished, by Piccadilly Circus today: a traffic maelstrom, deluged by visitors and flanked by flashing advertisement panels.

At the centre of Piccadilly Circus stands the famous aluminium statue mistakenly called Eros as it actually portrays his twin brother, **Anteros**. To add to the confusion, the figure is officially the *Angel of Christian Charity* and dedicated to the philanthropist and social reformer Lord Shaftesbury. The sculpture was at first cast in gold but later replaced by newfangled aluminium, the first outdoor statue in that lightweight metal.

Churchill War Rooms
Museum

(Map p64; www.iwm.org.uk/visits/churchill-war-rooms; Clive Steps, King Charles St, SW1; adult/child £21/10.50; ⊗9.30am-6pm; ⊖Westminster) Winston Churchill helped coordinate the Allied resistance against Nazi Germany on a Bakelite telephone from

Fourth Plinth Commission

Three of the four plinths at Trafalgar Sq's corners are occupied by notables: King George IV on horseback, and military men General Sir Charles Napier and Major General Sir Henry Havelock. One, originally intended for a statue of William IV, remained largely vacant for more than a century and a half. The Royal Society of Arts conceived the **Fourth Plinth Project** (Fourth Plinth Commission; Map p64; www.london.gov.uk/what-we-do/arts-and-culture/art-and-design/fourth-plinth; ⊖Charing Cross) in 1999, deciding to use the empty space for works by contemporary artists.

The Invisible Enemy Should Not Exist, by Michael Rakowitz, on the Fourth Plinth
AC MANLEY / SHUTTERSTOCK ©

this underground complex during WWII. The **Cabinet War Rooms** remain much as they were when the lights were switched off in 1945, capturing the drama and dogged spirit of the time, while the multimedia **Churchill Museum** affords intriguing insights into the life and times of the resolute, cigar-smoking wartime leader.

Tate Britain
Gallery

(Map p64; ☏020-7887 8888; www.tate.org.uk/visit/tate-britain; Millbank, SW1; ⊗10am-6pm, to 9.30pm on selected Fri; ⊖Pimlico) **FREE** The older and more venerable of the two Tate siblings celebrates British works from 1500 to the present, including those from Blake, Hogarth, Gainsborough, Whistler, Constable and Turner, as well as vibrant modern and contemporary pieces from Lucian Freud,

Barbara Hepworth, Francis Bacon and Henry Moore. Join a free 45-minute **thematic tour** (⊙11am, noon, 2pm & 3pm daily) and 15-minute **Art in Focus** (⊙1.15pm Tue, Thu & Sat) talks.

The stars of the show at Tate Britain are, undoubtedly, the light infused visions of JMW Turner in the Clore Gallery. After he died in 1851, his estate was settled by a decree declaring that whatever had been found in his studio – 300 oil paintings and about 30,000 sketches and drawings – would be bequeathed to the nation. The collection at the Tate Britain constitutes a grand and sweeping display of his work, including classics such as *The Scarlet Sunset* and *Norham Castle, Sunrise*.

There are also seminal works from Constable, Gainsborough and Reynolds, as well as the Pre-Raphaelites, including William Holman Hunt's *The Awakening Conscience*, John William Waterhouse's *The Lady of Shalott*, *Ophelia* by John Everett Millais and Edward Burne-Jones's *The Golden Stairs*. Look out also for Francis Bacon's *Three Studies for Figures at the Base of a Crucifixion*. Tate Britain hosts the prestigious and often controversial Turner Prize for

Contemporary Art from October to early December every year.

The Tate Britain also has a program of ticketed exhibitions that changes every few months; consult the website for details of the latest exhibition.

Royal Academy of Arts Gallery

(Map p64; ☑020-7300 8000; www.royal academy.org.uk; Burlington House, Piccadilly, W1; adult/child from £13.50/free, exhibition prices vary; ⊙10am-6pm Sat-Thu, to 10pm Fri; ☻Green Park) Britain's oldest society devoted to fine arts was founded in 1768 and moved to Burlington House exactly a century later. The collection contains drawings, paintings, architectural designs, photographs and sculptures by past and present academicians, such as Joshua Reynolds, John Constable, Thomas Gainsborough, JMW Turner, David Hockney and Lord Norman Foster.

Somerset House Historic Building

(Map p64; ☑020-7845 4600; www.somerset house.org.uk; The Strand, WC2; ⊙galleries 10am-6pm, courtyard 7.30am-11pm, terrace 8am-11pm; ☻Temple, Covent Garden) Designed by William Chambers in 1775

From left: The statue of Anteros at Piccadilly Circus (p69); St Paul's Cathedral; Somerset House

for government departments and royal societies – in fact, the world's first office block – Somerset House now contains several fabulous galleries. In the North Wing near the Strand entrance, the **Courtauld Gallery** (Map p64; http://courtauld.ac.uk; adult/child £8/free, temporary exhibitions vary; ⏱10am-6pm) displays a wealth of 14th- to 20th-century art, including masterpieces by Rubens, Botticelli, Cézanne, Degas, Renoir, Seurat, Manet, Monet, Leger and others. The **Embankment Galleries** in the South Wing are devoted to temporary (mostly photographic, design and fashion) exhibitions; prices and hours vary.

For a fortnight every summer, Somerset House turns its stunning courtyard into an open-air **cinema** (www.somersethouse.org.uk/film; tickets from £20) screening an eclectic mix of film premieres, cult classics and popular requests.

Madame Tussauds — Museum

(Map p78; ☎0870 400 3000; www.madame-tussauds.com/london; Marylebone Rd, NW1; adult/child 4-15yr £35/30; ⏱10am-6pm; ⊖Baker St) It may be kitschy and pricey, but Madame Tussauds makes for a fun-filled day. There are photo ops with your dream celebrity (be it Daniel Craig, Lady Gaga, Benedict Cumberbatch, Audrey Hepburn or the Beckhams), the Bollywood gathering (sparring studs Hrithik Roshan and Salman Khan) and the Royal Appointment (the Queen, Harry and Meghan, William and Kate). Book online for much cheaper rates and check the website for seasonal opening hours.

◉ The City

London's historic core is a tale of two cities: packed with office workers during the week and eerily quiet at weekends. The current millennium has seen a profusion of daring skyscrapers sprout from the City's fringes, but the essential sights have been standing for hundreds of years: St Paul's Cathedral and the Tower of London.

St Paul's Cathedral — Cathedral

(Map p74; ☎020-7246 8357; www.stpauls.co.uk; St Paul's Churchyard, EC4; adult/child £18/8; ⏱8.30am-4.30pm Mon-Sat; ⊖St Paul's) In a superb position that's been a place

DAVID BANK × GETTY IMAGES ©

Sir John Soane's Museum

This little **museum** (Map p64; ☎020-7405 2107; www.soane.org; 12 Lincoln's Inn Fields, WC2; ☺10am-5pm Wed-Sun; ☻Holborn) **FREE** is one of the most atmospheric and fascinating in London. The building was the beautiful, bewitching home of architect Sir John Soane (1753–1837), which he left brimming with his vast architectural and archaeological collection, as well as intriguing personal effects and curiosities.

DANIEL LANGE / SHUTTERSTOCK ©

of Christian worship for over 1400 years (and pagan before that), St Paul's is one of London's most magnificent buildings. For Londoners, the vast dome towering over Ludgate Hill is a symbol of resilience and pride, standing tall for more than 300 years. Viewing Sir Christopher Wren's masterpiece from the inside and climbing to the top for sweeping views of the capital is an exhilarating experience.

The cathedral was designed by Wren after the Great Fire and built between 1675 and 1710; it opened the following year. The site is ancient hallowed ground, with four other cathedrals preceding Wren's English baroque masterpiece here, the first dating from 604.

The world's second-largest cathedral dome is famed for surviving Luftwaffe incendiary bombs in the 'Second Great Fire of London' of December 1940, becoming an icon of London resilience during the Blitz. Outside in the churchyard, north of the church, is a simple and elegant **monument to the people of London**, honouring the 32,000 Londoners killed.

Inside, rising 68m above the floor, is the dome, supported by eight huge columns. It actually consists of three parts: a plastered brick inner dome, a nonstructural lead outer dome visible on the skyline and a brick cone between them holding it all together. The walkway around its base, accessed via 257 steps from a staircase on the western side of the southern transept, is called the **Whispering Gallery**, because if you talk close to the wall, your words will carry to the opposite side, 32m away. A further 119 steps brings you to the exterior **Stone Gallery**, 152 iron steps above which is the **Golden Gallery** at the very top, with unforgettable views of London.

The crypt has memorials to around 300 of the great and the good, including Wellington and Nelson, whose body lies directly below the dome. But the most poignant is to Wren himself. On a simple slab bearing his name, part of a Latin inscription translates as: 'If you seek his memorial, look around you'.

As part of its 300th anniversary celebrations in 2011, St Paul's underwent a £40 million renovation project that gave the church a deep clean. It's not looked this good since they cut the blue ribbon opening the cathedral in 1711.

There's no charge to attend a service. To hear the cathedral choir, attend the 11.30am Sunday Eucharist or Evensong (5pm Monday to Saturday and 3.15pm Sunday), but check the website as a visiting choir may appear for the latter.

Otherwise, the standard admission price includes a free video- and audio guide. Free 1½-hour guided tours depart four times a day (10am, 11am, 1pm and 2pm); reserve a place at the tour desk, just past the entrance. Around twice a month, 60-minute tours (£8) also visit the astonishing Library, Geometric Staircase and Great Model, and include impressive views down the nave from above the Great West Doors; check the website for dates and hours and book well ahead. Filming and photography is not

St Bartholomew-the-Great

permitted within the cathedral. Book online for cheaper rates.

Tower Bridge
Bridge

(Map p74; ⊖Tower Hill) One of London's most recognisable sights, familiar from dozens of movies, Tower Bridge doesn't disappoint in real life. Its neo-Gothic towers and sky-blue suspension struts add extraordinary elegance to what is a supremely functional structure. London was a thriving port in 1894 when it was built as a much-needed crossing point in the east, equipped with a then-revolutionary steam-driven bascule (counterbalance) mechanism that could raise the roadway to make way for oncoming ships in just three minutes.

A lift leads up from the northern tower to the **Tower Bridge Exhibition** (Map p74; ☏020-7403 3761; www.towerbridge.org. uk; adult/child £9.80/4.20, incl the Monument £12/5.50; ⊗10am-5.30pm Apr-Sep, 9.30am-5pm Oct-Mar; ⊖Tower Hill), where the story of building the bridge is recounted. Tower Bridge was designed by architect Horace Jones, who was also responsible for

Smithfield and Leadenhall markets, and completed by engineer John Wolfe Barry. The bridge is still operational, although these days it's electrically powered and rises mainly for pleasure craft. It does so around 1000 times a year and as often as 10 times a day in summer; consult the Exhibition website for times to watch it in action.

St Bartholomew-the-Great
Church

(Map p74; ☏020-7600 0440; www.great stbarts.com; West Smithfield, EC1; adult/child £5/3; ⊗8.30am-5pm Mon-Fri, 10.30am-4pm Sat, 8.30am-8pm Sun; ⊖Barbican) Dating to 1123 and adjoining one of London's oldest hospitals, St Bartholomew-the-Great is one of London's most ancient churches. The Norman arches and profound sense of history lend this holy space an ancient calm, while approaching from nearby Smithfield Market through the restored 13th-century half-timbered archway is like walking back in time. The church was originally part of an Augustinian priory, but became the parish church of Smithfield in 1539 when Henry VIII dissolved the monasteries.

The City, the South Bank & East London

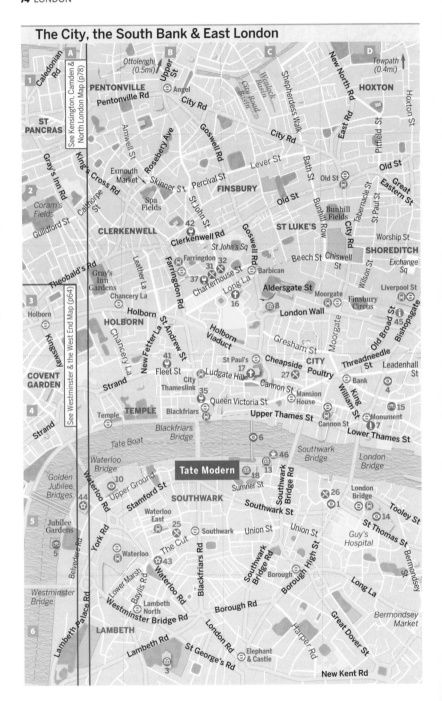

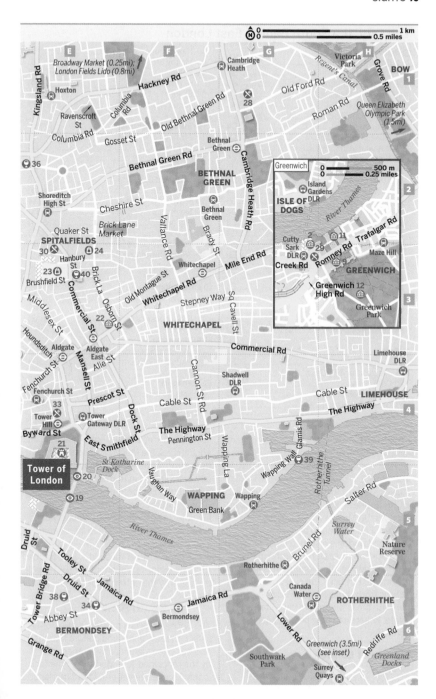

N

0 _____ 1 km
0 _____ 0.5 miles

Broadway Market (0.25mi);
London Fields Lido (0.8mi)

Victoria
Park

BOW

Cambridge
Heath

Hoxton

Hackney Rd

Old Ford Rd

Grove Rd

Regent's Canal

28

Old Ford Rd

Roman Rd

Queen Elizabeth
Olympic Park
(1.5mi)

Ravenscroft
St

Columbia
Rd

Old Bethnal Green Rd

Columbia Rd

Gosset St

Bethnal
Green

36

Bethnal Green Rd

**BETHNAL
GREEN**

Greenwich

0 _____ 500 m
0 _____ 0.25 miles

Shoreditch
High St

Cheshire St

Bethnal
Green

Cambridge Heath Rd

Island
Gardens

DLR

River Thames

**ISLE OF
DOGS**

Quaker St

Brick Lane
Market

Vallance Rd

Brady St

Cutty
Sark

DLR

2

29

11

Trafalgar Rd

SPITALFIELDS

30

24

Whitechapel

Mile End Rd

Creek Rd

Romney Rd

9

Maze Hill

GREENWICH

Hanbury
St

Brick La

Osborn St

23

40

Old Montague St

Whitechapel Rd

Greenwich
High Rd

12

Brushfield St

Stepney Way

Greenwich
Park

Middlesex St

Commercial St

22

WHITECHAPEL

Sq Cavell St

Houndsditch

Aldgate

Aldgate
East

Alie St

Commercial Rd

Limehouse
DLR

Fenchurch St

Mansell St

Prescot St

Cable St

Shadwell
DLR

Cable St

LIMEHOUSE

Fenchurch St

33

Cannon St Rd

Glamis Rd

The Highway

Tower
Hill

Tower
Gateway DLR

Dock St

The Highway

4

Byward St

East Smithfield

Pennington St

Wapping La

Wapping Wall

39

Rotherhithe
Tunnel

Salter Rd

21

St Katharine
Docks

Vaughan Way

WAPPING

Wapping

Surrey
Water

**Tower of
London**

20

Green Bank

Nature
Reserve

19

River Thames

Brunel Rd

5

Druid St

Tooley St

Rotherhithe

Tower Bridge Rd

Druid St

Jamaica Rd

Canada
Water

ROTHERHITHE

38

34

Jamaica Rd

Abbey St

Bermondsey

Lower Rd

Redriffe Rd

6

BERMONDSEY

Grange Rd

Southwark
Park

Greenwich (3.5mi)
(see inset)

Surrey
Quays

Greenland
Docks

The City, the South Bank & East London

Monument
Monument

(Map p74; ☏020-7403 3761; www.themonument.
org.uk; Fish St Hill, EC3; adult/child £5/2.50, incl
Tower Bridge Exhibition £12/5.50; ◷9.30am-
5.30pm Apr-Sep, to 5pm Oct-Mar; ◉Monument)
Sir Christopher Wren's 1677 column, known
simply as the Monument, is a memorial to
the Great Fire of London of 1666, whose
impact on London's history cannot be over-
stated. An immense Doric column made
of Portland stone, the Monument is 4.5m
wide and 60.6m tall – the exact distance
it stands from the bakery in Pudding Lane
where the fire is thought to have started.

Note, tickets can only be purchased
with cash.

Museum of London
Museum

(Map p74; ☏020-7001 9844; www.museumof
london.org.uk; 150 London Wall, EC2; ◷10am-

6pm; ◉Barbican) **FREE** As entertaining as it is
educational, the Museum of London meanders through the various incarnations of the
city, stopping off in Roman Londinium and
Saxon Ludenwic before eventually ending
up in the 21st-century metropolis. Interesting objects and interactive displays work
together to bring each era to life, without
ever getting too whiz-bang, making this one
of the capital's best museums. Free themed
tours take place throughout the day; check
the signs by the entrance for times.

◎ The South Bank

The South Bank is a must-visit area for art
lovers, theatre-goers and culture hounds,
and has been significantly re-energised
by the renowned Tate Modern. Come for
iconic Thames views, great food markets,

first-rate pubs, dollops of history, striking examples of modern architecture, and a sprinkling of fine bars and restaurants.

London Eye   Viewpoint

(Map p74; ☑0871 222 4002; www.londoneye. com; adult/child £27/22; ☺11am-6pm Sep-May, 10am-8.30pm Jun-Aug; ☻Waterloo, Westminster) Standing 135m high in a fairly flat city, the London Eye affords views 25 miles in every direction, weather permitting. Interactive tablets provide great information (in six languages) about landmarks as they appear in the skyline. Each rotation – or 'flight' – takes a gracefully slow 30 minutes. At peak times (July, August and school holidays) it can feel like you'll spend more time in the queue than in the capsule; book premium fast-track tickets to jump the queue.

Shakespeare's
Globe   Historic Building

(Map p74; ☑020-7902 1500; www.shake spearesglobe.com; 21 New Globe Walk, SE1; adult/ child £17/10; ☺9.30am-5pm; ♿; ☻Blackfriars, London Bridge) Unlike other venues for Shakespearean plays, the new Globe was designed to resemble the original as closely as possible, which means having the arena open to the fickle London skies, leaving the 700 'groundlings' (standing spectators) to weather London's spectacular downpours. Visits to the Globe include tours of the theatre (half hourly) as well as access to the exhibition space, which has fascinating exhibits on Shakespeare and theatre in the 17th century.

The Shard   Notable Building

(Map p74; www.theviewfromtheshard.com; 32 London Bridge St, SE1; adult/child £30.95/24.95; ☺10am-10pm; ☻London Bridge) Puncturing the skies above London, the dramatic splinter-like form of the Shard has rapidly become an icon of London. The viewing platforms on floors 69 and 72 are open to the public and the views are, as you'd expect from a 244m vantage point, sweeping, but they come at a hefty price – book online at least a day in advance to make a big saving.

◎ Kensington & Hyde Park

Splendidly well groomed, Kensington is one of London's most handsome neighbourhoods. You'll find three fine museums here – the V&A, the Natural History Museum and the Science Museum – as well as excellent dining and shopping, graceful parklands and elegant streets of grand period architecture.

Victoria & Albert Museum   Museum

(Map p78; www.vam.ac.uk; Cromwell Rd, SW7; ☺10am-5.45pm Sat-Thu, to 10pm Fri; ☻South Kensington) FREE The Museum of Manufactures, as the V&A was known when it opened in 1852, was part of Prince Albert's legacy to the nation in the aftermath of the successful Great Exhibition of 1851. It houses the world's largest collection of decorative arts, from Asian ceramics to Middle Eastern rugs, Chinese paintings, Western furniture, fashion from all ages and modern-day domestic appliances. The (ticketed) temporary exhibitions are another highlight, covering anything from David Bowie retrospectives to designer Alexander McQueen, special materials and trends.

There are more than 100 galleries in the museum, so pick carefully or join a free one-hour guided tour; there are several a day (they meet close to the information desk in the main hall) on a variety of themes, including introductory tours, medieval and Renaissance tours, and theatre and performance tours.

Natural History Museum   Museum

(Map p78; www.nhm.ac.uk; Cromwell Rd, SW7; ☺10am-5.50pm; ☻South Kensington) FREE This colossal and magnificent-looking building is infused with the irrepressible Victorian spirit of collecting, cataloguing and interpreting the natural world. The **Dinosaurs Gallery** (Blue Zone) is a must for children, who gawp at the animatronic T-Rex, fossils and excellent displays. Adults for their part will love the intriguing Treasures exhibition in the **Cadogan Gallery** (Green Zone), which houses a host of unrelated objects each telling its own unique story, from a chunk of moon rock to a dodo skeleton.

Kensington, Camden & North London

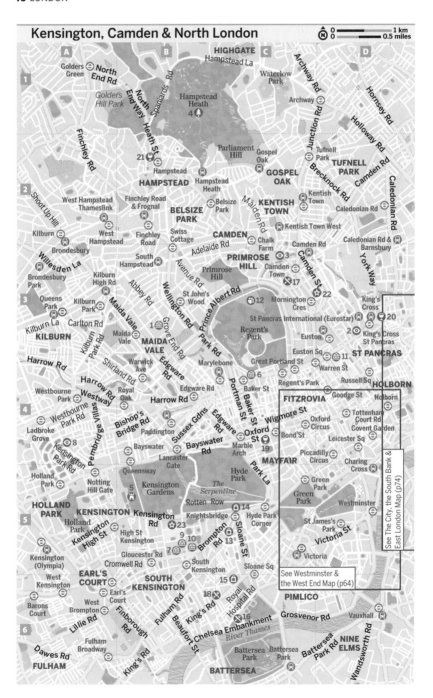

Kensington, Camden & North London

Also in the Green Zone, the **Mineral Gallery** is a breathtaking display of architectural perspective leading to the **Vault**, where you'll find the **Aurora Collection** of almost 300 coloured diamonds. In the Orange Zone, the vast **Darwin Centre** focuses on taxonomy, showcasing 28 million insects and six million plants in a giant cocoon; glass windows allow you to watch scientists at work.

At the centre of the museum is **Hintze Hall**, which resembles a cathedral nave – quite fitting, as it was built in a time when the natural sciences were challenging the biblical tenets of Christian orthodoxy. In 2017, after 81 years in the Mammals Hall, the Blue Whale skeleton you see on entering the hall was relocated here, with the famous cast of a diplodocus skeleton (nicknamed Dippy) making way for the colossal marine mammal (Dippy has gone on a long tour of the UK until late 2020). The transfer itself was a painstaking engineering project, disassembling and preparing the whale's 4.5-tonne bones for reconstruction in a dramatic diving posture that greets visitors to the museum.

The NHM hosts regular exhibitions (admission fees apply), some of them on a recurrent basis. **Wildlife Photographer of the Year** (Map p78; adult/child £13.50/8, family £28-38; ⊙Oct-Sep), for example, with its show-stopping images, is now in its 50th year, and **Sensational Butterflies** (Map p78; per person £5.85, family £19.80; ⊙Apr-Sep), a tunnel tent on the East Lawn that swarms with the colourful flying insects, has become a firm summer favourite.

A slice of English countryside in SW7, the beautiful **Wildlife Garden** (⊙Apr-Nov), next to the West Lawn, encompasses a range of British lowland habitats, including a meadow with farm gates and a bee tree where a colony of honey bees fills the air.

The museum is transforming its outdoor spaces, tripling the Wildlife Garden in size, creating a piazza in the eastern grounds and adding a geological and palaeontological timeline walk.

From Halloween to January, a section by the East Lawn of the museum is transformed into a glittering and highly popular **ice rink**, complete with a hot drinks stall. Book your slot well ahead.

The entire museum and its gardens cover a huge 5.7 hectares and contain 80 million specimens from across the natural world. More than five million visitors come each year, so queues can often get long, especially during the school holidays.

Science Museum
Museum

(Map p78; ☑020-7942 4000; www.science museum.org.uk; Exhibition Rd, SW7; ⊙10am-6pm; ⊖South Kensington) FREE With seven

From left: British Library; Hampstead Heath; London Aquatics Centre (p82)

floors of interactive and educational exhibits, this scientifically spellbinding museum will mesmerise adults and children alike, covering everything from early technology to space travel. A perennial favourite is **Exploring Space**, a gallery featuring genuine rockets and satellites and a full-size replica of the *Eagle*, the lander that took Neil Armstrong and Buzz Aldrin to the moon in 1969. The **Making the Modern World Gallery** next door is a visual feast of locomotives, planes, cars and other revolutionary inventions.

Kensington Palace
Palace

(Map p78; www.hrp.org.uk/kensington -palace; Kensington Gardens, W8; adult/child £19.50/9.70 (cheaper weekdays after 2pm); ☺10am-6pm Mar-Oct, to 4pm Nov-Feb; ☻High St Kensington) Built in 1605, Kensington Palace became the favourite royal residence under William and Mary of Orange in 1689, remaining so until George III became king and moved out. Today, it's still a royal residence, with the likes of the Duke and Duchess of Cambridge (Prince William and his wife Catherine) and the Duke and Duchess of Sussex (Prince Harry and Meghan) living

there. A large part of the palace is open to the public, however, including the King's and Queen's State Apartments.

◉ North London

North London is framed by Camden's famous eponymous market, its unrivalled music scene and excellent pubs. There's plenty here for quiet enjoyment, too, including gorgeous green spaces as well as canal walks.

British Library
Library

(Map p78; www.bl.uk; 96 Euston Rd, NW1; ☺galleries 9.30am-6pm Mon & Wed-Fri, to 8pm Tue, to 5pm Sat, 11am-5pm Sun; ☻King's Cross St Pancras) **FREE** Consisting of low-slung red-brick terraces and fronted by a large plaza featuring an oversized statue of Sir Isaac Newton, Colin St John Wilson's British Library building is a love-it-or-hate-it affair (Prince Charles likened it to a secret-police academy). Completed in 1997, it's home to some of the greatest treasures of the written word, including the *Codex Sinaiticus* (the first complete text of the New Testament), Leonardo da Vinci's notebooks and a copy of the Magna Carta (1215).

RON ELLIS / SHUTTERSTOCK ©

Wellcome Collection Museum

(Map p78; www.wellcomecollection.org; 183 Euston Rd, NW1; ⊙10am-6pm Tue, Wed & Fri-Sun, to 10pm Thu; ⊖Euston Sq, Euston) FREE Focusing on the interface of art, science and medicine, this clever and resourceful museum is fascinating. The heart of the museum is Sir Henry Wellcome's collection of medical curiosities (saws for amputation, forceps through the ages, sex aids and amulets etc), which illustrate the universal fascination with health and the body across civilisations. In the **Medicine Now** gallery, interactive displays and provocative artworks are designed to make you ponder about humanity and the human body.

ZSL London Zoo Zoo

(Map p78; www.zsl.org/zsl-london-zoo; Outer Circle, Regent's Park, NW1; adult/child £29.75/22; ⊙10am-6pm Apr-Sep, to 5.30pm Mar & Oct, to 4pm Nov-Feb; 🚼; ☐274) Established in 1828, these 15-hectare zoological gardens are among the oldest in the world. The emphasis nowadays is firmly placed on conservation, education and breeding, with fewer animals and bigger enclosures.

Highlights include **Land of the Lions**, **Gorilla Kingdom**, **Tiger Territory**, the walk-through **In with the Lemurs** and **Butterfly Paradise**. Feeding sessions and talks take place throughout the day. The zoo also organises various experiences, such as Keeper for a Day or sleepovers in the Bug House.

Hampstead Heath Park

(Map p78; www.cityoflondon.gov.uk; ⊖Hampstead Heath, Gospel Oak) Sprawling Hampstead Heath, with its rolling woodlands and meadows, feels a million miles away – despite being approximately four – from the City of London. Covering 320 hectares, most of it woods, hills and meadows, it's home to about 180 bird species, 23 species of butterflies, grass snakes, bats and a rich array of flora. It's a wonderful place for a ramble, especially to the top of **Parliament Hill**, which offers expansive views across the city.

⊚ East London

Anyone with an interest in multicultural London needs to visit the East End. There's standout ethnic cuisine, some interesting museums and galleries, excellent pubs, canal-side eating and drinking, some of London's hippest neighbourhoods, and the vast redeveloped expanse of Queen Elizabeth Olympic Park to explore.

Queen Elizabeth Olympic Park   Park

(www.queenelizabetholympicpark.co.uk; E20; ⊕Stratford) The glittering centrepiece of London's 2012 Olympic Games, this vast 227-hectare expanse includes the main Olympic venues as well as playgrounds, walking and cycling trails, gardens, and a diverse mix of wetland, woodland, meadow and other wildlife habitats as an environmentally fertile legacy for the future. The main focal point is **London Stadium** (☑020-8522 6157; www.london-stadium.com; tours adult/child £19/11; ☺tours 10am-4.15pm; ⌂DLR Pudding Mill Lane), with a Games capacity of 80,000, scaled back to 54,000 seats for its new role as the home ground for West Ham United FC.

Other signature buildings include the **London Aquatics Centre** (☑020-8536 3150; www.londonaquaticscentre.org; Carpenters Rd, E20; adult/child from £5.20/3; ☺6am-10.30pm; ⊕Stratford), **Lee Valley VeloPark** (☑0300 003 0613; www.visitleevalley.org.uk/velopark; Abercrombie Rd, E20; 1hr taster £40, pay & ride from £4, bike & helmet hire adult/child from £12/8; ☺9am-10pm; ⌂DLR Stratford International), **ArcelorMittal Orbit** (☑0333 800 8099; www.arcelormittalorbit.com; 3 Thornton St, E20; adult/child £12.50/7.50, with slide £17.50/12.50; ☺11am-5pm Mon-Fri, 10am-6pm Sat & Sun; ⊕Stratford) and the **Copper Box Arena** (☑020-8221 4900; http://copperboxarena.org.uk; Copper St, E20; badminton 1hr £11, gym day pass £10; ☺7am-10pm; ⊕Hackney Wick), a 6000-seat indoor venue for sports and concerts. Then there's the **BeachEast** (www.beacheast.co.uk; Stratford Waterfront, E20; adult/child £2/1; ☺noon-9pm Mon-Fri, 10am-9pm Sat & Sun late Jul-early Sep; ⊕Stratford), an artificial sandy beach on the River Lea, and **Here East**, a vast 'digital campus' covering an area equivalent to 16 football fields.

For a different perspective on the park, or if you're feeling lazy, take a tour through its waterways with **Lee & Stort Boats** (☑0845 116 2012; www.leeandstortboats.co.uk; Stratford waterfront pontoon, E20; adult/child £9/4; ☺daily Apr-Sep, Sat & Sun Mar & Oct; ⊕Stratford).

Royal Observatory

LUKASZ PAJOR / SHUTTERSTOCK ©

Whitechapel Gallery Gallery

(Map p74; ☑020-7522 7888; www.whitechapel
gallery.org; 77-82 Whitechapel High St, E1;
⊘11am-6pm Tue, Wed & Fri-Sun, to 9pm Thu;
⊖Aldgate East) FREE A firm favourite of art
students and the avant-garde cognoscenti,
this ground-breaking gallery doesn't have
a permanent collection but is devoted to
hosting edgy exhibitions of contemporary
art. It made its name by staging exhibitions
by both established and emerging artists, including the first UK shows by Pablo Picasso,
Jackson Pollock, Mark Rothko and Frida
Kahlo. The gallery's ambitiously themed
shows change every couple of months
(check online) and there's often also live
music, talks and films on Thursday evenings.

◉ Greenwich & South London

Regal riverside Greenwich complements its
village feel with some grand architecture,
grassy parkland and riverside pubs.

Royal Observatory Historic Building

(Map p74; ☑020-8312 6565; www.rmg.co.uk/
royal-observatory; Greenwich Park, Blackheath
Ave, SE10; adult/child £10/6.50, incl Cutty Sark
£20/11.50; ⊘10am-5pm Sep-Jun, to 6pm Jul &
Aug; ⊠DLR Cutty Sark, DLR Greenwich, Greenwich) Rising south of Queen's House, idyllic
Greenwich Park (☑0300 061 2380; www.
royalparks.org.uk; King George St, SE10; ⊘6am-
around sunset; ⊠DLR Cutty Sark, ⊠Greenwich,
Maze Hill) climbs up the hill, affording
stunning views of London from the Royal
Observatory, which Charles II had built in
1675 to help solve the riddle of longitude. To
the north is lovely **Flamsteed House** and
the **Meridian Courtyard**, where you can
stand with your feet straddling the western
and eastern hemispheres; admission is by
ticket. The southern half contains the highly
informative and free **Weller Astronomy
Galleries** and the **Peter Harrison Planetar-
ium** (☑020-8312 6608; www.rmg.co.uk/whats-
on/planetarium-shows; adult/child £8/5.50).

Cutty Sark Museum

(Map p74; ☑020-8312 6608; www.rmg.co.uk/
cuttysark; King William Walk, SE10; adult/
child £13.50/7; ⊘10am-5pm Sep-Jun, to 6pm

Abbey Road Studios

Beatles aficionados can't possibly visit
London without making a pilgrimage to
this famous recording **studio** (Map p78;
www.abbeyroad.com; 3 Abbey Rd, NW8; ⊖St
John's Wood) in St John's Wood. The studios themselves are off-limits, so you'll
have to content yourself with examining
the decades of fan graffiti on the fence
outside. Stop-start local traffic is long
accustomed to groups of tourists lining
up on the zebra crossing to re-enact the
cover of the fab four's 1969 masterpiece
Abbey Road. In 2010 the crossing was
rewarded with Grade II heritage status.

CLAUDIO DIVIZIA / SHUTTERSTOCK ©

Jul & Aug; ⊠DLR Cutty Sark) The last of the
great clipper ships to sail between China
and England in the 19th century, the fully
restored *Cutty Sark* endured massive fire
damage in 2007 that occurred during a
£25 million restoration. The exhibition in
the ship's hold tells its story as a tea clipper
at the end of the 19th century. Launched in
1869 in Scotland, she made eight voyages
to China in the 1870s, sailing out with a
mixed cargo and coming back with tea.

Old Royal Naval College Historic Building

(Map p74; www.ornc.org; 2 Cutty Sark Gardens,
SE10; ⊘10am-5pm, grounds 8am-11pm; ⊠DLR
Cutty Sark) FREE Sir Christopher Wren's
baroque masterpiece in Greenwich and
indeed Britain's largest ensemble of
baroque architecture, the Old Royal Naval
College contains the Neoclassical **Chapel**

Emirates Air Line

Capable of ferrying 2400 people per hour across the Thames in either direction, this **cable car** (www.emiratesairline.co.uk; 27 Western Gateway, E16; one-way adult/child £4.50/2.30, with Oyster Card £3.40/1.70; ⊙7am-11pm Mon-Fri, 8am-11pm Sat, 9am-11pm Sun Apr-Sep, 7am-9pm Mon-Thu, to 11pm Fri, 8am-11pm Sat, 9am-9pm Sun Oct-Mar; ⊠Royal Victoria DLR, ⊖North Greenwich) makes quick work of the journey from the Greenwich Peninsula to the Royal Docks. Although it's mostly patronised by tourists for the views over the river – and the views are ace – it's also listed on the London Underground map as part of the transport network, meaning you can pay with your Oyster Card and nab a discount while you're at it.

and the extraordinary **Painted Hall** (☎020-8269 4799). The entire Old Royal Naval College, including the Chapel, the **Visitor Centre** (www.ornc.org/visitor-centre; Pepys Bldg, King William Walk; ⊙10am-5pm, to 6pm Jun-Sep), and the grounds, can be visited for free. Volunteers lead free 45-minute tours throughout each day from the Visitor Centre.

National Maritime Museum   Museum
(Map p74; ☎020-8312 6565; www.rmg.co.uk/national-maritime-museum; Romney Rd, SE10; ⊙10am-5pm; ⊠DLR Cutty Sark) **FREE** Narrating the long, briny and eventful history of seafaring Britain, this excellent museum's exhibits are arranged thematically, with

highlights including *Miss Britain III* (the first boat to top 100mph on open water) from 1933, the 19m-long golden state barge built in 1732 for Frederick, Prince of Wales, the huge ship's propeller and the colourful figureheads installed on the ground floor. Families will love these, as well as the ship simulator and the 'All Hands' children's gallery on the 2nd floor.

Imperial War Museum   Museum
(Map p74; ☎020-7416 5000; www.iwm.org.uk; Lambeth Rd, SE1; ⊙10am-6pm; ⊖Lambeth North) **FREE** Fronted by a pair of intimidating 15in naval guns, this riveting museum is housed in what was the Bethlehem Royal Hospital, a psychiatric hospital also known as Bedlam. Although the museum's focus is on military action involving British or Commonwealth troops largely during the 20th century, it rolls out the carpet to war in the wider sense. Highlights include the state-of-the-art **First World War Galleries** and **Witnesses to War** in the forecourt and atrium above.

TOURS

Guide London   Tours
(Association of Professional Tourist Guides; ☎020-7611 2545; www.guidelondon.org.uk; half-/full day £165/270) Hire a prestigious Blue Badge Tourist Guide, know-it-all guides who have studied for two years and passed a dozen written and practical exams to do their job. They can tell you stories behind the sights that you'd only hear from them or whisk you on a themed tour – from royalty and The Beatles to parks and shopping. Go by car, public transport, bike or on foot.

Original Tour   Bus
(www.theoriginaltour.com; adult/child £32/15; ⊙8.30am-8.30pm) A 24-hour hop-on, hop-off bus service with a river cruise thrown in, as well as three themed walks: Changing of the Guard, Rock 'n' Roll and Jack the Ripper. Buses run every five to 20 minutes; you can buy tickets on the bus or online. There's also a 48-hour ticket available (adult/child £41/19.50), with an extended river cruise.

Crown River Cruises   Boating

(☎020-7936 2033; www.crownrivercruise.
co.uk; adult/child one way £9.90/4.95, return
£13.15/6.58; ⏰11am-6.30pm late May-early Sep,
to 5pm Apr, May, Sep & Oct, to 3pm Nov-Mar)
Vessels travel east from Westminster Pier
to St Katharine's Pier near the Tower of
London and back, calling at Embankment,
Festival and Bankside piers. You can travel
just one way, make the return trip or use
the boat as a hop-on, hop-off service
to visit sights on the way. Tours depart
half-hourly late May to early September,
and every 40 minutes the rest of the year.

Big Bus Tours   Bus

(☎020-7808 6753; www.bigbustours.com;
adult/child £35/18; ⏰every 20min 8.30am-6pm
Apr-Sep, to 5pm Oct & Mar, to 4.30pm Nov-Feb)
Informative commentaries in 12 languages.
The ticket includes a free river cruise with
City Cruises and three thematic walking
tours (royal London, film locations, myster-
ies). Good online booking discounts available. Onboard wi-fi. The ticket is valid for
24 hours; for an extra £8 (£4 for children),
you can upgrade to a 48-hour ticket.

🅐 SHOPPING

From charity-shop finds to designer bags,
there are thousands of ways to spend your
hard-earned cash in London. Many of the
big-name shopping attractions, such as
Harrods, Hamleys, Camden Market and Old
Spitalfields Market, have become must-
sees in their own right. Chances are that
with so many temptations, you'll give your
wallet a full workout.

Fortnum & Mason   Department Store

(Map p64; ☎020-7734 8040; www.fortnum
andmason.com; 181 Piccadilly, W1; ⏰10am-8pm
Mon-Sat, 11.30am-6pm Sun; 🚇Piccadilly Circus)
With its classic eau-de-Nil (pale green)
colour scheme, 'the Queen's grocery
store' established in 1707 refuses to yield
to modern times. Its staff – men and
women – still wear old-fashioned tailcoats
and its glamorous food hall is supplied with
hampers, cut marmalade, speciality teas,
superior fruitcakes and so forth. Fortnum &
Mason remains the quintessential London
shopping experience.

A tour boat on the River Thames

JEFF GREENBERG / AGE FOTOSTOCK ©

Claridge's Foyer & Reading Room (p88)

Harrods   Department Store

(Map p78; ☎020-7730 1234; www.harrods. com; 87-135 Brompton Rd, SW1; ☺10am-9pm Mon-Sat, 11.30am-6pm Sun; ☻Knightsbridge) Garish and stylish in equal measure, perennially crowded Harrods is an obligatory stop for visitors, from the cash-strapped to the big spenders. The stock is astonishing, as are many of the price tags. High on kitsch, the 'Egyptian Elevator' resembles something out of an Indiana Jones epic, while the memorial fountain to Dodi and Di (lower ground floor) merely adds surrealism.

Harvey Nichols   Department Store

(Map p78; www.harveynichols.com; 109-125 Knightsbridge, SW1; ☺10am-8pm Mon-Sat, 11.30am-6pm Sun; ☻Knightsbridge) At London's temple of high fashion, you'll find Chloé and Balenciaga bags, the city's best denim range, a massive make-up hall with exclusive lines and great jewellery. The food hall and in-house restaurant, **Fifth Floor**, are, you guessed it, on the 5th floor. From 11.30am to midday, it's browsing time only.

John Sandoe Books   Books

(Map p78; ☎020-7589 9473; www.johnsandoe.com; 10 Blacklands Tce, SW3; ☺9.30am-6.30pm Mon-Sat, 11am-5pm Sun; ☻Sloane Sq) The perfect antidote to impersonal book superstores, this atmospheric three-storey bookshop in 18th-century premises is a treasure trove of literary gems and hidden surprises. It's been in business for six decades and loyal customers swear by it, while knowledgeable booksellers spill forth with well-read pointers and helpful advice.

Liberty   Department Store

(Map p64; ☎020-7734 1234; www.liberty. co.uk; Great Marlborough St, W1; ☺10am-8pm Mon-Sat, noon-6pm Sun; ☻Oxford Circus) An irresistible blend of contemporary styles in an old-fashioned mock-Tudor atmosphere (1875), Liberty has a huge cosmetics department and an accessories floor, along with a breathtaking lingerie section, all at sky-high prices. A classic London gift or souvenir is a Liberty fabric print, especially in the form of a scarf.

EATING

Once the butt of many a culinary joke, London has transformed itself over the last few decades and today is a global dining destination. World-famous chefs can be found at the helm of several top-tier restaurants, but it is the sheer diversity on offer that is head-spinning: from Afghan to Zambian, London delivers an A to Z of world cuisine.

The West End

Shoryu   Noodles £

(Map p64; www.shoryuramen.com; 9 Regent St, SW1; mains £10-14.50; ⏱11.15am-midnight Mon-Sat, to 10.30pm Sun; ⊖Piccadilly Circus) Compact, well-mannered and central noodle-parlour Shoryu draws in reams of noodle diners to feast at its wooden counters and small tables. It's busy, friendly and efficient, with helpful and informative staff. Fantastic *tonkotsu* (pork-broth ramen) is the name of the game here, sprinkled with nori (dried, pressed seaweed), spring onion, *nitamago* (soft-boiled eggs) and sesame seeds. No bookings.

Palomar   Israeli ££

(Map p64; ☎020-7439 8777; http://thepalomar. co.uk; 34 Rupert St, W1; mains £9-17; ⏱noon-2.30pm & 5.30-11pm Mon-Sat, 12.30-3.30pm & 6-9pm Sun; 🛜; ⊖Piccadilly Circus) The buzzing vibe at this good-looking celebration of modern-day Jerusalem cuisine (in all its permutations) is infectious, but the noise in the back dining room might drive you mad. Choose instead the counter seats at the front. The 'Yiddish-style' chopped chicken-liver pâté, the Jerusalem-style polenta and the 'octo-hummus' are all fantastic, but portions are smallish, so it's best to share several dishes.

Gymkhana   Indian ££

(Map p64; ☎020-3011 5900; www.gymkhana london.com; 42 Albemarle St, W1; mains £10-38, 4-course lunch/dinner £28.50/40; ⏱noon-2.30pm & 5.30-10.15pm Mon-Sat; 🛜; ⊖Green Park) The rather sombre setting is all British Raj – ceiling fans, oak ceiling, period cricket

 Hamleys: The World's Oldest Toy Store?

Claiming to be the world's oldest (and some say, the largest) toy store, **Hamleys** (Map p64; ☎0371 704 1977; www.hamleys.com; 188-196 Regent St, W1; ⏱10am-9pm Mon-Fri, 9.30am-9pm Sat, noon-6pm Sun; ⊖Oxford Circus) moved to its address on Regent St in 1881. From the basement's Star Wars Collection and ground floor where staff blow bubbles and glide foam boomerangs through the air with practised nonchalance, to Lego World and a cafe on the 5th floor, it's a rich layer cake of playthings.

photos and hunting trophies – but the menu is lively, bright and inspiring. For lovers of variety, there is a six-course tasting meat/vegetarian menu (£70/65). The bar is open to 1am.

Brasserie Zédel   French ££

(Map p64; ☎020-7734 4888; www.brasserie zedel.com; 20 Sherwood St, W1; mains £9.75-25.75; ⏱11.30am-midnight Mon-Sat, to 11pm Sun; 🛜; ⊖Piccadilly Circus) This brasserie in the renovated art deco ballroom of a former hotel is the Frenchest eatery west of Calais. Favourites include *choucroute alsacienne* (sauerkraut with sausages and charcuterie; £15.50) or a straight-up *steak haché* (chopped steak) with pepper sauce and *frites* (£9.75). Set menus (£9.95/13.25 for two/three courses) and plats du jour (£15.75) offer excellent value in a terrific setting.

👓 Sky Garden at the 'Walkie Talkie'

The City's sixth-tallest building didn't get off to a good start when it opened in 2014. Officially called 20 Fenchurch St it was quickly dubbed the 'Walkie Talkie' by unimpressed Londoners, and its highly reflective windows melted the bodywork of several cars parked below. However, the opening of this 155m-high, three-storey, **public garden** (Map p74; ✐020-7337 2344; www.skygarden.london; L35-37, 20 Fenchurch St, EC3; ◷10am-6pm Mon-Fri, 11am-9pm Sat & Sun; ⊖Monument) FREE in the glass dome at the top has helped win naysayers over. Entry is free, but you'll need to book a slot in advance.

DRIMAFILM / SHUTTERSTOCK ©

Claridge's Foyer & Reading Room   British £££

(Map p64; ✐020-7107 8886; www.claridges. co.uk; 49-53 Brook St, W1; afternoon tea £60, with champagne £70; ◷afternoon tea 2.45-5.30pm; ⊛; ⊖Bond St) Extend that pinkie finger to partake in afternoon tea within the classic art deco foyer and Reading Room of this landmark hotel, where the gentle clink of fine porcelain and champagne glasses could be a defining memory of your trip to London. The setting is gorgeous and dress is elegant, smart casual (ripped jeans and baseball caps won't get you served).

Portrait   Modern European £££

(Map p64; ✐020-7312 2490; www.npg.org.uk/ visit/shop-eat-drink.php; 3rd fl, National Portrait Gallery, St Martin's Pl, WC2; mains £19.50-28, 2-/3-course menu £27.95/31.50; ◷10-11am, 11.45am-3pm & 3.30-4.30pm daily, 6.30-8.30pm Thu-Sat; ⊛; ⊖Charing Cross) This stunningly located restaurant above the excellent National Portrait Gallery (p68) comes with dramatic views over Trafalgar Sq and Westminster. It's a fine choice for tantalising food and the chance to relax after a morning or afternoon of picture-gazing at the gallery. The breakfast/brunch (10am to 11am) and afternoon tea (3.30pm to 4.30pm) come highly recommended. Booking is advisable.

👁 The City

Wine Library   Buffet ££

(Map p74; ✐020-7481 0415; www.winelibrary. co.uk; 43 Trinity Sq, EC3; buffet £18; ◷buffet 11.30am-3.30pm, shop 10am-6pm Mon, to 8pm Tue-Fri; ⊖Tower Hill) This is a great place for a light but boozy lunch opposite the Tower. Buy a bottle of wine at retail price from the large selection (£9.50 corkage fee) and then head into the vaulted cellar to snack as much as you like from the selection of delicious pâtés, charcuterie, cheeses, bread and salads.

Café Below   Cafe ££

(Map p74; ✐020-7329 0789; www.cafebelow. co.uk; Cheapside, EC2; mains £11-16.50; ◷7.30am-2.30pm Mon-Fri; ⊖Mansion House) This very atmospheric cafe-restaurant in the crypt of St Mary-le-Bow church offers a tasty range of international dishes. Summer sees tables set up outside in the shady courtyard.

👁 The South Bank

Anchor & Hope   Gastropub ££

(Map p74; www.anchorandhopepub.co.uk; 36 The Cut, SE1; mains £12-20; ◷noon-2.30pm Tue-Sat, 6-10.30pm Mon-Sat, 12.30-3.15pm Sun; ⊖Southwark) A stalwart of the South Bank food scene, the Anchor & Hope is a quintessential gastropub: elegant but not formal, and utterly delicious (European fare with a British twist). The menu changes daily but think salt-marsh lamb shoulder cooked for seven hours; wild rabbit with anchovies, almonds and rocket; and panna cotta with rhubarb compote.

Roast bone marrow and parsley salad at St John (p91)

Skylon
Modern European ££

(Map p74; ✆020-7654 7800; www.skylon -restaurant.co.uk; 3rd fl, Royal Festival Hall, Southbank Centre, Belvedere Rd, SE1; 3-course menu grill/restaurant £25/30; ⊙grill noon-11pm Mon-Sat, to 10.30pm Sun, restaurant noon-2.30pm & 5-10.30pm Mon-Sat, 11.30am-4pm Sun; 🖙; 🚇Waterloo) This excellent restaurant inside the Royal Festival Hall (p96) is divided into grill and fine-dining sections by a large **bar** (Map p74; ⊙noon-1am Mon-Sat, to 10.30pm Sun; 🖙). The decor is cutting-edge 1950s: muted colours and period chairs (trendy then, trendier now), while floor-to-ceiling windows bathe you in magnificent views of the Thames and the city. Booking is advised.

Arabica Bar & Kitchen
Middle Eastern £££

(Map p74; ✆020-3011 5151; www.arabicabar andkitchen.com; 3 Rochester Walk, Borough Market, SE1; dishes £6-14; ⊙noon-11pm Mon-Fri, 9am-11.30pm Sat, noon-9pm Sun; 🍴; 🚇London Bridge) Pan–Middle Eastern cuisine is a well-rehearsed classic these days, but Arabica Bar & Kitchen has managed to bring something fresh to its table: the decor is contemporary and bright, the food delicate and light, and there's an emphasis on sharing (two to three small dishes per person). The downside of this tapas approach is that the bill adds up quickly.

⊗ Kensington & Hyde Park

Pimlico Fresh
Cafe £

(Map p64; ✆020-7932 0030; 86 Wilton Rd, SW1; mains from £4.50; ⊙7.30am-7.30pm Mon-Fri, 9am-6pm Sat & Sun; 🚇Victoria) This friendly two-room cafe will see you right whether you need breakfast (French toast, bowls of porridge laced with honey or maple syrup), lunch (homemade quiches and soups, 'things' on toast) or just a good old latte and cake.

Rabbit
Modern British ££

(Map p78; ✆020-3750 0172; www.rabbit -restaurant.com; 172 King's Rd, SW3; mains £6-24, set lunch £13.50; ⊙noon-midnight Tue-Sat, noon-6pm Sun, 6-11pm Mon; 🍴; 🚇Sloane Sq) Three brothers grew up on a farm. One became a farmer, another a butcher, while the third worked in hospitality. So they pooled their skills and came up with Rabbit, a breath of fresh air in upmarket Chelsea. The restaurant rocks the agri-chic (yes) look, and the creative, seasonal Modern British cuisine is fabulous. The drinks list is just as good, with a great selection of wines from the family vineyard in Sussex, and local beers and ciders.

Dinner by Heston Blumenthal
Modern British £££

(Map p78; ☑020-7201 3833; www.dinnerby heston.com; Mandarin Oriental Hyde Park, 66 Knightsbridge, SW1; 3-course set lunch £45, mains £30-49; ◷noon-2pm & 6-10.15pm Mon-Fri, noon-2.30pm & 6-10.30pm Sat & Sun; ; ◉Knightsbridge) Sumptuously presented Dinner is a gastronomic tour de force, taking diners on a journey through British culinary history (with inventive modern inflections). Dishes carry historical dates to convey context, while the restaurant interior is a design triumph, from the glass-walled kitchen and its overhead clock mechanism to the large windows looking onto the park. Book ahead.

Also on hand is a 16th-century Tudor-style private room that seats 12 guests, who dine at an extravagant Sapele and Rosewood oval table. Set lunches are available Monday to Friday.

Gordon Ramsay
French £££

(Map p78; ☑020-7352 4441; www.gordon ramsayrestaurants.com/restaurant-gordon-ramsay; 68 Royal Hospital Rd, SW3; 3-course lunch/dinner £65/110; ◷noon-2.30pm & 6.30-11pm Mon-Fri; ; ◉Sloane Sq) One of Britain's finest restaurants and London's longest-running with three Michelin stars, this is hallowed turf for those who worship at the altar of the stove. It's a treat right from the taster to the truffles, but you won't get much time to savour it all. Bookings are made in specific sittings and you dare not linger; book as late as you can to avoid that rushed feeling. The blowout Menu Prestige (£145) is seven courses of perfection.

⊗ Clerkenwell, Shoreditch & Spitalfields

Polpo
Italian £

(Map p74; ☑020-7250 0034; www.polpo.co.uk; 3 Cowcross St, EC1M; dishes £4-12; ◷11.30am-11pm Mon-Thu & Sat, to midnight Fri, to 4pm Sun;

⊖Farringdon) Occupying a sunny spot on semipedestrianised Cowcross St, this sweet little place serves rustic Venetian-style meatballs, *pizzette* (small pizzas), grilled meat and fish dishes. Portions are larger than your average tapas but a tad smaller than a regular main – the perfect excuse to sample more than one of the exquisite dishes. Exceptional value for money.

St John   British ££

(Map p74; ☑020-7251 0848; www.stjohngroup. uk.com/spitalfields; 26 St John St, EC1M; mains £14.80-24.90; ☺noon-3pm & 6-11pm Mon-Fri, 6-11pm Sat, 12.30-4pm Sun; ⊖Farringdon) Whitewashed brick walls, high ceilings and simple wooden furniture don't make for a cosy dining space but they do keep diners free to concentrate on St John's famous nose-to-tail dishes. Serves are big, hearty and a celebration of England's culinary past. Don't miss the signature roast bone marrow and parsley salad (£8.90).

Hawksmoor   Steak £££

(Map p74; ☑020-7426 4850; www.thehawks moor.com; 157 Commercial St, E1; mains £20-50; ☺noon-2.30pm & 5-10.30pm Mon-Sat, noon-9pm Sun; ☎; ⊖Liverpool St) You could easily miss discreetly signed Hawksmoor, but confirmed carnivores will find it worth seeking out. The dark wood, bare bricks and velvet curtains make for a handsome setting in which to gorge yourself on the best of British beef. The Sunday roasts (£20) are legendary.

⊗ Greenwich & South London

Greenwich Market   Market £

(Map p74; www.greenwichmarketlondon.com/ food-and-drink; College Approach, SE10; ☺10am-5.30pm; ℙ⊅; ℝDLR Cutty Sark) Perfect for snacking your way through a world atlas of food while browsing the other market stalls. Come here for delicious food to take away, from Spanish tapas and Thai curries to sushi, Ethiopian vegetarian, French crêpes, dim sum, Mexican burritos and lots more.

⊗ North London

Hook Camden Town   Fish & Chips £

(Map p78; www.hookrestaurants.com; 65 Park-way, NW1; mains £8-12; ☺noon-3pm & 5-10pm Mon-Thu, noon-10.30pm Fri & Sat, to 9pm Sun; ⊞; ⊖Camden Town) ⚑ In addition to working entirely with sustainable small fisheries and

SIMON LEIGH / ALAMY STOCK PHOTO ©

| ★ Top Five Places to Eat |
| Dinner by Heston Blumenthal |
| Gordon Ramsay |
| Rabbit (p89) |
| Claridge's Foyer & Reading Room (p88) |
| Hook Camden Town |

From left: Cocktails at a bar in London; Ice-cream at Chin Chin Labs (p92); baked goods at Ottolenghi (p92)

ALISON WRIGHT / GETTY IMAGES ©

local suppliers, Hook makes all its sauces on-site and wraps its fish in recycled materials, supplying diners with extraordinarily fine-tasting morsels. Totally fresh, the fish arrives in panko breadcrumbs or tempura batter, with seaweed salted chips. Craft beers and fine wines are also on hand.

Chin Chin Labs
Ice Cream £

(Map p78; www.chinchinlabs.com; 49-50 Camden Lock Pl, NW1; ice cream £4-5; ⊗noon-7pm; ⊜Camden Town) This is food chemistry at its absolute best. Chefs prepare the ice-cream mixture and freeze it on the spot by adding liquid nitrogen. Flavours change regularly and match the seasons (spiced hot cross bun, passionfruit and coconut, for instance). Sauces and toppings are equally creative. Try the ice-cream sandwich if you can: ice cream wedged inside gorgeous brownies or cookies.

Ottolenghi
Bakery, Mediterranean ££

(☎020-7288 1454; www.ottolenghi.co.uk; 287 Upper St, N1; breakfast £5.90-12.50, mains lunch/ dinner from £18.80/11.90; ⊗8am-10.30pm Mon-Sat, 9am-7pm Sun; ✐; ⊜Highbury & Islington)

Mountains of meringues tempt you through the door of this deli-restaurant, where a sumptuous array of baked goods and fresh salads greets you. Meals are as light and bright as the brilliantly white interior design, with a strong influence from the eastern Mediterranean.

🚇 East London

Towpath
Cafe £

(☎020-7254 7606; rear 42-44 De Beauvoir Cres, N1; mains £7-9.50; ⊗9am-5pm Tue & Wed, to 9.30pm Thu-Sun; ⊜Haggerston) Occupying four small units on the Regent's Canal towpath, this simple cafe is a super place to sit in the sun and watch the ducks and narrowboats glide by. The coffee and food are excellent, too, with delicious cookies and brownies on the counter and cooked dishes chalked up on the blackboard daily.

Corner Room
Modern British ££

(Map p74; ☎020-7871 0460; www.townhall hotel.com/food-and-drink/corner_room; Patriot Sq, E2; mains £13-14, 2-/3-course lunch £19/23; ⊗7-10am & noon-4pm Mon-Fri, 7.30-10.30am & noon-2.30pm Sat & Sun, 6-9.45pm Sun-Wed,

Meringues at Ottolenghi

6-10.15pm Thu-Sat; ⊖Bethnal Green) Someone put this baby in the corner, but we're certainly not complaining. Tucked away on the 1st floor of the Town Hall Hotel, this relaxed restaurant serves expertly crafted dishes with complex yet delicate flavours, highlighting the best of British seasonal produce.

DRINKING & NIGHTLIFE

The metropolis offers a huge variety of venues to wet your whistle in – from cosy neighbourhood pubs to glitzy all-night clubs, and everything in between.

The West End

American Bar
Bar

(Map p78; www.thebeaumont.com/dining/american-bar; The Beaumont, Brown Hart Gardens, W1; ⊙11.30am-midnight Mon-Sat, to 11pm Sun; 🖱; ⊖Bond St) Sip a bourbon or a classic cocktail in the 1930s art deco ambience of this stylish bar at the hallmark Beaumont hotel. It's central, period and like a gentleman's club, but far from stuffy. Only a few years old, the American Bar feels like it's been pouring drinks since the days of the flapper and jazz age.

Dukes London
Cocktail Bar

(Map p64; ☑020-7491 4840; www.dukeshotel.com/dukes-bar; Dukes Hotel, 35 St James's Pl, SW1; ⊙2-11pm Mon-Sat, 4-10.30pm Sun; 🖱; ⊖Green Park) Sip to-die-for martinis like royalty in a gentleman's-club-like ambience at this tucked-away classic bar where white-jacketed masters mix up some awesomely good preparations. Ian Fleming used to frequent the place, perhaps perfecting his 'shaken, not stirred' James Bond maxim. Smokers can ease into the secluded Cognac and Cigar Garden to light up cigars purchased here.

American Bar
Cocktail Bar

(Map p64; ☑020-7836 4343; www.fairmont.com/savoy-london/dining/americanbar; Savoy, The Strand, WC2; ⊙11.30am-midnight Mon-Sat, noon-midnight Sun; ⊖Covent Garden) Home of the Hanky Panky, White Lady and other

Blackfriar: The Ex-Monastery Pub

Built in 1875 on the site of a Dominican monastery (hence the name and the corpulent chap above the door), this prominent **pub** (Map p74; ☑020-7236 5474; www.nicholsonspubs.co.uk; 174 Queen Victoria St, EC4; ⊙10am-11pm Mon-Fri, 9am-11pm Sat, noon-10.30pm Sun; ⊖Blackfriars) was famously saved from demolition in the 1960s by poet Sir John Betjeman. The unusual monastic-themed friezes date from an art nouveau makeover in 1905. It serves a good selection of ales, along with speciality sausages and chops.

classic infusions created on-site, the seriously dishy and elegant American Bar is an icon of London, with soft blue and rust art deco lines and live piano music. Cocktails start at £17.50 and peak at a stupefying £5000 (the Original Sazerac, containing Sazerac de Forge cognac from 1857).

Lamb & Flag
Pub

(Map p64; ☑020-7497 9504; www.lambandflagcoventgarden.co.uk; 33 Rose St, WC2; ⊙11am-11pm Mon-Sat, noon-10.30pm Sun; ⊖Covent Garden) Everybody's favourite pub in central London, pint-sized Lamb & Flag is full of charm and history, and is on the site of a pub that dates from at least 1772. Rain or shine, you'll have to elbow your way to the bar through the merry crowd drinking outside. Inside are brass fittings and creaky wooden floors.

 ## Prospect of Whitby

Once known as the Devil's Tavern due to its unsavoury clientele, the **Prospect** (Map p74; ☑020-7481 1095; www.greene kingpubs.co.uk; 57 Wapping Wall, E1; ☺noon-11pm Mon-Thu, 11am-midnight Fri & Sat, noon-10.30pm Sun; ☎; ☻Wapping) first opened its doors in 1520, although the only part of the original pub remaining is the flagstone floor. Famous patrons have included Charles Dickens and Samuel Pepys. There's a smallish terrace overlooking the Thames, a restaurant upstairs, open fires in winter and a pewter-topped bar.

VISITBRITAIN / BRITAIN ON VIEW / GETTY IMAGES ©

☺ The City
Ye Olde Cheshire Cheese   Pub
(Map p74; ☑020-7353 6170; Wine Office Court, 145 Fleet St, EC4; ☺11.30am-11pm Mon-Fri, noon-11pm Sat; ☻Chancery Lane) Rebuilt in 1667 after the Great Fire, this is one of London's most famous pubs, accessed via a narrow alley off Fleet St. Over its long history, Dr Johnson, Thackeray and Dickens have all supped in its gloriously gloomy surrounds. The vaulted cellars are thought to be remnants of a 13th-century Carmelite monastery.

Sky Pod   Bar
(Map p74; ☑0333 772 0020; www.skygarden. london; L35, 20 Fenchurch St, EC3; ☺7am-11pm Mon, to midnight Tue, to 1am Wed-Fri, 8am-1am Sat, 8am-11pm Sun; ☻Monument) You'll need a booking for the Sky Garden (p88) to

access this rooftop bar, and if you'd like a guaranteed table to sit at, you're best to book one at the same time. The views are extraordinary, although it does get cold up here in winter. Note, it doesn't admit patrons in shorts, sportswear, trainers or flip-flops after 5pm.

☺ The South Bank
Little Bird Gin   Cocktail Bar
(Map p74; www.littlebirdgin.com; Maltby St, SE1; ☺5-10pm Thu & Fri, 10am-10pm Sat, 11am-4pm Sun; ☻London Bridge) This South London–based distillery opens a pop-up bar in a workshop at **Maltby Street Market** (Map p74; www.maltby.st; ☺9am-4pm Sat, 11am-4pm Sun; ☻Bermondsey) to ply merry punters with devilishly good cocktails (£5 to £7), served in jam jars or apothecary's glass bottles.

Oblix   Bar
(Map p74; www.oblixrestaurant.com; 32nd fl, Shard, 31 St Thomas St, SE1; ☺noon-11pm; ☻London Bridge) On the 32nd floor of the Shard (p77), Oblix offers mesmerising vistas of London. You can come for anything from a coffee (£3.50) to a cocktail (from £13.50) and enjoy virtually the same views as the official viewing galleries of the Shard (but at a reduced cost and with the added bonus of a drink). Live music every night from 7pm.

Anspach & Hobday   Microbrewery
(Map p74; www.anspachandhobday.com; 118 Druid St, SE1; ☺5-9.30pm Fri, 10.30am-6.30pm Sat, 12.30-5pm Sun; ☻London Bridge) It's all about porter at this microbrewery, although lighter ales are also brewed. Beer aficionados will love trying brews from the experimental range; beers come in large 750ml bottles and are rotated regularly. There's a nice outdoor seating area.

☺ Clerkenwell, Shoreditch & Spitalfields
Zetter Townhouse Cocktail Lounge   Cocktail Bar
(Map p74; ☑020-7324 4545; www.thezetter townhouse.com; 49-50 St John's Sq, EC1; ☺7.30am-12.45am; ☎; ☻Farringdon) Tucked

away behind an unassuming door on St John's Sq, this ground-floor bar is decorated with plush armchairs, stuffed animal heads and a legion of lamps. The cocktail list takes its theme from the area's distilling history – recipes of yesteryear plus homemade tinctures and cordials are used to create interesting and unusual tipples. House cocktails are all £11.

Fabric   Club

(Map p74; ☎0207 336 8898; www.fabric london.com; 77a Charterhouse St, EC1M; cover £5-25; ⊗11pm-7am Fri, to 8am Sat, to 5.30am Sun; ⊖Farringdon, Barbican) London's leading club, Fabric's three separate dance floors in a huge converted cold store opposite Smithfield meat market draw impressive queues (buy tickets online). FabricLive (on selected Fridays) rumbles with drum 'n' bass and dubstep, while Fabric (usually on Saturdays but also on selected Fridays) is the club's signature live DJ night. Sunday's WetYourSelf! delivers house, techno and electronica.

Cargo   Bar, Club

(Map p74; www.cargo-london.com; 83 Rivington St, EC2A; ⊗noon-1am Mon-Thu, to 3am Fri & Sat, to midnight Sun; ⊖Shoreditch High St) Cargo is one of London's most eclectic clubs. Under its brick railway arches you'll find a dance floor, a bar and an outside terrace adorned with two original Banksy images. The music policy (hip-hop, pop, R&B and club classics) is varied, with plenty of up-and-coming bands also in the line-up. Food is available throughout the day.

⊙ North London

Bar Pepito   Wine Bar

(Map p78; www.camino.uk.com/location/ bar-pepito; 3 Varnishers Yard, The Regent's Quarter, N1; ⊗5pm-midnight Mon-Fri, 6pm-midnight Sat; ⊖King's Cross St Pancras) This tiny, intimate Andalusian bodega specialises in sherry and tapas. Novices fear not: the staff are on hand to advise. They're also experts at food pairings (top-notch ham and cheese selections). To go the whole hog, try a tasting flight of selected sherries with snacks to match.

Little Bird Gin

TJSLL / GETTY IMAGES ©

KAMIRA / SHUTTERSTOCK ©

Shakespeare's Globe (p50)

Holly Bush   Pub

(Map p78; www.hollybushhampstead.co.uk; 22 Holly Mount, NW3; ⊙noon-11pm Mon-Sat, to 10.30pm Sun; 🛜👪🐾; ⊖Hampstead) This beautiful Grade II–listed Georgian pub opens to an antique interior, with open fires in winter. It has a knack for making you stay longer than you planned. Set above Heath St, in a secluded hilltop location, it's reached via the Holly Bush Steps.

⭐ ENTERTAINMENT

Whatever it is that sets your spirits soaring or your booty shaking, you'll find it in London. The city's been a world leader in theatre ever since a young man from Stratford-upon-Avon set up shop here in the 16th century. And if London started swinging in the 1960s, its live rock and pop scene has barely let up since.

Ronnie Scott's   Jazz

(Map p64; ☎020-7439 0747; www.ronnie scotts.co.uk; 47 Frith St, W1; ⊙7pm-3am Mon-Sat, 1-4pm & 8pm-midnight Sun; ⊖Leicester Sq, Tottenham Court Rd) Ronnie Scott's jazz club opened in 1965 and became widely known as Britain's best. Support acts are at 7pm, with main gigs at 8.15pm (8pm Sunday) and a second house at 11.15pm Friday and Saturday (check ahead). The more informal Late, Late Show runs from 1am to 3am. Expect to pay from £25; the Late, Late Show and Sunday lunch shows are just £10.

Royal Festival Hall   Concert Venue

(Map p74; ☎020-7960 4200; www.southbank centre.co.uk; Southbank Centre, Belvedere Rd, SE1; 🛜; ⊖Waterloo) Royal Festival Hall's amphitheatre seats 2500 and is one of the best places for catching world- and classical-music artists. The sound is fantastic, the programming impeccable and there are frequent free gigs in the wonderfully expansive foyer.

Old Vic   Theatre

(Map p74; ☎0844 871 7628; www.oldvic theatre.com; The Cut, SE1; ⊖Waterloo) Matthew Warchus, director of *Matilda the Musical* and the film *Pride*, took the theatrical helm of this London theatre in

April 2015. His aim was to bring eclectic programming to the theatre: expect new writing, as well as dynamic revivals of old works and musicals.

KOKO   Live Music

(Map p78; www.koko.uk.com; 1a Camden High St, NW1; ⊖Mornington Cres) Once the legendary Camden Palace, where Charlie Chaplin, the Goons and the Sex Pistols performed, and where Prince played surprise gigs, KOKO is maintaining its reputation as one of London's better gig venues. The theatre has a dance floor and decadent balconies, and attracts an indie crowd. There are live bands most nights and hugely popular club nights on Saturdays.

 INFORMATION

DANGERS & ANNOYANCES

London is a fairly safe city for its size, but exercise common sense.

● Several high-profile terrorist attacks have afflicted London in recent years, but the risk to individual visitors is remote. Report anything suspicious to the police by calling 999 (emergency) or 101 (nonemergency).

● Keep an eye on your handbag and wallet, especially in bars and nightclubs, and in crowded areas such as the Underground.

● Be discreet with your tablet/smartphone – snatching happens.

● If you're getting a cab after a night's clubbing, go for a black taxi or a licensed minicab firm.

MONEY

ATMs are widespread. Major credit cards are accepted everywhere. The best place to change money is in post-office branches, which do not charge a commission.

TOURIST INFORMATION

Visit London (www.visitlondon.com) can fill you in on everything from attractions and events to tours and accommodation. Kiosks are dotted about the city and can also provide maps and brochures; some branches are able to book theatre tickets.

 # LGBTIQ+ London

The city of Oscar Wilde, Virginia Woolf and Elton John is a world gay capital on par with New York and San Francisco, with visible gay, lesbian and transgender communities and enlightened laws to protect them. The West End, particularly Soho, is the visible centre of gay and lesbian London, with venues clustered around Old Compton St and its surrounds.

Village (Map p64; ☎020-7478 0530; www.village-soho.co.uk; 81 Wardour St, W1; ⊗5pm-2am Mon-Thu, to 3am Fri & Sat, to 11.30pm Sun; ⊖Piccadilly Circus) The Village is always up for a party, whatever the night of the week. There are karaoke nights, 'discolicious' nights, go-go-dancer nights – take your pick. And if you can't wait until the clubs open to strut your stuff, there's a dance floor downstairs, complete with pole, of course. Open till 3am on the last weekend of the month.

She Soho (Map p64; ☎020-7287 5041; www.she-soho.com; 23a Old Compton St, W1D; ⊗4-11.30pm Mon-Thu, noon-midnight Fri & Sat, noon-10.30pm Sun; ⊖Leicester Sq) This intimate and dimly lit basement bar has DJs, comedy, cabaret, burlesque, live music and party nights. Open till 3am on the last Friday and Saturday of the month. Everybody is welcome at this friendly lesbian spot.

Heaven (Map p64; http://heaven-live.co.uk; Villiers St, WC2; ⊗11pm-5am Mon, to 4am Thu & Fri, 10.30pm-5am Sat; ⊖Embankment, Charing Cross) This perennially popular mixed/gay club under the arches beneath Charing Cross Station is host to excellent live gigs and club nights. Monday's Popcorn (mixed dance party, with an all-welcome door policy) offers one of the best weeknight's clubbing in the capital. The celebrated G-A-Y takes place here on Thursday (G-A-Y Porn Idol), Friday (G-A-Y Camp Attack) and Saturday (plain ol' G-A-Y).

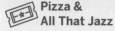

Pizza & All That Jazz

Pizza Express Jazz Club (Map p64; 📞020-7439 4962; www.pizzaexpresslive.com/venues/soho-jazz-club; 10 Dean St, W1; tickets £15-40; ⊖Tottenham Court Rd) has been one of the best jazz venues in London since opening in 1969. It may be a strange arrangement, in a basement beneath a branch of the chain restaurant, but it's highly popular. Lots of big names perform here and artists such as Norah Jones, Gregory Porter and the late Amy Winehouse played here in their early days.

Jazz trumpeter performing
JAAPO / SHUTTERSTOCK ©

There aren't a huge number of Visit London **tourist offices** (www.visitlondon.com/tag/tourist-information-centre) in town, but they can be found at several places:

Heathrow Airport (Terminal 1, 2 & 3 Underground station concourse; ⊗7.30am-8.30pm)

King's Cross St Pancras Station (Western Ticket Hall, Euston Rd N1; ⊗8am-6pm)

Liverpool Street Station (Map p74; Liverpool St Station; ⊗8am-6pm; ⊖Liverpool St)

Piccadilly Circus Underground Station (Map p64; Piccadilly Circus Underground Station; ⊗9am-4pm)

Victoria Station (Map p64; Victoria Station; ⊗8am-6pm; ⊖Victoria)

GETTING THERE & AWAY

Air Most people arrive in London by air, but an increasing number of visitors coming from Europe let the train take the strain, while buses from across the Continent are a further option.

The city has five airports: Heathrow, which is the largest, to the west; Gatwick to the south; Stansted to the northeast; Luton to the northwest; and London City in the Docklands.

Most trans-Atlantic flights land at Heathrow (average flight time from the US East Coast is between 6½ and 7½ hours, 10 to 11 hours from the West Coast; slightly longer on the return).

Visitors from Europe are more likely to arrive at Gatwick, Stansted or Luton (the latter two are used exclusively by low-cost airlines such as easyJet and Ryanair). Most flights to Continental Europe last from one to three hours.

Rail Check National Rail (www.nationalrail.co.uk) for timetables and fares.

Eurostar (www.eurostar.com) High-speed passenger rail service linking London St Pancras International with Paris, Brussels and Lille, with up to 19 daily departures. Fares vary greatly, from £29 one-way standard class to around £245 one-way for a fully flexible business premier ticket (prices based on return journeys). Direct links between London and Amsterdam and Rotterdam commenced in 2018.

GETTING AROUND

The cheapest way to get around London is with an Oyster Card or a UK contactless card (foreign cardholders should check for contactless charges first).

Tube (London Underground) The fastest and most efficient way of getting around town. First/last trains operate from around 5.30am to 12.30am and 24 hours on Friday and Saturday on five lines.

Train The DLR and Overground network are ideal for zooming across more distant parts of the city. Trains run from a number of stations to more distant destinations in and around London.

Bus The London bus network is very extensive and efficient; while bus lanes free up traffic, buses can still be slow going.

Taxis Black cabs are ubiquitous, but not cheap. Available around the clock.

Bicycle Santander Cycles are great for shorter journeys around central London.

Where to Stay

Landing the right accommodation is integral to your London experience, and there's no shortage, from hip hostels to boutique B&Bs and prestigious five-star properties.

Neighbourhood	Atmosphere
The West End	Close to main sights; great transport links; wide range of accommodation in all budgets; good restaurants.
The City	Near St Paul's and Tower of London; good transport links; handy central location; quality hotels; some cheaper weekend rates.
The South Bank	Near Tate Modern, London Eye and Southbank Centre; cheaper than West End; excellent pubs and views.
Kensington & Hyde Park	Excellent for South Kensington museums and shopping; great accommodation range; stylish area; good transport.
Clerkenwell, Shoreditch & Spitalfields	Hip area with great bars and nightlife; excellent for boutique hotels.
East London	Markets, multicultural feel; great restaurants and traditional pubs.
North London	Leafy; vibrant nightlife; pockets of village charm; excellent boutique hotels and hostels; great gastropubs; quiet during the week.
West London	Good shopping, markets and pubs; excellent boutique hotels; good transport.
Greenwich & South London	Great boutique options; leafy escapes; near top Greenwich sights.

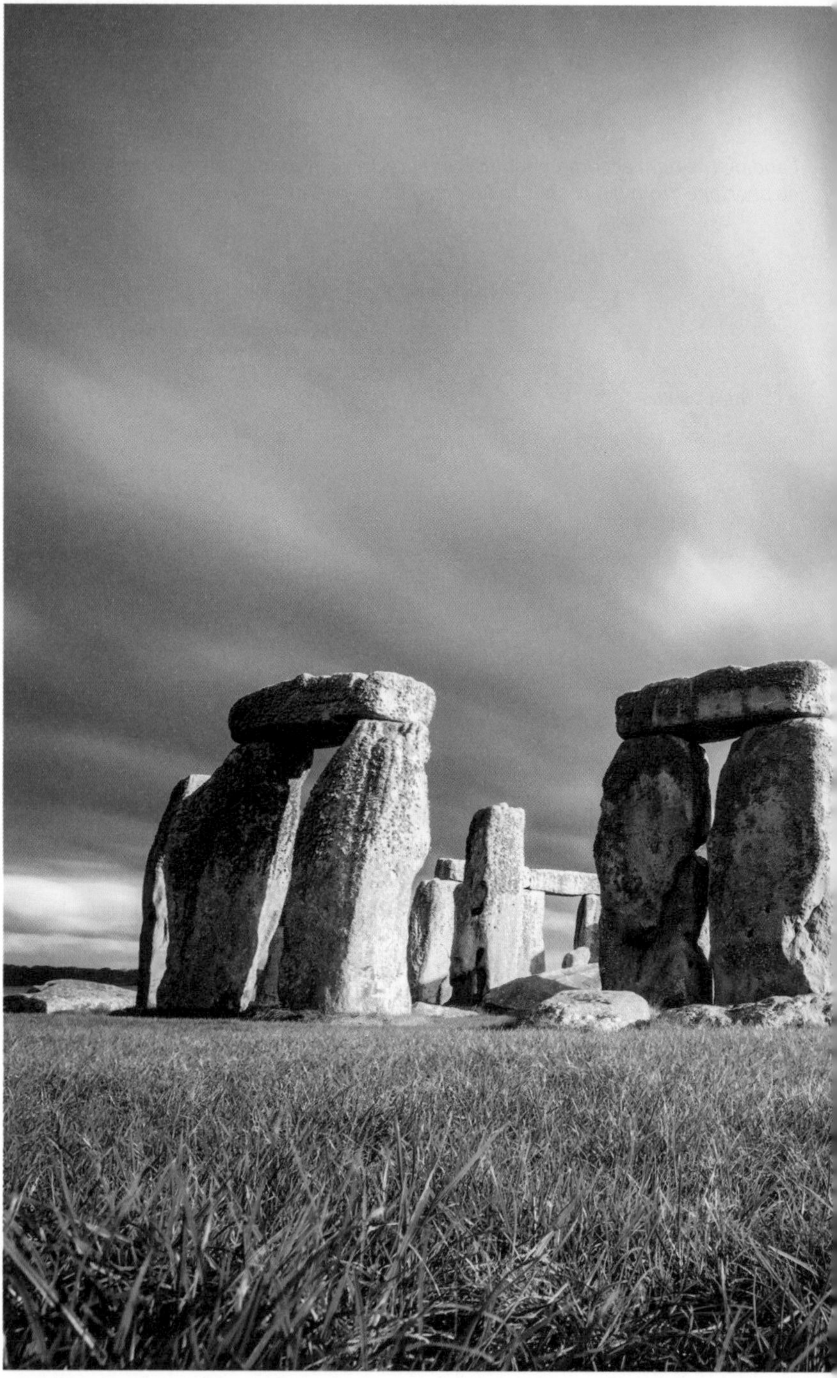

STONEHENGE

Stonehenge at a Glance...

The verdant landscape in which Stonehenge sits is rich in the reminders of ritual and packed with not-to-be-missed sights. Dotted with more mysterious stone circles and processional avenues than anywhere else in Britain, it's a place that teases the imagination. Here you'll experience the prehistoric majesty of Stonehenge itself, the serene 800-year-old cathedral at Salisbury and the supremely stately homes at Stourhead and Longleat. It's an area crammed full of English charm waiting to be explored.

Two Days Around Stonehenge

Arrive early on day one to delight in a less-crowded **Stonehenge** (p104). Next have a (perhaps picnic) lunch, then go walking through the wider landscape with its powerful ruins. On your second day, tour **Salisbury Cathedral** (p108), taking in the soaring spire and panoramic tower views. After studying the remarkable **Magna Carta** (p108), explore **Salisbury Museum** (p108).

Four Days Around Stonehenge

Head off to stunning **Stourhead** (p108) on day three, to roam around an exquisite house and its spectacular grounds – give yourself enough time to explore. Then it's back to Salisbury for a drink at the ancient, (purportedly) haunted **Haunch of Venison** (p109). The following morning, motor over to **Longleat** (p108) to drive through its zoo. After spotting African animals, tour the stately home, then nip back to Salisbury for dinner at **Charter 1227** (p109) or **Anokaa** (p109).

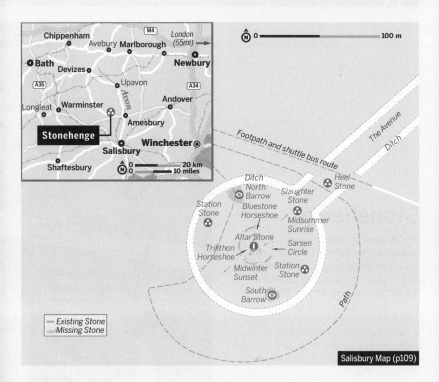

Existing Stone
Missing Stone

Salisbury Map (p109)

Arriving in Stonehenge

Stonehenge is 10 miles north of Salisbury. The Stonehenge Tour bus (adult/child £30/20) leaves Salisbury's railway station half-hourly from June to August, and hourly between September and May. Tickets include admission to Stonehenge.

Salisbury's transport connections are good, with frequent train and bus services to London and the southwest.

Where to Stay

Salisbury has a good range of places to sleep, from characterful B&Bs to sleek hotels. It makes an ideal base for exploring Stonehenge and its outlying sights.

Stonehenge

You've seen the photos, now prepare to be dazzled by Britain's most recognisable archaeological site. This compelling ring of monolithic stones has been attracting a steady stream of pilgrims, poets and philosophers for 5000 years and it's still a mystical, ethereal place – a haunting echo from Britain's ancient past and a reminder of those who once walked the ceremonial avenues across Salisbury Plain.

Great For...

❶ Need to Know

EH; ☏0370 333 1181; www.english-heritage.
org.uk; near Amesbury; adult/child same-
day tickets £19.50/11.70, advance booking
£17.50/10.50; ⊙9am-8pm Jun-Aug, 9.30am-
7pm Apr, May & Sep, 9.30am-5pm Oct-Mar; Ⓟ

★ **Top Tip**

Book your Stone Circle Access Visits (p106) months in advance for a rare chance to walk inside the stone circle itself.

An ultramodern makeover at Stonehenge has brought an impressive visitor centre and the closure of an intrusive road (now restored to grassland). The result is a far stronger sense of historical context.

Planning

Admission to Stonehenge is through timed tickets – at peak periods secure yours two weeks in advance. Note that visitors normally can't get inside the stone circle itself. However, if you book an unforgettable Stone Circle Access **experience** (☑0370 333 0605; www.english-heritage.org.uk; adult/child £38.50/23.10), you can wander around the core of the site, getting up-close views of the iconic bluestones and trilithons. Each visit only takes 26 people; book at least three months in advance.

Access

A pathway frames the ring of massive stones, which are 1.5 miles from the visitor centre. A fleet of trolley buses makes the 10-minute trip – if you can, walk; it's much more atmospheric. Admission is free for English Heritage and National Trust members.

Visitor Centre

Stonehenge's swish new **visitor centre** sees you standing in the middle of an atmospheric 360-degree projection of the stone circle through the ages and seasons – complete with midsummer sunrise and swirling star-scape. Engaging audiovisual displays detail the transportation of the stones and the building stages, while 300 finds from the wider site include

Stonehenge's visitor centre

bone pins and arrowheads. There's also a striking recreation of the face of a Neolithic man whose body was found nearby.

From 3000 BC

The first phase of building started around 3000 BC, when the outer circular bank and ditch were erected. A thousand years later, an inner circle of granite stones, known as bluestones, was added. It's thought these mammoth 4-tonne blocks were hauled from the Preseli Mountains in South Wales, some 250 miles away – an extraordinary feat for builders equipped with only simple

☑ Don't Miss

The Slaughter Stone, Heel Stone and Avenue, which provide intriguing glimpses into Stonehenge's place in what was a much wider ceremonial landscape.

tools. It's believed a system of ropes, sledges and rollers fashioned from tree trunks was used.

From 1500 BC

Around 1500 BC, Stonehenge's main stones were dragged to the site, erected in a circle and crowned by massive lintels to make the trilithons (two vertical stones topped by a horizontal one). The sarsen (sandstone) stones were cut from rock found on the Marlborough Downs, 20 miles from the site. It's estimated dragging one of these 50-tonne stones across the countryside would require about 600 people.

Also around this time, the bluestones from 500 years earlier were rearranged as an inner bluestone horseshoe with an altar stone at the centre. Outside this the trilithon horseshoe of five massive sets of stones was erected. Three of these are intact; the other two have just a single upright. Then came the major sarsen circle of 30 massive vertical stones, of which 17 uprights and six lintels remain.

The Wider Site

Much further out, another circle was delineated by the 58 Aubrey Holes, named after John Aubrey, who discovered them in the 1600s. Just inside this circle are the South and North Barrows, each originally topped by a stone. The inner horseshoes are aligned to coincide with sunrise at the midsummer solstice, prompting claims that the site was some kind of astronomical calendar.

Prehistoric pilgrims would have entered the site via the Avenue, whose entrance to the circle is marked by the Slaughter Stone and the Heel Stone, located slightly further out to the north east. The visitor centre has leaflets detailing walking routes through the wider 6500-acre World Heritage Site.

✕ Take a Break

The visitor centre has a large cafe serving sandwiches, soup, drinks and cakes; you can eat inside or in the picnic area.

Salisbury

Centred on a majestic cathedral that's topped by the tallest spire in England, Salisbury makes an appealing Wiltshire base. The city's streets form an architectural timeline ranging from medieval walls to Georgian mansions and Victorian villas.

◎ SIGHTS

Salisbury Cathedral   Cathedral

(📞01722-555120; www.salisburycathedral.org.uk; The Close; requested donation adult/child £7.50/3; ⏰9am-5pm Mon-Sat, noon-4pm Sun) England is endowed with countless stunning churches, but few can hold a candle to the grandeur and sheer spectacle of 13th-century Salisbury Cathedral. This early English Gothic–style structure has an elaborate exterior decorated with pointed arches and flying buttresses, and a sombre, austere interior designed to keep its congregation suitably pious. Its statuary and tombs are outstanding; don't miss the daily **tower tours** (📞01722-555120; www.salisburycathedral.org.uk; The Close; adult/child £13.50/8.50; ⏰2-5 tours daily, May-Sep) and the cathedral's original, 13th-century copy of the Magna Carta.

The cathedral was built between 1220 and 1258. In the north aisle look out for a fascinating **medieval clock** dating from 1386, probably the world's oldest working timepiece. The cathedral's crowning glory however is its 123m **spire**, added in the mid-14th century – the tallest in Britain and an enormous technical challenge for its medieval builders, weighing around 6500 tonnes. Look closely and you'll see the additional weight has buckled the four central piers of the **nave**. Sir Christopher Wren surveyed the cathedral in 1668 and calculated that the spire was leaning by 75cm (a brass plate in the floor of the nave is used to measure any shift).

The cathedral really comes into its own during **evensong** (⏰5.30pm Mon-Sat, 4.30pm Sun, during term time only).

Magna Carta   Museum

(www.salisburycathedral.org.uk; The Close; ⏰9.30am-5pm Mon-Sat, noon-4pm Sun Apr-Oct, 9.30am-4.30pm Mon-Sat, noon-3.45pm Sun Nov-Mar) The Magna Carta on display in Salisbury is one of only four surviving original copies. A historic agreement made in 1215 between King John and his barons, it acknowledged the fundamental principle that the monarch was not above the law. It's a still-powerful document, beautifully written and remarkably well preserved. It's displayed in an interactive exhibit in Salisbury Cathedral's 13th-century Chapter House.

Salisbury Museum   Museum

(📞01722-332151; www.salisburymuseum.org.uk; 65 The Close; adult/child £8/4; ⏰10am-5pm Mon-Sat year-round, plus noon-5pm Sun Jun-Sep) The hugely important archaeological finds here include the Stonehenge Archer, the bones of a man found in the ditch near the stone circle – one of the arrows found alongside probably killed him. With gold coins dating from 100 BC and a Bronze Age gold necklace, it's a powerful introduction to Wiltshire's prehistory.

Stourhead   Historic Building

(NT; 📞01747-841152; www.nationaltrust.org.uk; Mere; adult/child £16.60/8.30; ⏰11am-4.30pm early Mar–early Nov, to 3.30pm mid-Nov–late Dec; 🅿) Overflowing with vistas, temples and follies, Stourhead is landscape gardening at its finest. The Palladian house has some fine Chippendale furniture and paintings by Claude and Gaspard Poussin, but it's a sideshow to the magnificent 18th-century gardens (open 9am to 5pm), which spread out across the valley. Stourhead is off the B3092, 30 miles west of Salisbury.

Longleat   Zoo

(📞01985-844400; www.longleat.co.uk; near Warminster; all-inclusive ticket adult/child £35/26, house & grounds £19/14; ⏰10am-5pm Feb–mid-Oct, to 7pm late Jul & Aug; 🅿) Half ancestral mansion, half wildlife park, Longleat was transformed into Britain's first safari park in 1966, turning Capability Brown's landscaped grounds into an amazing drive-through zoo populated by a menagerie of animals more at home in the African wilderness than the fields of Wiltshire. There's a throng of attractions, too: the historic house, animatronic dinosaur exhibits, narrow-gauge railway, mazes, pets' corner, butterfly garden and bat cave.

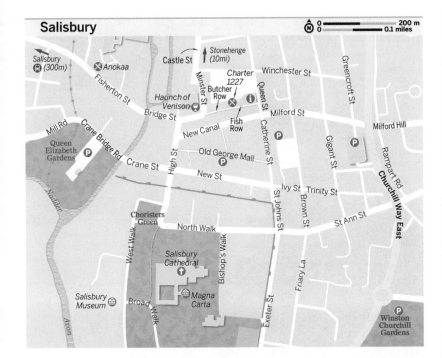

Salisbury

It's just off the A362, 25 miles west of Salisbury. Save around 10% by booking tickets online.

EATING

Anokaa   Indian ££
(☏01722-414142; www.anokaa.com; 60 Fisherton St; mains £14-19; ⊙noon-2pm & 5.30-11pm; 🅟) The pink-neon sign signals what's in store here: a modern, multilayered take on high-class Indian cuisine. The spice and flavour combos make the ingredients sing, the meat-free menu makes vegetarians gleeful, and the lunchtime buffet (£9) makes everyone smile.

Charter 1227   British £££
(☏01722-333118; www.charter1227.co.uk; 6 Ox Row, Market Pl; mains £15-30; ⊙noon-2.30pm & 6-9.30pm Tue-Sat) Ingredients that speak of classic English dishes have a firm foothold here – feast on duck confit, beef fillet or roast lamb; the cooking and presentation are assured. Canny locals eat at lunchtime or between 6pm and 7pm Tuesday to Thursday, when mains are capped at £10 to £15.

🍷 DRINKING & NIGHTLIFE

Haunch of Venison   Pub
(www.haunchpub.co.uk; 1 Minster St; ⊙11am-11pm Mon-Sat, to 6pm Sun) Featuring wood-panelled snugs, spiral staircases and crooked ceilings, this 14th-century drinking den is packed with atmosphere – and ghosts. One is a cheating whist player whose hand was severed in a game – look out for his mummified bones on display.

ℹ INFORMATION

Tourist Office (☏01722-342860; www.visit salisbury.co.uk; Fish Row; ⊙9am-5pm Mon-Fri, 10am-4pm Sat, 10am-2pm Sun; 🖥)

ℹ GETTING THERE & AWAY

Bus National Express (www.nationalexpress.com) services to/from Salisbury include Bath (£11, 1¼ hours, one daily) and London Victoria via Heathrow (£10, three hours, three daily Monday to Saturday).

Train Salisbury has regular services to Bath (£10, one hour) and London Waterloo (£42, 1½ hours).

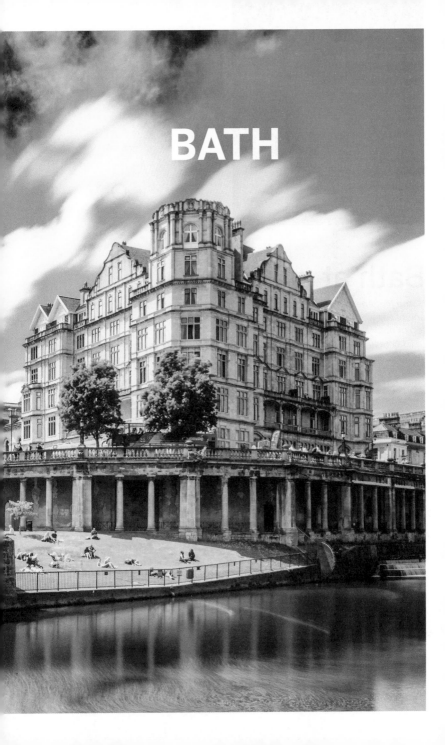

BATH

In This Chapter

Bath at a Glance...

Home to some of the nation's grandest Georgian architecture – not to mention one of the world's best-preserved Roman bathhouses – this chic city, founded on top of natural hot springs, has been a tourist draw for nigh on 2000 years. Bath's heyday really began during the 18th century, when local entrepreneur Ralph Allen and his team of father-and-son architects, John Wood the Elder and Younger, turned this sleepy backwater into the toast of Georgian society, and constructed fabulous landmarks such as the Circus and Royal Crescent.

Two Days in Bath

Start by touring the **Roman Baths** (p115), then sip some spring water and sample afternoon tea in the **Pump Room** (p121), before a stylish supper at **Acorn** (p121). On day two, Bath's glorious architecture awaits: first the Royal Crescent – ducking inside **No 1** (p117) – then the **Circus** (p117), stopping at the Circus **restaurant** (p121) for lunch. Next up, **shopping** (p119), then dinner at local favourite **Chequers** (p122).

Four Days in Bath

On day three, clamber up Bath Abbey's **tower** (p118), then discover the **Jane Austen Centre** (p118). Take in a barmy comedy **walk** (p119) before dropping by live-music pub, the **Bell Inn** (p122). After starting day four with a lazy cruise down the **Avon** (p119), continue chilling out at **Thermae Bath Spa** (p119); saving the roof-top swim until dusk. End with still more indulgence at **Menu Gordon Jones** (p122).

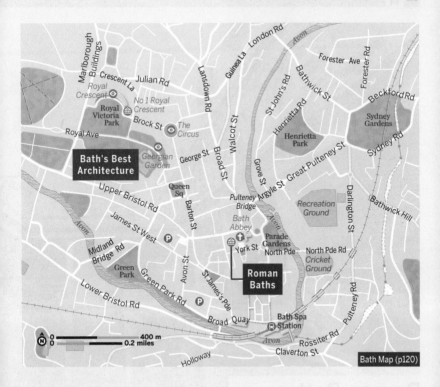

Map labels:
Marlborough Buildings · Crescent La · Julian Rd · Guinea La · London Rd · Avon · Forester Ave · Forester Rd · Royal Crescent · No 1 Royal Crescent · Lansdown Rd · St John's Rd · Bathwick St · Beckford Rd · Royal Victoria Park · Brock St · The Circus · Henrietta Rd · Sydney Gardens · Royal Ave · Georgian Garden · George St · Broad St · Walcot St · Henrietta Park · Sydney Rd · **Bath's Best Architecture** · Upper Bristol Rd · Queen Sq · Barton St · Grove St · Pulteney Bridge · Argyle St · Great Pulteney St · Recreation Ground · Darlington St · Bathwick Hill · James St West · Bath Abbey · Avon · York St · Parade Gardens · North Pde · North Pde Rd · Cricket Ground · Midland Bridge Rd · Green Park · Green Park Rd · Avon St · St James's Pde · **Roman Baths** · Pulteney Rd · Lower Bristol Rd · Broad Quay · Bath Spa Station · Rossiter Rd · Holloway · Claverton St · Bath Map (p120)

0 / 0 · 400 m / 0.2 miles

Arriving in Bath

Bus National Express coaches run to London (£20, 2½ hours, hourly). Two-hourly services also go to London Heathrow (£25, three hours).

Car Bath is 115 miles (2½ hours) from London and 34 miles (one hour) from Stonehenge.

Train Direct services include London Paddington (£35, 1½ hours, half-hourly) and Salisbury (for Stonehenge; £18, one hour, hourly).

Where to Stay

Bath has a wide range of hotels and B&Bs, and gets extremely busy in the height of summer when prices peak. Be aware, they also rise by anything from £10 to £60 a room at weekends year-round. Few hotels have on-site parking, although some offer discounted rates at municipal car parks.

Roman Baths

In typically ostentatious style, Romans built a bathhouse complex above Bath's hot springs. Set alongside a temple to a goddess with healing powers, they now form one of the best-preserved Roman-era spas in the world.

Great For...

☑ **Don't Miss**

Sampling a free glass of Bath's disconcertingly warm spring waters in the on-site restaurant.

You could say Bath the city originated with these Roman baths – legend has it that King Bladud, a Trojan refugee and father of King Lear, founded Bath some 2800 years ago when his pigs were cured of leprosy by a dip in the muddy swamps. The Romans established the town of Aquae Sulis in AD 44, building the extensive baths complex and a temple to the goddess Sulis-Minerva.

The Great Bath

The heart of the complex is the Great Bath, a lead-lined pool filled with steaming, geothermally heated water to a depth of 1.6m. It emerges at a toasty 46°C (115°F) from the so-called 'Sacred Spring'. Though now open-air, the bath would originally have been covered by a 45m-high, barrel-vaulted roof.

❶ Need to Know

📱01225-477785; www.romanbaths.co.uk; Abbey Churchyard; adult/child/family £17.50/10.25/48; ⏱9.30am-5pm Nov-Feb, 9am-5pm Mar–mid-Jun, Sep & Oct, 9am-9pm mid-Jun–Aug

✗ Take a Break

The bath's Georgian Pump Room Restaurant (p121) is an elegant spot for light bites and afternoon tea.

★ Top Tip

Saver tickets covering the Fashion Museum (p118) and the Roman Baths cost adult/child/family £22.50/12.25/58.

The Pools

More bathing pools and changing rooms are situated to the east and west, with excavated sections revealing the hypocaust system that heated the bathing rooms. After luxuriating in the baths, Romans would have reinvigorated themselves with a dip in the circular cold-water pool, which now has life-size films of bathers projected on to the walls.

The King's Bath

The King's Bath was added sometime during the 12th century around the site of the original Sacred Spring. Every day, 1.5 million litres of hot water still pour into the pool. Beneath the Pump Room are the remains of the Temple of Sulis-Minerva.

The Museum

Look out for the famous gilded bronze head of Minerva and a striking carved Gorgon's Head, as well as some of the 12,000-odd Roman coins thrown into the spring as votive offerings to the goddess.

The Wider Complex

The complex of buildings around the baths were built in stages during the 18th and 19th centuries. The two John Woods designed the buildings around the Sacred Spring, while the famous Pump Room was built by their contemporaries, Thomas Baldwin and John Palmer, in neoclassical style, complete with soaring Ionic and Corinthian columns.

Tours

Admission also includes an entertaining audio guide. Free hourly guided tours start at the Great Bath.

Bath's Best Architecture

Most cities would count themselves blessed to have a site as special as the Roman Baths, but Bath also boasts beautiful, 18th-century buildings dotted all around the compact centre.

Great For...

☑ **Don't Miss**

The view of the other side of the famous Circus terrace from the restored Georgian Garden.

In the early 18th century Ralph Allen and the celebrated dandy Richard 'Beau' Nash made Bath the centre of fashionable society. Allen developed the quarries at nearby Coombe Down and employed the two John Woods (father and son) to create Bath's signature buildings.

During WWII, Bath was hit by the Luftwaffe during the so-called Baedeker raids, which targeted historic cities in an effort to sap British morale. It didn't work, and in 1987 Bath became the only city in Britain to be declared a Unesco World Heritage Site in its entirety.

Royal Crescent

Bath's glorious Georgian architecture doesn't get any grander than this semi-circular **terrace** of majestic town houses

Aerial view of Royal Crescent

GEORGECLERK / GETTY IMAGES ©

the rooms on display are the drawing room, several bedrooms and the huge kitchen. Costumed guides add to the heritage atmosphere.

The Circus

The **Circus** is a Georgian masterpiece. Built to John Wood the Elder's design and completed in 1768, it's said to have been inspired by the Colosseum. Arranged over three equal terraces, the 33 mansions overlook a garden populated by plane trees. Famous residents have included Thomas Gainsborough, Clive of India, David Livingstone and the American actor Nicholas Cage.

The Georgian Garden

These tiny, walled **gardens** (☎01225-394041; off Royal Ave; ☺9am-7pm) **FREE** feature period plants and gravel walkways. They've been carefully restored and provide an intriguing insight into what would have sat behind the Circus' grand facades.

overlooking the green sweep of Royal Victoria Park. Designed by John Wood the Younger (1728–82) and built between 1767 and 1775, the houses appear perfectly symmetrical from the outside, but the owners were allowed to tweak the interiors, so no two houses are quite the same.

No 1 Royal Crescent

For a revealing glimpse into the splendour and razzle-dazzle of Georgian life, head inside the beautifully restored house at **No 1 Royal Crescent** (☎01225-428126; www. no1royalcrescent.org.uk; 1 Royal Cres; adult/ child/family £10.30/5.10/25.40; ☺10am-5pm), given to the city by the shipping magnate Major Bernard Cayzer, and since restored using only 18th-century materials. Among

⦿ SIGHTS

Bath Abbey   Church
(☎01225-422462; www.bathabbey.org; Abbey
Churchyard; suggested donation adult/child £4/2;
⊙9.30am-5.30pm Mon, 9am-5.30pm Tue-Fri, to
6pm Sat, 1-2.30pm & 4.30-6pm Sun) Looming
above the city centre, Bath's huge abbey
church was built between 1499 and 1616,
making it the last great medieval church
raised in England. Its most striking feature
is the west facade, where angels climb up
and down stone ladders, commemorating a
dream of the founder, Bishop Oliver King.

Jane Austen Centre   Museum
(☎01225-443000; www.janeausten.co.uk; 40 Gay
St; adult/child £12/6.20; ⊙9.45am-5.30pm Apr-
Oct, 10am-4pm Sun-Fri, 9.45am-5.30pm Sat Nov-
Mar) Bath is known to many as a location in
Jane Austen's novels, including *Persuasion*
and *Northanger Abbey*. Although Austen
lived in Bath for only five years, from 1801 to

> *Bath is known to many as a
> location in Jane Austen's novels*

Jane Austen Centre

1806, she remained a regular visitor and a
keen student of the city's social scene. Here,
guides in Regency costumes regale you with
Austen-esque tales as you tour memorabilia relating to the writer's life in Bath.

Museum of Bath
Architecture   Museum
(☎01225-333895; www.museumofbath
architecture.org.uk; The Vineyards, off the Paragon;
adult/child £5.50/2.50; ⊙2-5pm Tue-Fri, 10.30am-
5pm Sat & Sun mid-Feb–Nov) The stories behind
the building of Bath's most striking structures are explored here, using antique tools,
displays on Georgian construction methods
and a 1:500 scale model of the city.

Fashion Museum   Museum
(☎01225-477789; www.fashionmuseum.co.uk;
Assembly Rooms, 19 Bennett St; adult/child £9/7;
⊙10.30am-5pm Mar-Oct, to 4pm Nov-Feb) The
world-class collections on display in this
museum, within the basement of the city's
Georgian Assembly Rooms, include costumes from the 17th to late-20th centuries.
Some exhibits change annually; check the
website for the latest.

Pulteney Bridge   Bridge

Elegant Pulteney Bridge has spanned the River Avon since the late 18th century and continues to be a much-loved and much-photographed Bath landmark (the view from Grand Parade, southwest of the bridge, is the best). Browse the shops that line both sides of the bridge or have a rest and a Bath bun in the Bridge Coffee Shop.

🏃 ACTIVITIES

Thermae Bath Spa   Spa

(✏01225-331234; www.thermaebathspa.com; Hot Bath St; spa £36-40, treatments from £65; ☺9am-9.30pm, last entry 7pm) Taking a dip in the Roman Baths might be off limits, but you can still sample the city's curative waters at this fantastic modern spa complex, housed in a shell of local stone and plate glass. The showpiece is the open-air rooftop pool, where you can bathe in naturally heated, mineral-rich waters with a backdrop of Bath's cityscape – a don't-miss experience, best enjoyed at dusk.

🎯 TOURS

Bizarre Bath Comedy Walk   Walking

(www.bizarrebath.co.uk; adult/student £10/7; ☺8pm Apr-Oct) A fabulously daft city tour mixing street theatre and live performance that bills itself as 'hysterical rather than historical'. Leaves nightly from outside the tourist office. There's no need to book.

Bath City Sightseeing   Bus

(Bath Bus Company; ✏01225-444102; www.bathbuscompany.com; adult/child/family £15/9.50/43; ☺10am-5pm, reduced services Jan-Mar) Two hop-on/hop-off city tours on open-topped buses, with multi-language commentary. Tickets last 24 hours, or two consecutive days.

Pulteney Cruisers   Boating

(✏01225-863600; www.bathboating.com; Pulteney Bridge; adult/child £9/4; ☺mid-Mar–Oct) Runs between five and 11 hour-long boat trips on the River Avon each day.

 ### Bath Abbey Tower Tours

The 50 minute **tours** (✏01225-422462; www.bathabbey.org; adult/child £8/4; ☺10am-5pm Apr-Aug, 10am-4pm Sep & Oct, 11am-4pm Nov-Mar, closed Sun) of Bath Abbey's tower see you standing above the Abbey's fan vaulted ceiling, sitting behind the clock face and visiting the ringing and bell chamber. The views from the roof of the city and surrounding countryside are superb. Tours can only be booked at the Abbey shop, and only on the day. Tours leave on the hour Monday to Friday, and on the half hour on Saturday. There are no tours on Sunday. Children have to be at least five years old.

Bath as seen from the top of Bath Abbey Tower
NIGEL JARVIS / SHUTTERSTOCK ©

🛍 SHOPPING

Bath's shops are some of the best in the west. The city's main shopping centre is **SouthGate** (www.southgatebath.com; ☺shops 9am-6pm Mon-Wed, Fri & Sat, 9am-7pm Thu, 11am-5pm Sun), where you'll find all the major chain stores.

High-quality, independent shops line the narrow lanes just north of Bath Abbey and Pulteney Bridge. Milsom St is good for upmarket fashion, while Walcot St has food shops, design stores, vintage-clothing retailers and artisans' workshops.

🍴 EATING

Bertinet Bakery   Bakery £

(www.bertinet.com/bertinetbakery; 1 New Bond St Pl; baked goods £2.50-5; ☺8am-5pm Mon-Fri, 8.30am-5.30pm Sat) The flavoursome fillings

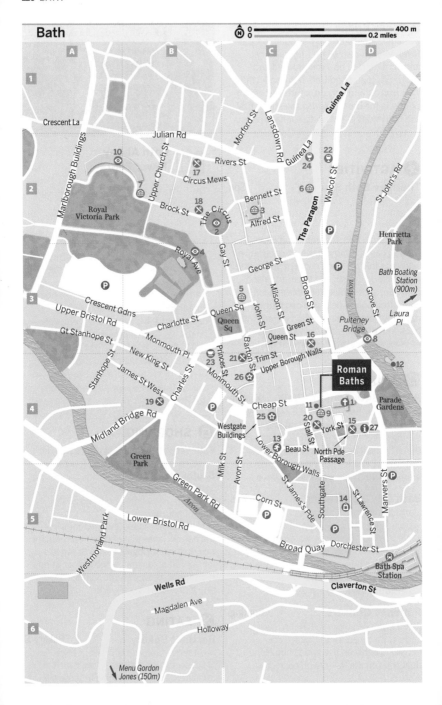

Bath

N 0 ___ 400 m
0 ___ 0.2 miles

Bath

and light pastry of the pasties at baker Richard Bertinet's take-out shop could change your view of that foodstuff for good. You'll also be tempted by rich quiches, cheese-studded croissants, French-inspired cakes and irresistible pistachio swirls.

Thoughtful Bread Company
Bakery £

(☏01225-471747; www.thethoughtfulbread company.com; 19 Barton St; ☺8am-5pm Tue-Fri, 8am-4pm Sat & Sun) ✔ Come lunchtime they could well be queuing out the door of this snug artisan bakery, where chunky loaves sit alongside delicate macaroons and salted-caramel bombs. It also has a stall at Bath's Saturday **farmers market** (www.greenparkstation.co.uk; Green Park; ☺9am-1.30pm Sat) ✔ – come early as it sells out fast.

The Circus
Modern British ££

(☏01225-466020; www.thecircusrestaurant. co.uk; 34 Brock St; mains lunch £12-15, dinner £16-23; ☺10am-midnight Mon-Sat; ☑) Chef Ali Golden has turned this bistro into one of Bath's destination addresses. Her taste is for British dishes with a Continental twist, à la British food writer Elizabeth David:

rabbit, Wiltshire lamb and West Country fish are all infused with herby flavours and rich sauces. It occupies an elegant town house near the Circus. Reservations recommended.

Acorn
Vegetarian ££

(☏01225-446059; www.acornvegetarian kitchen.co.uk; 2 North Pde Passage; lunch 2/3 courses £18/23, dinner 2/3 courses £28/37; ☺noon-3pm & 5.30-9.30pm, to 3.30pm & 10pm Sat; ☑) ✔ Proudly proclaiming 'plants taste better', Bath's premier vegetarian restaurant tempts you inside with aromas reflecting its imaginative, global-themed cuisine. The wine flights (two/three courses £15/22) matched to the set dinner menus are good value; or opt for a pear Bellini (£7) to get the liquid refreshments under way.

Pump Room Restaurant
Cafe ££

(☏01225-444477; www.romanbaths.co.uk; Stall St; snacks £7-9, mains £13-17; ☺9.30am-5pm) Elegance is everywhere in this tall, Georgian room, from the string trio and Corinthian columns to the oil paintings and glinting chandeliers. It sets the scene perfectly for morning coffee, classic lunches and the dainty sandwiches and cakes of its famous afternoon tea (£26 to £35 per person).

Mayor's Guide Tours of Bath

Excellent historical tours provided free by the Mayor's Corp of Honorary **Guides** (www.bathguides.org.uk; ⊙10.30am & 2pm Sun-Fri, 10.30am Sat) **FREE**; tours cover about 2 miles and are wheelchair accessible. They leave from within the Abbey Churchyard, outside the Pump Room. There are extra tours at 7pm on Tuesdays and Thursdays May to August.

Pump Room (p121)
CHRISTIAN MUELLER / SHUTTERSTOCK ©

Chequers   Gastropub ££
(☑01225-360017; www.thechequersbar.com; 50 Rivers St; mains £14-25; ⊙bar noon-11pm, food noon-2.30pm & 6-9pm) A discerning crowd inhabits Chequers, a Georgian pub that's now morphed into a classy gastro-pub. Here the menu ranges from well-executed bar-food favourites to relative rarities such as mallard and smoked eel, and partridge with quince.

Menu Gordon Jones   Modern British £££
(☑01225-480871; www.menugordonjones.co.uk; 2 Wellsway; 5-course lunch £50, 6-course dinner £55; ⊙12.30-2pm & 7-9pm Tue-Sat) If you enjoy dining with an element of surprise, then Gordon Jones' restaurant will be right up your culinary boulevard. Menus are dreamt up daily and showcase the chef's taste for experimental ingredients (expect mushroom mousse and Weetabix ice cream) and eye-catching presentation (test tubes and paper bags). It's superb value given the skill on show. Reservations essential.

DRINKING & NIGHTLIFE

Colonna & Smalls   Cafe
(☑07766 808067; www.colonnaandsmalls. co.uk; 6 Chapel Row; ⊙8am-5.30pm Mon-Fri, from 8.30am Sat, 10am-4pm Sun; 🖀) If you're keen on caffeinated beans, this is a cafe not to miss. A mission to explore coffee means there are three guest espresso varieties and smiley staff happy to share their expertise. They'll even tell you that black filter coffee – yes, filter coffee – is actually the best way to judge high-grade beans.

Star   Pub
(☑01225-425072; www.abbeyales.co.uk; 23 The Vineyards, off the Paragon; ⊙noon-2.30pm & 5.30-11pm Mon-Fri, noon-midnight Sat, to 10.30pm Sun) Few pubs are registered relics, but the Star is just that, and it still has many of its 19th-century bar fittings. It's the brewery tap for Bath-based Abbey Ales; some ales are served in traditional jugs, and you can even ask for a pinch of snuff in the 'smaller bar'.

Bell   Pub
(www.thebellinnbath.co.uk; 103 Walcot St; ⊙11.30am-11pm Mon-Thu, to midnight Fri & Sat, noon-10.30pm Sun; 🖀) Get chatting to Bath's bohemian muso crowd around the real fire at this laid-back locals' favourite. Conversation starters include the table football, bar billiards, backgammon and chess, and there's live music ranging from acoustic, country and folk to blues.

ENTERTAINMENT

Theatre Royal   Theatre
(☑01225-448844; www.theatreroyal.org.uk; Sawclose) Bath's historic theatre dates back 200 years. Major touring productions appear in the main auditorium and smaller shows take place in the Ustinov Studio.

There's also the egg – an award-winning space for children's and young people's shows.

Theatre Royal

Little Theatre Cinema

Cinema

(☎0871 9025735; www.picturehouses.com; St Michael's Pl) Bath's excellent art-house cinema screens fringe films and foreign-language flicks in art deco surrounds.

ℹ INFORMATION

Bath Tourist Office (☎01225-614420; www.visitbath.co.uk; 2 Terrace Walk; ⊗9.30am-5.30pm Mon-Sat, 10am-4pm Sun, closed Sun Nov-Jan) Advice and information, plus an accommodation booking service.

ℹ GETTING AROUND

Bicycle A 10-minute walk from the centre, **Bath Bike Hire** (☎01225-447276; www.bath-narrowboats.co.uk; Sydney Wharf; adult/child per day £15/10; ⊗9am-5pm) is handy for the canal and railway paths. **Take Charge Bikes** (☎01225-789568; www.takechargebikes.co.uk; 1 Victoria Bldgs, Lower Bristol Rd; per day £30; ⊗9am-5pm Mon-Fri, to 4pm Sat) Rents electric bikes.

Bus Bus U1 Runs from the bus station, via High St and Great Pulteney St, up Bathwick Hill, past the YHA to the university every 20 minutes (£2.50).

Car Bath has serious traffic problems, especially at rush hour. **Park & Ride** (☎01225-394041; return Mon-Fri £3.40, Sat & Sun £3; ⊗6.15am-8.30pm Mon-Sat, 9.30am-6pm Sun) services are in operation. There's a good, central car park underneath the SouthGate shopping centre (two/eight hours £3.50/11).

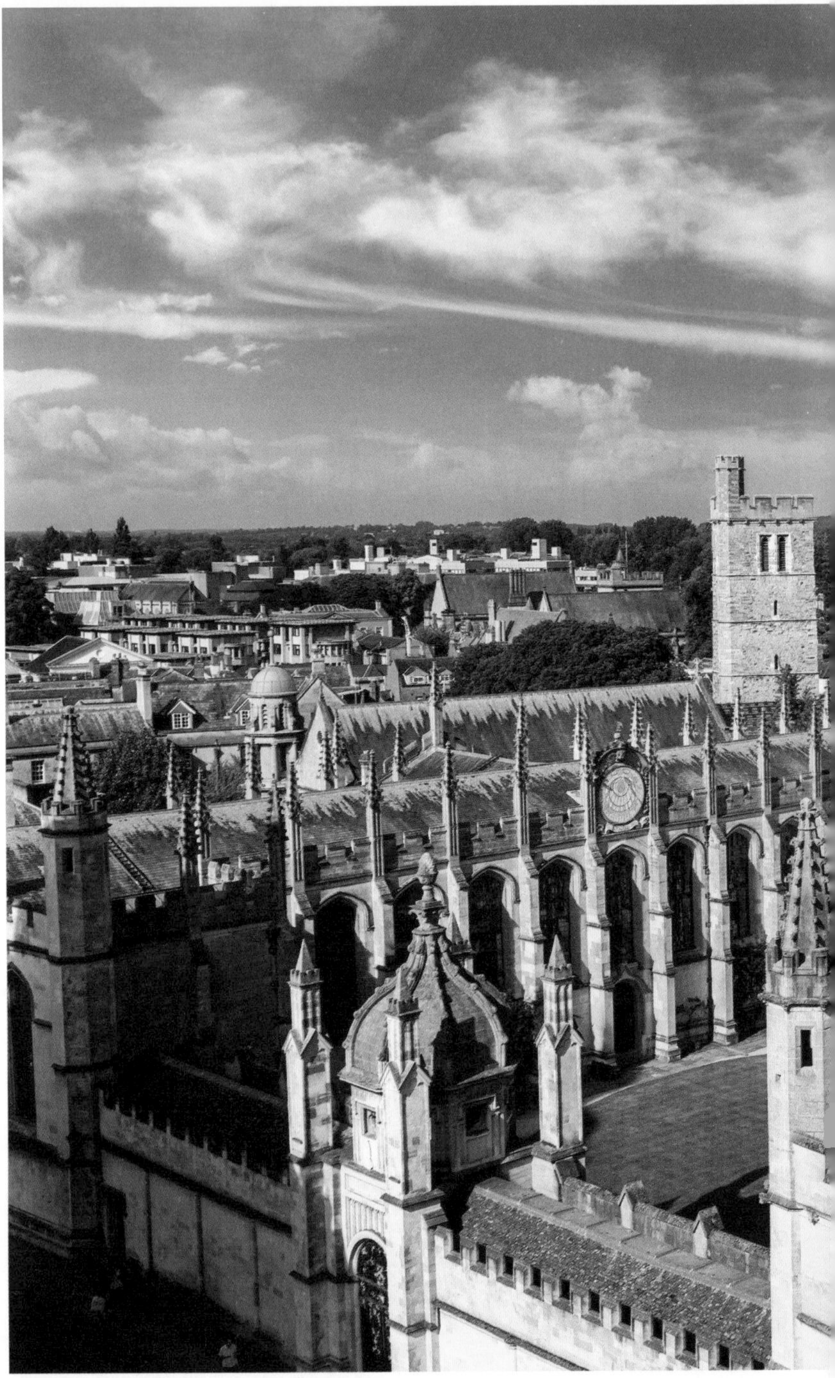
S-F / SHUTTERSTOCK ©

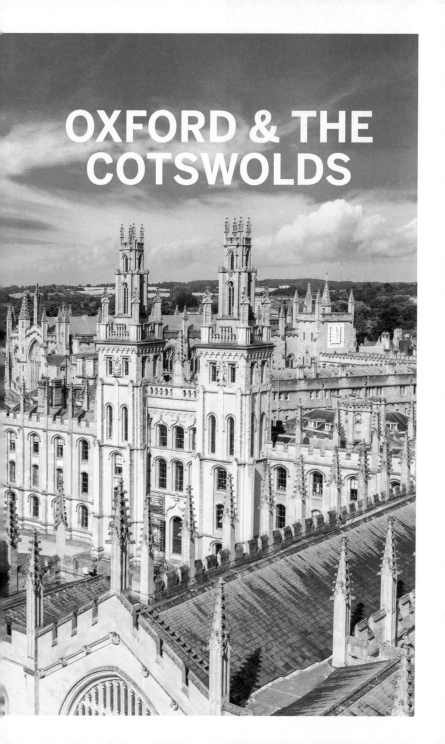

OXFORD & THE COTSWOLDS

Oxford & the Cotswolds at a Glance...

One of the world's most famous university cities, Oxford is steeped in history and studded with grandiose buildings, yet maintains a vibrant atmosphere, thanks in part to large student numbers. A few miles west, rolling gracefully across six counties, the Cotswolds are a delightful tangle of charming villages, thatch-roofed cottages and ancient mansions of gold-coloured stone. Like exposed beams, cream teas and cuisine full of local produce? Then the Cotswolds are calling.

Two Days in Oxford & the Cotswolds

Start day one gently – stroll through **college quads** (p128), marvel at fine buildings, sip pints in **pubs** (p143). Then head to **Turl St Kitchen** (p141) for a fine feed. On day two, take in the city's other sights, targeting the **Bodleian Library** (p138), the **Ashmolean Museum** (p138) and the **Pitt Rivers Museum** (p139). After a drink at the famous **Lamb & Flag** (p143), twiddle your chopsticks at **Edamamé** (p141).

Four Days in Oxford & the Cotswolds

On day three, immerse yourself in the ornate beauty of **Blenheim Palace** (p137), taking time to explore the exquisite, less-visited grounds. For supper, repair to the **Magdalen Arms** (p142) back in town. Next morning, begin your Cotswolds road trip, touring **Stow-on-the-Wold** (p134) and the **Slaughters** (p134) for starters. Foodie treats come courtesy of **Daylesford Organic** (p134) or **Mount Inn** (p144).

Previous page: All Souls College (p131)

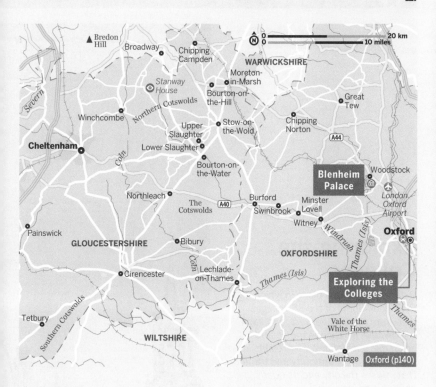

Arriving in Oxford & the Cotswolds

Oxford's excellent transport connections include rail services to London Paddington (£9.50 to £26.50, 1¼ hours), and National Express bus connections to Bath (£11.30, two hours) and London Victoria (£16, two hours).

Oxford Bus Company (www.oxford bus.co.uk) services go to Heathrow (£23, 1½ hours) and Gatwick (£28, two hours) airports. Trains and buses run to key Cotswolds towns, but it's easier to explore the villages by car.

Where to Stay

In Oxford, book ahead between May and September and on weekends. If stuck, there are plenty of B&Bs along Iffley, Abingdon, Banbury and Headington Rds. Budget accommodation options are clustered near the train station.

The Cotswolds overflow with exquisite hotels, but have fewer budget options (except in walker-friendly Winchcombe and Chipping Campden). Book ahead, especially during festivals and between May and August.

Brasenose College (p131)

Exploring the Colleges

Oxford is a glorious place in which to wander. Some of the 38 colleges date from the 13th century, and each is individual in its appearance and academic specialities. This results in an enchanting air of antiquity and tradition that infuses the city and its quads, halls, chapels and inns.

Great For...

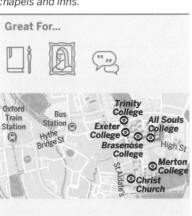

ℹ Need to Know

Visiting hours change with terms and exam schedules. Check www.ox.ac.uk for full details.

★ **Top Tip**

Take your time: atmosphere and details are the appeal here. Lingering and looking bring rewards.

Much of Oxford's centre is taken up by elegant university buildings. The gorgeous architecture and compact geography make strolling between them a joy.

Christ Church

The largest of all of Oxford's colleges, and the one with the grandest quad, **Christ Church** (☑01865-276492; www.chch.ox.ac.uk; St Aldate's; adult/child Jul & Aug £10/9, Sep-Jun £8/7; ☺10am-5pm Mon-Sat, from 2pm Sun, last admission 4.15pm) is also its most popular. It was founded in 1524 by Cardinal Thomas Wolsey. Past students include Albert Einstein, John Locke, WH Auden, Charles Dodgson (Lewis Carroll), and no fewer than 13 British prime ministers.

The main entrance to Christ Church, Tom Gate, stands immediately below the imposing 17th-century **Tom Tower**. Sir Christopher Wren, who studied at Christ Church, was responsible for its topmost portions. Pass by at 9.05pm, and you'll hear 101 chimes from its 6-tonne bell, Great Tom, to commemorate the curfew inflicted on the college's original students.

The college's imposing **Great Hall**, with its hammer-beam roof and distinguished portraits of past scholars, was replicated in film studios as the Hogwarts dining hall for the Harry Potter films. The grand fan-vaulted staircase that leads from it is where Professor McGonagall welcomed Harry in *Harry Potter and the Philosopher's Stone*.

Merton College

Founded in 1264, **Merton** (☑01865-276310; www.merton.ox.ac.uk; Merton St; adult/child £3/free; ☺2-5pm Mon-Fri, from 10am Sat & Sun) is the oldest of Oxford's colleges. Its celebrated architectural features include large gargoyles, the charming 14th-century

Bodleian Library (p138)

Mob Quad, and a 13th-century chapel. The Old Library is the oldest medieval library in use; it's said that Tolkien, a Merton English professor, spent many hours here writing *The Lord of the Rings* and that the trees in the Fellows' Garden inspired the ents of Middle Earth. Other literary alumni include TS Eliot and Louis MacNeice.

All Souls College

One of the wealthiest and most peaceful Oxford colleges, **All Souls** (01865-279379; www.asc.ox.ac.uk; High St; 2-4pm Sun-Fri, closed Aug) FREE was founded in 1438 as a centre of prayer and learning. Much of the college facade dates from the 1440s and

> ☑ **Don't Miss**
>
> Christ Church's Harry Potter film connections: seek out the Great Hall and its sweeping staircase.

JJFARQ / SHUTTERSTOCK ©

the smaller Front Quad is largely unchanged in five centuries. Most eye-catching are the twin mock-Gothic towers on the North Quad; it also contains a 17th-century sundial designed by Christopher Wren.

Brasenose College

The main draw at **Brasenose** (01865-277830; www.bnc.ox.ac.uk; Radcliffe Sq; £2; 10-11.30am & 2-5pm Mon-Fri, 9.30-10.30am & 2-5pm Sat & Sun) is a chapel with a fine painted, vaulted ceiling. A small elegant college, it was founded in 1509. Famous alumni include *Lord of the Flies* author William Golding, Monty Python's Michael Palin and British prime minister David Cameron.

Exeter College

Founded in 1314, **Exeter** (01865-279600; www.exeter.ox.ac.uk; Turl St; 2-5pm) FREE is known for its elaborate 17th-century dining hall, which celebrated its 400th birthday in 2018, and ornate Victorian Gothic chapel which holds a tapestry created by former students William Morris and Edward Burne Jones, *The Adoration of the Magi*. Exeter also inspired former student Philip Pullman to create fictional Jordan College in *His Dark Materials*.

Trinity College

Founded in 1555, the highlight of this small **college** (01865-279900; www.trinity.ox.ac. uk; Broad St; adult/child £3/2; 9.30am-noon & 2pm-dusk) is a lovely 17th-century garden quad, designed by Christopher Wren. Its exquisitely carved chapel is one of the city's most beautiful and a masterpiece of English baroque. Famous students have included Cardinal Newman and British Prime Minister, William Pitt the Elder.

> ✕ **Take a Break**
>
> After strolling around Christ Church's Great Hall and Tom Quad, peel off into the nearby streets for a drink or a snack at the ancient and atmospheric **Bear Inn** (01865-728164; www.bearoxford. co.uk; 6 Alfred St; 11am-11pm Mon-Thu, to midnight Fri & Sat, 11.30am-10.30pm Sun).

Lower Slaughter (p134)

Driving the Cotswolds

The Cotswolds lie just west of Oxford, a bewitching network of winding country lanes that link ancient market towns, time-warped villages and majestic stately homes. The landscape is England's second-largest protected area after the Lake District and the gentle yet dramatic hills are perfect for touring by car.

Great For...

❶ Need to Know

The most popular villages can be besieged by traffic and visitors, especially in summer. Visit the main centres early in the morning or late in the evening.

★ **Top Tip**

Stretch your trip to two or three days to really soak up the local life.

The Slaughters

The picture-postcard villages of Upper and Lower Slaughter have maintained their unhurried medieval charm. The village names have nothing to do with abattoirs; they are derived from the Old English 'sloughtre', meaning slough or muddy place. Today the River Eye is contained within limestone banks and meanders peacefully through the two villages, past classic gold-tinged Cotswolds houses and the **Old Mill** (☎01451-820052; www.oldmill-lowerslaughter.com; Lower Slaughter; adult/child £2.50/1; ⏰10am-6pm Mar-Oct, to dusk Nov-Feb), now home to a cafe, crafts shop and small museum.

Stow-on-the-Wold & Daylesford Organic

The highest town in the Cotswolds (244m), Stow is anchored by a large market square surrounded by handsome buildings and steep-walled alleyways, originally used to funnel sheep into the fair. The town is famous for its twice-yearly **Stow Horse Fair** (⏰mid-May & late Oct), but it attracts plenty of visitors year-round.

Four miles east of Stow, **Daylesford Organic** (☎01608-731700; www.daylesford.com; Daylesford; ⏰8am-8pm Mon-Sat, 10am-4pm Sun) 🍴 is a country-chic temple to the Cotswolds' organic movement. The award-winning agricultural operation includes a gleaming food hall crammed with Daylesford-brand produce and an excellent cafe-restaurant that dishes up a daily-changing menu of organic treats (£13 to £19).

Chipping Campden

Pretty Chipping Campden boasts an array of fine terraced houses and ancient inns,

Stow-on-the-Wold

most made of beautiful honey-coloured Cotswolds stone. There are particularly striking thatch-roofed cottages along Westington, at the southwestern end of town.

One of the grandest residences is 14th-century **Grevel House** (High St; ⊘closed to the public) – look out for its splendid Perpendicular Gothic–style gabled window and sundial.

Stanway House

This magnificent Jacobean **mansion** (☏01386-584469; www.stanwayfountain.co.uk;

NIGEL JARVIS / SHUTTERSTOCK ©

Stanway; adult/child £9/4; ⊘2-5pm Tue & Thu Jun-Aug), hidden behind a triple-gabled gatehouse, has beautiful baroque water gardens featuring Britain's tallest fountain, which erupts, geyser-like, to 300ft. The manor has been the private home of the Earls of Wemyss for 500 years and has a delightful, lived-in charm with much of its original furniture and character intact.

Winchcombe

In Winchcombe, butchers, bakers and independent shops still line the main streets. The capital of the Anglo-Saxon kingdom of Mercia, it was one of the major towns in the Cotswolds until the Middle Ages. Today reminders of this past can be seen in Winchcombe's dramatic stone and half-timbered buildings, and the picturesque cottages on Vineyard St and Dents Tce.

Set on Winchcombe's southeast edge, the magnificent **Sudeley Castle** (☏01242-604244; www.sudeleycastle.co.uk; adult/child £16.50/7.50; ⊘10am-5pm mid-Mar–Oct; P♿) has welcomed many a monarch over its thousand-year history, including Richard III, Henry VIII and Charles I. It's most famous as the home and final resting place of Catherine Parr (Henry VIII's widow), who lived here with her fourth husband, Thomas Seymour. You'll find Catherine's tomb in the castle's Perpendicular Gothic St Mary's Church, making this the only private house in England where a queen is buried.

The 10 splendid gardens include spectacular avenues of sculpted yews and an intricate knot garden. The rose-filled Queen's Garden gets its name from having been strolled in by four English queens: Anne Boleyn, Katherine Parr, Lady Jane Grey and Elizabeth I.

EDWIN BUTTER / SHUTTERSTOCK ©

Blenheim Palace

One of Britain's greatest stately homes, Blenheim Palace is a monumental baroque fantasy. With ornate architecture and lush parklands, it's also the birthplace of Prime Minister, Sir Winston Churchill.

Blenheim Palace was designed by Sir John Vanbrugh and Nicholas Hawksmoor, and built between 1705 and 1722. The land and funds to build the house were granted to John Churchill, Duke of Marlborough, by a grateful Queen Anne, after his victory over the French at the 1704 Battle of Blenheim. Sir Winston Churchill was born here in 1874. Now a Unesco World Heritage Site, Blenheim is still home to the 12th duke.

The Great Hall

Beyond majestic oak doors, the house is stuffed with statues, tapestries, ostentatious furniture, priceless china, and giant oil paintings in elaborate gilt frames. Visits start in the Great Hall, a soaring space topped by a 20m-high ceiling adorned with images of the first duke. To the right upon entering is the Churchill Exhibition,

Great For...

☑ Don't Miss

Exploring the impressive grounds – full of features they were landscaped by Lancelot 'Capability' Brown.

State Dining Room

DE AGOSTINI / S. VANNINI / GETTY IMAGES ©

ⓘ Need to Know

☏01993-810530; www.blenheimpalace.com; Woodstock; adult/child £26/14.50, park & gardens only £16/7.40; ⊙palace 10.30am-5.30pm, park & gardens 9am-6.30pm or dusk; Ⓟ

✕ Take a Break

Blenheim's Orangery Restaurant serves everything from three-course lunches to afternoon tea.

★ Top Tip

Free, 45-minute guided tours depart every 30 minutes, except Sunday, when there are guides in all rooms.

dedicated to the life, work, paintings and writings of Sir Winston Churchill. The British war-time prime minister was a descendant of the Dukes of Marlborough and is buried nearby in Bladon graveyard.

House Highlights

Must-sees include the famous Blenheim Tapestries, a set of 10 large wall hangings commemorating the first duke's triumphs; the State Dining Room, with its painted walls and trompe l'oeil ceilings; and the magnificent Long Library, overlooked by an elaborate 1738 statue of Queen Anne.

The Untold Story

Upstairs, the Untold Story exhibit sees a ghostly chambermaid leading you through a series of tableaux recreating important scenes from the palace's history.

Tours

As well as free, 45-minute guided tours of the house (Monday to Saturday), from February to September, you can also join tours (adult/child £6/5) of the Duke's private apartments, the palace's bedrooms or the household staff areas.

The Grounds

If the crowds in the house become too oppressive, escape into the vast, lavish gardens and park lands, parts of which were landscaped by the great Capability Brown. A minitrain (50p) takes visitors to the Pleasure Gardens, which feature a yew maze, adventure playground, lavender garden and butterfly house.

For quieter and longer strolls, there are glorious walks of up to 4.5 miles, leading past lakes to an arboretum, rose garden, cascade and temple, and Vanbrugh's Grand Bridge.

Oxford

◎ SIGHTS

Bodleian Library
Library

(☑01865-287400; www.bodleian.ox.ac.uk/
bodley; Catte St; Divinity School £1, with audio
tour £3.50, guided tours £6-14; ☺9am-5pm Mon-
Sat, from 11am Sun) At least five kings, dozens
of prime ministers and Nobel laureates,
and luminaries such as Oscar Wilde, CS
Lewis and JRR Tolkien have studied in
Oxford's Bodleian Library, a magnificent
survivor from the Middle Ages. Wander into
its central 17th-century quad, and you can
admire its ancient buildings for free, while it
costs just £1 to enter the most impressive
of these, the 15th-century Divinity School.
To see the rest of the complex, though,
you'll have to join a guided tour.

Ashmolean Museum
Museum

(☑01865-278000; www.ashmolean.org; Beaumont St; ☺10am-5pm Tue-Sun, to 8pm last Fri of
month) **FREE** Britain's oldest public museum,
Oxford's wonderful Ashmolean Museum is
surpassed only by the British Museum in

London. It was established in 1683, when
Elias Ashmole presented Oxford University
with a collection of 'rarities' amassed by the
well-travelled John Tradescant, gardener
to Charles I. A new exhibition celebrates
Ashmole's 400th birthday by displaying
original treasures including the hat worn
by the judge who presided over the trial of
Charles I, and a mantle belonging to 'Chief
Powhatan', the father of Pocahontas.

Radcliffe Camera
Library

(☑01865-287400; www.bodleian.ox.ac.uk;
Radcliffe Sq; tours £14; ☺Bodleian tours 9.15am
Wed & Sat, 11.15am & 1.15pm Sun) Surely
Oxford's most photographed landmark, the
sandy-gold Radcliffe Camera is a beautiful,
light-filled, circular, columned library. Built
between 1737 and 1749 in grand Palladian
style, as 'Radcliffe Library', it's topped by
Britain's third-largest dome. It's only been a
'camera', which simply means 'room', since
1860, when it lost its independence and
became what it remains, a reading room
of the Bodleian Library. The only way for
nonmembers to see the interior is on an
extended 1½-hour tour of the Bodleian.

Ashmolean Museum

Pitt Rivers Museum   Museum

(📞01865-270927; www.prm.ox.ac.uk; South Parks Rd; ⏱noon-4.30pm Mon, from 10am Tue-Sun; 🚼) **FREE** If exploring an enormous room full of eccentric and unexpected artefacts sounds like your idea of the perfect afternoon, welcome to the amulets-to-zithers extravaganza that is the Pitt Rivers museum. Tucked behind Oxford's **natural-history museum** (📞01865-272950; www.oum.ox.ac.uk; Parks Rd; ⏱10am-5pm; 🚼) **FREE**, and dimly lit to protect its myriad treasures, it's centred on an anthropological collection amassed by a Victorian general, and revels in exploring how differing cultures have tackled topics like 'Smoking and Stimulants' or 'Treatment of Dead Enemies'.

Museum of the History of Science   Museum

(📞01865-277293; www.mhs.ox.ac.uk; Broad St; ⏱noon-5pm Tue-Sun) **FREE** Students of science will swoon at this fascinating museum, stuffed to the ceilings with awesome astrolabes, astonishing orreries and early electrical apparatus. Housed in the lovely 17th-century building that held the original Ashmolean Museum, it displays everything from cameras that belonged to Lewis Carroll and Lawrence of Arabia to a wireless receiver used by Marconi in 1896 and a blackboard that was covered with equations by Einstein in 1931, when he was invited to give three lectures on relativity.

University Church of St Mary the Virgin   Church

(📞01865-279111; www.university-church.ox.ac.uk; High St; church free, tower £4; ⏱9am-5pm Mon-Sat, from noon Sun Sep-Jun, 9am-6pm daily Jul & Aug) The ornate 14th-century spire of Oxford's university church is arguably the dreamiest of the city's legendary 'dreaming spires'. Otherwise, this is famous as the site where three Anglican bishops, including the first Protestant archbishop of Canterbury, Thomas Cranmer, were tried for heresy in 1556, during the reign of Mary I. All three were later burned at the stake on Broad St. Visitors can climb the church's 1280 tower (£4) for excellent views of the adjacent Radcliffe Camera (p138).

Magdalen Bridge Boathouse: Worth a Punt

Punting, the quintessential Oxford experience, is all about lounging back in a flat-bottomed boat and sipping Pimms (the classic, cooling English summer drink) as you watch the city's glorious architecture drift by. Right beside Magdalen Bridge, this **boathouse** (📞01865-202643; www.oxfordpunting.co.uk; High St; chauffeured 4-person punts per 30min £32, punt rental per hour £22; ⏱9.30am-dusk Feb-Nov) is the most central location to hire a punt, chauffeured or otherwise. From here you can either head downstream around the Botanic Garden and Christ Church Meadow, or upstream around Magdalen Deer Park.

Punting in front of Magdalen Bridge
ZOONAR / GRAHAM MULROO / AGE FOTOSTOCK ©

Bridge of Sighs   Bridge

(Hertford Bridge; New College Lane) As you stroll along New College Lane, look up at the steeped Bridge of Sighs linking the two halves of Hertford College. Completed in 1914, it's sometimes erroneously referred to as a copy of the famous bridge in Venice, but it looks much more like that city's Rialto Bridge.

🎯 TOURS

Oxford Official Walking Tours   Walking

(📞01865-686441; www.experienceoxfordshire.org; 15-16 Broad St; adult/child from £14/10; ⏱10.45am & 1pm, extra tours 11am & 2pm during busy periods; 🚼) Comprehensive two-hour tours of the city and its colleges, plus several themed

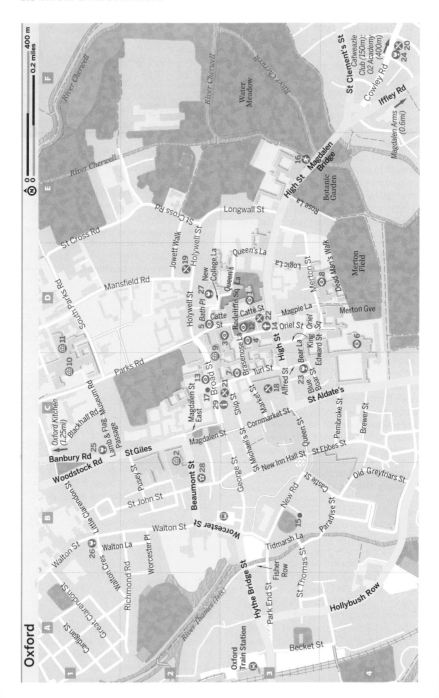

Oxford

Oxford

tours, including one devoted to *Alice's Adventures in Wonderland* and Harry Potter, another to CS Lewis and JRR Tolkien, and a third to Inspector Morse. Check online for details, or book at the tourist office (p144).

Oxford Walking Tours　　Walking
(🖉07790 734387; www.oxfordwalkingtours. com; Trinity College, Broad St; adult/child £13/6; ⊙11am, noon, 1pm, 2pm, 3pm & 4pm; 👪) These informative 90-minute tours, covering the story of Oxford and its university, set off hourly, year-round, from the gates of Trinity College. Rates include admission to the Bodleian's Divinity School and certain colleges, usually including New College. They also offer a weekly literary tour (2pm Wednesday, adult/child £15/8); ghost tours to varying schedules (£13/6); and Tolkien tours on request.

✕ EATING

Edamamé　　Japanese £
(🖉01865-246916; www.edamame.co.uk; 15 Holywell St; mains £7-10.50; ⊙11.30am-2.30pm Wed, 11.30am-2.30pm & 5-8.30pm Thu-Sat, noon-3.30pm Sun; 🖉) No wonder a constant stream of students squeeze in and out of

this tiny diner – it's Oxford's top spot for delicious, gracefully simple Japanese cuisine. Changing noodle and curry specials include fragrant chicken miso ramen, tofu stir-fries, or mackerel with soba noodles; it only serves sushi or sashimi on Thursday evenings. No bookings; arrive early and be prepared to wait.

Covered Market　　Market £
(www.oxford-coveredmarket.co.uk; Market St; ⊙vary, some close Sun; 🛜🖉👪) A haven for impecunious students, this indoor marketplace holds 20 restaurants, cafes and takeaways. Let anyone loose here, and something's sure to catch their fancy. Brown's no-frills cafe, famous for its apple pies, is the longest-standing veteran. Look out, too, for Georgina's, serving quiches and burgers upstairs; Burt's superlative Cookies; two excellent pie shops; and good Thai and Chinese options.

Turl Street Kitchen　Modern British ££
(🖉01865-264171; www.turlstreetkitchen. co.uk; 16-17 Turl St; mains £10-16; ⊙8-10am, noon-2.30pm & 6.30-10pm; 🖉) 🍃 Whatever time you drop into this laid-back, not-quite-scruffy, seductively charming all-day bistro, with its fairy lights and faded-wood tables,

Oxford Ghost Trail

For a theatrical and entertaining voyage through Oxford's uncanny underbelly, plus the occasional magic trick, take a 1¾-hour **tour** (📞07941-041811; www.ghosttrail. org; Oxford Castle; adult/child £10/7; ☉6.30pm Fri & Sat; 👶) with Victorian undertaker Bill Spectre. No bookings needed, audience participation more than likely.

Bridge of Sighs (p139)
ACOBA / SHUTTERSTOCK ©

you can expect to eat well. Fresh local produce is thrown into creative combinations, with the changing menu featuring the likes of roasted beetroot, braised lamb, or, on Sunday, roast beef and Yorkshire pudding. It also serves good cakes and coffee.

Vaults & Garden   Cafe £

(📞01865-279112; www.thevaultsandgarden. com; University Church of St Mary the Virgin, Radcliffe Sq; mains £7-10.50; ☉9am-6pm; 🛜🅿) ✔ This beautiful lunch venue spreads from the vaulted 14th-century Old Congregation House of the University Church into a garden facing the Radcliffe Camera. Come early, and queue at the counter to choose from wholesome organic specials such as leek-and-potato soup, tofu massaman curry, or slow-roasted lamb *tajine* (North African hot pot). Breakfast and afternoon tea (those scones!) are equally good.

Spiced Roots   Caribbean ££

(📞01865-249888; www.spicedroots.com; 64 Cowley Rd; mains £12-17.50; ☉6-10pm Tue & Wed, noon-3pm & 6-10pm Thu-Sat, noon-8pm Sun; 🅿) From black rice with pomegranate to oxtail with mac cheese and plantains – and, of course, spicy jerk chicken – everything is just perfection at this flawless new Caribbean restaurant. There are plenty of vegetarian options too, as well as curried fish or goat, while adding a cocktail or two from the thatched rum bar is pretty much irresistible.

Magdalen Arms   British ££

(📞01865-243159; www.magdalenarms.co.uk; 243 Iffley Rd; mains £14-42; ☉5-11pm Mon, from 10am Tue-Sat, 10am-10.30pm Sun; 🅿👶) A mile beyond Magdalen Bridge, this extra-special neighbourhood gastropub has won plaudits from the national press. A friendly, informal spot, it offers indoor and outdoor space for drinkers, and dining tables further back. From vegetarian specials such as broad-bean tagliatelle to the fabulous sharing-size steak-and-ale pie – well, it's a stew with a suet-crust lid, really – everything is delicious, with gutsy flavours.

On the first Saturday of each month it holds a flea market outside, starting at 9.30am.

Oxford Kitchen   Modern British £££

(📞01865-511149; www.theoxfordkitchen. co.uk; 215 Banbury Rd; set menus £22.50-65; ☉noon-2.30pm & 6-9.30pm Tue-Sat) Oxford's not renowned for high-end, cutting-edge cuisine, so if you're crying out for a few foams, mousses, funny-shaped plates and bumpy slates, make haste to Summertown's contemporary Oxford Kitchen. We jest; it's modern British food, served as set menus ranging from £22.50 for a weekday lunch up to the £65 weekend tasting menu, is superb.

🍷 DRINKING & NIGHTLIFE

Turf Tavern   Pub

(📞01865-243235; www.turftavern-oxford.co.uk; 4-5 Bath Pl; ☉11am-11pm; 🛜) Squeezed down an alleyway and subdivided into endless nooks and crannies, this medieval rabbit warren dates from around 1381. The definitive Oxford pub, this is where Bill Clinton famously 'did not inhale'; other patrons have included Oscar Wilde, Stephen Hawking and Margaret Thatcher. Home to a fabulous array of real ales and ciders, it's always pretty crowded, but there's outdoor seating, too.

Lamb & Flag   Pub

(12 St Giles; ⊙noon-11pm Mon-Sat, to 10.30pm Sun; 🛜) This relaxed 17th-century tavern remains one of Oxford's nicest pubs for a sturdy pint or glass of wine. Thomas Hardy wrote (and set) parts of *Jude the Obscure* at these very tables, while CS Lewis and JRR Tolkien shifted their custom here in later years. The food's nothing special, but buying a pint helps fund scholarships at St John's College.

Raoul's   Cocktail Bar

(📞01865-553732; www.raoulsbar.com; 32 Walton St; ⊙4pm-midnight Sun-Tue, to 1am Fri & Sat) A long-established local favourite, Jericho's finest retro-look bar is renowned for its expertly mixed cocktails – typically priced at around £7.50, and infused with fresh fruit – along with its moody booths, laid-back lounge music, and 'watering can' sharing concoctions.

Café Tarifa   Bar

(📞01865-256091; www.cafe-tarifa.co.uk; 56-60 Cowley Rd; ⊙5pm-midnight Mon-Thu, to 1am Fri, 10am-1am Sat, 10am-11pm Sun; 🛜) Inspired by the eponymous Spanish kitesurfing centre, this low-key lounge spot is big on neo-Moorish style, with cushioned booths, low-slung tables, tile-patterned sinks and cushy beanbags. There's a wide selection of cocktails, plus a menu of tapas and Mediterranean snacks, movie nights and live music.

✪ ENTERTAINMENT

Creation Theatre   Theatre

(📞01865-766266; www.creationtheatre.co.uk) This ambitious theatre company produces highly original shows – often Shakespeare, but also anything from *Dracula* to *The Wind in the Willows* – that are bursting with magic, quirk and special effects. It then performs them in all sorts of non-traditional venues, including city parks, the Westgate Shopping Centre, various colleges and Oxford Castle.

Oxford Playhouse   Theatre

(📞01865-305305; www.oxfordplayhouse.com; Beaumont St) Oxford's main stage for quality drama also hosts an impressive selection of touring music, dance and theatre

Oxford Playhouse

The Cotswolds' Best Eateries

Wheatsheaf (☎01451-860244; www.cotswoldswheatsheaf.com; West End; mains £14.50-24; ☺8-10am, noon-3pm & 6-9pm Mon-Thu & Sun, to 10pm Fri & Sat; P ? ♦) Lively, stylish and laid-back, this beautifully revamped coaching inn serves excellent, elegant seasonal British dishes with a contemporary kick.

5 North St (☎01242-604566; www.5northstreetrestaurant.co.uk; 5 North St; 2-/3-course lunch £26/32, 3-/7-course dinner £54/74; ☺7-9pm Tue, 12.30-1.30pm & 7-9pm Wed-Sat, 12.30-1.30pm Sun; ♦) This veteran gourmet restaurant is a treat from start to finish, from its splendid 400-year-old timbered exterior to the elegant, inventive creations you find on your plate.

Badgers Hall (☎01386-840839; www.badgershall.com; High St; lunch mains £6-12, afternoon tea per person £6.50-25; ☺8am-5.30pm Thu-Sat; ♦) Set in a glorious old mansion facing the market hall, this definitive Cotswold tearoom is renowned for its no-holds-barred afternoon teas, served from 2.30pm onward.

Mount Inn (☎01386-584316; www.themountinn.co.uk; Stanton; mains £13-22; ☺noon-2pm & 6-9pm Mon-Sat, to 8pm Sun; P) Revelling in glorious hilltop views above pretty honey-washed Stanton, just off the Cotswolds Way 3.5 miles southwest of Broadway, this pub is idyllically located and serves hearty country favourites, prepared with contemporary flair.

Wheatsheaf

performances. The Burton Taylor Studio often features quirky student productions and other innovative pieces.

Catweazle Club Live Music

(www.catweazleclub.com; East Oxford Social Club, 44 Princes St; cover £6; ☺8pm Thu) This legendary weekly open-mic night has migrated from venue to venue. Now firmly ensconced at the East Oxford Social Club, it features an ever-changing panoply of musicians, poets, writers and all sorts of bohemian performers.

O2 Academy Live Music

(☎01865-813500; www.academymusicgroup.com/o2academyoxford; 190 Cowley Rd) Oxford's busiest club and live-music venue (previously known as the Venue and the Zodiac, way back when) hosts everything from big-name DJs and international touring artists to indie bands and hard rock.

INFORMATION

Tourist Office (☎01865-686430; www.experienceoxfordshire.org; 15-16 Broad St; ☺9am-5.30pm Mon-Sat, 10am-4pm Sun Jul & Aug, 9.30am-5pm Mon-Sat, 10am-4pm Sun Sep-Jun) Covers the whole of Oxfordshire. Sells Oxford guidebooks, makes reservations for local accommodation and walking tours, and sells tickets for events and attractions.

GETTING THERE & AWAY

Oxford's chaotic outdoor **bus station** is in the centre, on Gloucester Green near the corner of Worcester and George Sts. The main bus companies are **Oxford Bus Company** (☎01865-785400; www.oxfordbus.co.uk), **Stagecoach** (☎01865-772250; www.stagecoachbus.com) and **Swanbrook** (☎01452-712386; www.swanbrook.co.uk).

Oxford's main train station is conveniently located just west of the city centre.

ⓘ GETTING AROUND

Foot Oxford is a small city, so most visitors walk pretty much everywhere. It takes around 10 to 15 minutes to cross the centre on foot, while all the city's major attractions lie within half a mile of the centre.

Bicycle Cycling is the perfect way to get around this pocket-sized ancient city.

Car A car can be useful to explore the surrounding countryside, or reach rural pubs and restaurants, but it's a liability in the city centre.

Burford

Gliding down a steep hillside to an ancient (and still single-lane) crossing point on the River Windrush, 20 miles west of Oxford, Burford has hardly changed since its medieval glory days. Locals insist it's a town not a village, having received its charter in 1090, but it's a very small town, and a very picturesque one too, home to an appealing mix of stone cottages, gold-tinged Cotswold town houses, and the odd Elizabethan or Georgian treasure.

◎ SIGHTS

St John the Baptist's Church   Church

(www.burfordchurch.org; Church Lane; ⊙9am-5pm) Burford's splendid church, near the river, took over three centuries to build, from 1175 onwards. Its fan-vaulted ceiling, Norman west doorway and 15th-century spire remain intact. The star attraction is the macabre 1625 Tanfield tomb, depicting local nobleman Sir Lawrence Tanfield and his wife lying in finery above a pair of carved skeletons, one leg bone of which is said to be real.

Cotswold Wildlife Park   Zoo

(☑01993-823006; www.cotswoldwildlifepark. co.uk; Bradwell Grove; adult/child £16/10.50; ⊙10am-6pm Apr-Oct, to 5pm or dusk Nov-Mar, last admission 2hr before closing; P⛟) ✎ Younger visitors in particular will enjoy this hugely popular wildlife centre, 3 miles south of Burford. Its vast 250-species menagerie includes penguins, zebras, lions, reindeer, anacondas, endangered white rhinos and a giant tortoise. A miniature train takes the excitement up a notch.

⊗ EATING

Swan Inn   Modern British ££

(☑01993-823339; www.theswanswinbrook. co.uk; Swinbrook; mains £16-26; ⊙noon-2pm & 7-9pm; P) With a maze of lively rooms, roaring winter fires and bench tables overlooking a gorgeous orchard, this popular riverside gastropub, 3 miles east of Burford, oozes appeal. Its seasonal British menu mixes a pinch of creativity with quality, mostly local ingredients, offering original starters (like Stilton soufflé) and sharing platters alongside succulent meaty mains. Bookings recommended.

Huffkins   Bakery, Cafe ££

(☑01993-824694; www.huffkins.com; 98 High St; mains £6-15; ⊙9am-4.30pm Mon-Fri, to 5pm Sat, 10am-5pm Sun; ⛟) The original outlet of a Cotswolds chain that's been baking and serving delicious scones, cakes and pies since 1890, this lively, friendly cafe is usually packed with locals enjoying quiches, soups, macaroni cheese or burgers. It also offers all-day cooked breakfasts and full-blown afternoon teas. For a quick snack, pick up baked goods in its adjoining deli.

⊕ DRINKING & NIGHTLIFE

Several of Burford's lively pubs have pretty back gardens to enjoy in sunny weather.

❶ INFORMATION

Tourist Office (☑01993-823558; www.oxford shirecotswolds.org; 33a High St; ⊙9.30am-5pm Mon-Sat, 10am-5pm Sun) Information on local walks.

❶ GETTING THERE & AWAY

Bus Stagecoach and Swanbrook buses run to/from Burford, including to Oxford (route 853; £6.30, 45 minutes to 1¼ hours).

Car Standing conveniently just north of the A40, Burford is one of the easiest Cotswold towns to reach by road. It's often the first port of call for drivers coming from Oxford (20 miles east) or London (75 miles southeast).

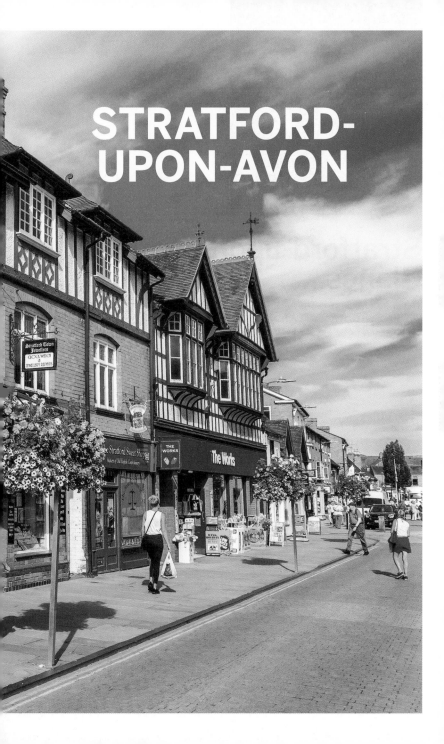

STRATFORD-UPON-AVON

Stratford-upon-Avon at a Glance...

The author of some of the most-quoted lines ever written in the English language, William Shakespeare, was born in Stratford in 1564 and died here in 1616. Experiences linked to his life in this unmistakably Tudor town range from the intriguing (his schoolroom) via the humbling (his grave) to the sublime (a performance at the Royal Shakespeare Company).

Two Days in Stratford-upon-Avon

Discover the Bard's home town on a two-hour guided **walk** (p154). Continue explorations at his **birthplace** (p152) and **classroom** (p152), before repairing to **Salt** (p156) for a lovely evening meal. On day two, take in the outlying Bard-related sights: **Anne Hathaway's Cottage** (p152) and **Mary Arden's Farm** (p152). For supper, it's back to town for more treats at **Townhouse** (p155).

Four Days in Stratford-upon-Avon

Start day three in grand style at the extravagantly Elizabethan **Charlecote Park** (p154), before a cruise down the **Avon** (p154) and dinner at **Edward Moon's** (p156). On your fourth day, shop for that perfect Shakespeare souvenir; have a pint at the oldest put in town, the **Old Thatch Tavern** (p156); then delight in an outstanding performance at the **Royal Shakespeare Company** (p157).

Previous page: Half-timbered houses in Stratford-upon-Avon

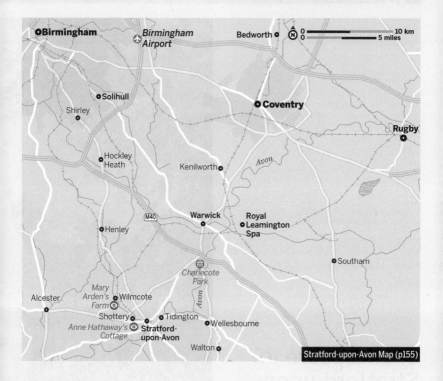

Stratford-upon-Avon Map (p155)

Arriving in Stratford-upon-Avon

Bus National Express coach services include those to London Victoria (£13.10, three hours, two daily) and Oxford (£10.10, one hour, one daily).

Car Stratford is 100 miles (two hours) northwest of London and 85 miles (two hours) north of Bath. Town car parks charge high fees.

Train Services include those to London Marylebone (£30.40, 2¾ hours, up to two per hour).

Where to Stay

B&Bs are plentiful, particularly along Grove Rd and Evesham Pl, but vacancies can be hard to find during the high season – check listings on www.shakespeare-country.co.uk. The tourist office can help with bookings.

Anne Hathaway's Cottage (p152)

Shakespeare in Stratford-upon-Avon

Stratford (the 'upon Avon' is dropped locally) is a delightful Tudor town that's fascinating to wander – even a short stroll here leads around a living, breathing map of Shakespeare's life. As well as being home to both his birth and burial place, the town also stages world-class performances of the Bard's plays.

Great For...

❶ Need to Know

The Shakespeare Birthplace Trust (www.shakespeare.org.uk) offers combined tickets (adult/child £22/14.50) to five key sights.

★ Top Tip

Visit the arboretum at Anne Hathaway's Cottage (p152) for examples of the trees mentioned in Shakespeare's plays.

Shakespeare's Birthplace

Start your Shakespeare quest at the **house** (☏01789-204016; www.shakespeare.org.uk; Henley St; adult/child £17.50/11.50; ⊙9am-5pm Apr-Aug, to 4.30pm Sep & Oct, 10am-3.30pm Nov-Mar) where the renowned playwright was born in 1564 and spent his childhood days. John Shakespeare owned the house for a period of 50 years. William, as the eldest surviving son, inherited it upon his father's death in 1601 and spent his first five years of marriage here. Behind a modern facade, the house has restored Tudor rooms, live presentations from famous Shakespearean characters and an engaging exhibition on Stratford's favourite son.

Shakespeare's Childhood

Shakespeare's alma mater, King Edward VI School (still a prestigious grammar school today), incorporates a vast black-and-white timbered building, dating from 1420, that was once the town's guildhall. Upstairs, in the Bard's former **classroom** (☏01789-203170; www.shakespearesschoolroom.org; King Edward VI School, Church St; adult/child £8/5; ⊙11am-5pm), you can sit in on mock-Tudor lessons, watch a short film and test yourself on Tudor-style homework.

Shakespeare's Family

Before tying the knot with Shakespeare, Anne Hathaway lived in Shottery, 1 mile west of the centre of Stratford, in a delightful thatched **cottage** (☏01789-338532; www.shakespeare.org.uk; Cottage Lane, Shottery; adult/child £12.50/8; ⊙9am-5pm Apr-Aug, to 4.30pm Sep & Oct, 10am-3.30pm Nov-Mar). As well as period furniture, the farmhouse has gorgeous gardens and an orchard and fine

arboretum. A footpath (no bikes allowed) leads to Shottery from Evesham Pl.

The childhood home of Mary Arden, Shakespeare's mother, can be found at Wilmcote, 3 miles west of Stratford. Aimed squarely at families, the working **farm** (☏01789-338535; www.shakespeare.org.uk; Station Rd, Wilmcote; adult/child £15/10; ⊙10am-5pm Apr-Aug, to 4.30pm Sep & Oct; 🐾) traces country life over the centuries, with nature trails, falconry displays and a collection of rare-breed farm animals. You can get here on the City Sightseeing bus (p154) or cycle via Anne Hathaway's Cottage, following the Stratford-upon-Avon Canal towpath.

Hall's Croft (☏01789-338533; www.shakespeare.org.uk; Old Town; adult/child £8.50/5.50; ⊙10am-5pm Apr-Aug, to 4.30pm Sep & Oct, 11am-3.30pm Nov-Feb), the

Hall's Croft

✕ Take a Break

The Townhouse (p155) is a delightful spot – pause the Shakespearean sightseeing for a while to feast in a 400-year-old building.

handsome Jacobean townhouse belonging to Shakespeare's daughter Susanna and her husband, respected doctor John Hall, stands south of the centre. The exhibition offers fascinating insights into medicine in the 16th and 17th centuries, and the lovely walled garden sprouts with aromatic herbs employed in medicinal preparations.

Later Years

When Shakespeare retired, he swapped the bright lights of London for a comfortable town house at **New Place** (☑01789-338536; www.shakespeare.org.uk; cnr Chapel St & Chapel Lane; adult/child £12.50/8; ☉10am-5pm Apr-Aug, to 4.30pm Sep & Oct, to 3.30pm Nov-Feb). The house has long been demolished, but an attractive Elizabethan knot garden occupies part of the grounds.

A major restoration project has uncovered Shakespeare's kitchen and incorporated new exhibits in a re-imagining of the house as it would have been. You can also explore the adjacent **Nash's House**, where Shakespeare's granddaughter Elizabeth lived.

Shakespeare's Grave

Set inside the **Holy Trinity Church** (☑01789-266316; www.stratford-upon-avon.org; Old Town; Shakespeare's grave adult/child £3/2; ☉9am-6pm Mon-Sat, 12.30-5pm Sun Apr-Sep, 9am-5pm Mon-Sat, 12.30-5pm Sun Mar & Oct, 9am-4pm Mon-Sat, 12.30-5pm Sun Nov-Feb) featuring handsome 16th-century tombs and carved choir stalls, the grave of William Shakespeare bears this ominous epitaph: 'cvrst be he yt moves my bones'.

TRABANTOS / SHUTTERSTOCK ©

◉ SIGHTS

Charlecote Park   Historic Building

(NT; ☑01789-470277; www.nationaltrust.org.
uk; Loxley Lane, Charlecote; house & garden
adult/child £11.45/5.70, garden only £7.60/3.80;
☺house 11am-4.30pm Thu-Tue mid-Mar–Oct,
noon-3.30pm Thu-Tue mid-Feb–mid-Mar, noon-
3.30pm Sat & Sun Nov & Dec, garden 10.30am-
5.30pm Mar-Oct, to 4.30pm Nov-Feb) A youthful
Shakespeare allegedly poached deer in the
grounds of this lavish Elizabethan pile on
the River Avon, 5 miles east of Stratford-
upon-Avon. Fallow deer still roam the
grounds today. The interiors were restored
from Georgian chintz to Tudor splendour in
1823. Highlights include Victorian kitchens,
filled with culinary moulds, and an original
1551 Tudor gatehouse.

Bus X17 runs to Charlecote hourly from
Stratford (£4.40, 30 minutes, two per hour
Monday to Friday, hourly Saturday and
Sunday).

Gower Memorial   Monument

(Bancroft Gardens, Bridge Foot) Aristocratic
sculptor Lord Ronald Gower is the master
behind this multisculpture homage to
Shakespeare, which features the characters of Hamlet (representing philosophy),
Prince Hal (history), Lady Macbeth (trage-
dy) and Falstaff (comedy) as well the Bard
himself. The figures and decorative bronze
work were cast in France in 1881; the final
statues were installed across from the
Holy Trinity Church in 1888 (Oscar Wilde
officiated at the unveiling). The memorial
shifted to its current location in Bancroft
Gardens in 1933.

American Fountain   Monument

(Market Sq, Rother St) Gifted by American
publisher George W Childs in 1887 to
mark Queen Victoria's Golden Jubilee, and
designed by Birmingham architect Jethro
Cossins, this ornate Victorian Gothic clock
tower was unveiled by Shakespearean
actor Henry Irving. Lions, eagles, owls
and Tudor roses adorn the tower; a fairy
sits atop each clock face representing *A
Midsummer Night's Dream*. Although the

fountain no longer runs, the clocks and bell
still work. The horse troughs, once filled
with water, now bloom with flowers.

☉ ACTIVITIES

Avon Boating   Boating

(☑01789-267073; www.avon-boating.co.uk;
The Boathouse, Swan's Nest Lane; river cruises
adult/child £6/4; ☺9am-dusk Easter-Oct) Avon
Boating runs 40-minute river cruises that
depart every 20 minutes from either side
of the main bridge. It also hires rowboats,
canoes and punts (per hour £6) and motorboats (per hour £40).

☉ TOURS

Stratford Town Walk   Walking

(☑07855 760377; www.stratfordtownwalk.co.uk;
town walk adult/child £6/3, ghost walk £7/5;
☺town walk 11am Mon-Fri, 11am & 2pm Sat & Sun,
ghost walk by reservation 7.30pm Sat) Popular
two-hour guided **town walks** depart from
Waterside, opposite Sheep St (prebook-
ing not necessary). Chilling **ghost walks**
lasting 90 minutes leave from the same
location but must be booked ahead.

City Sightseeing   Bus

(☑01789-299123; www.city-sightseeing.com;
adult/child 24hr £16.82/8.41, 48hr £25.52/13;
☺9.30am-5pm Apr-Sep, to 4pm Oct-Mar) Open-
top, hop-on/hop-off bus tours leave from
the tourist office on Bridge Foot, rolling to
each of the Shakespeare properties, and
making 11 stops in all. Buy tickets online, at
the tourist office or from the driver.

✖ EATING

Sheep St is rammed with upmarket eating
options, mostly aimed at theatre goers (look
out for good-value pre-theatre menus).

Fourteas   Cafe £

(☑01789-293908; www.thefourteas.co.uk;
24 Sheep St; dishes £4.60-7.55, afternoon tea
with/without Prosecco £20/15; ☺9.30am-5pm
Mon-Sat, 11am-4.30pm Sun) Breaking with
Stratford's Shakespearean theme, this tea-

Stratford-upon-Avon

Stratford-upon-Avon

◉ Sights
1 American Fountain	B1
2 Gower Memorial	D1
3 Hall's Croft	B3
4 Holy Trinity Church	C3
5 Shakespeare's Birthplace	B1
6 Shakespeare's New Place	C2
7 Shakespeare's School Room	C2

◉ Activities, Courses & Tours
8 Avon Boating	D2
City Sightseeing	(see 19)
9 Stratford Town Walk	C2

⊗ Eating
10 Edward Moon's	B2
11 Fourteas	C2

Rooftop Restaurant	(see 18)
12 Salt	B2
13 Townhouse	B2

⊖ Drinking & Nightlife
14 Dirty Duck	C2
15 Old Thatch Tavern	B1
16 Windmill Inn	B2

⊕ Entertainment
17 Other Place	C3
18 Royal Shakespeare Company	C2
Swan Theatre	(see 18)

ⓘ Information
19 Tourist Office	D1

room takes the 1940s as its inspiration with beautiful old teapots, framed posters and staff in period costume. As well as premium loose-leaf teas and homemade cakes, there are all-day breakfasts, soups, sandwiches (including a chicken and bacon 'Churchill club') and lavish afternoon teas.

Townhouse   Bistro **££**
(☑01789-262222; www.stratfordtownhouse.
co.uk; 16 Church St; mains £9.50-24; ⊘kitchen
noon-3pm & 5-10pm Mon-Fri, noon-10pm Sat, to
8pm Sun, bar 8am-midnight Mon-Sat, to 10.30pm
Sun; 🛜) Immerse yourself in Stratford's
historic charms at this lovely restaurant in

a four-century-old timber building. Rare-breed steaks and seafood dishes such as dressed crab with truffled mayo are specialities. Music students from Shakespeare's old grammar school across the way tinkle the ivories at 5.30pm Monday to Saturday, though the piano can be hard to hear over the bar noise.

Edward Moon's   British ££

(☎01789-267069; www.edwardmoon.com; 9 Chapel St; mains £12.25-17; ⊙noon-2.30pm & 5-9.30pm Mon-Fri, noon-3pm & 5-10pm Sat, noon-3pm & 5-9pm Sun; 🚸) Named after a famous travelling chef who cooked up the flavours of home for the British colonial service, this snug independent restaurant serves hearty English dishes, such as steak-and-ale pie and meltingly tender lamb shank with redcurrant gravy. Kids get a two-course menu for £6.95.

Salt   British £££

(☎01789-263566; www.salt-restaurant.co.uk; 8 Church St; 2-/3-course menus lunch £33.50/37, dinner £37/45; ⊙noon-2pm & 6.30-10pm Wed-Sat, noon-2pm Sun) Stratford's gastronomic star is this intimate, beam-ceilinged bistro. In the semi-open kitchen, owner-chef Paul Foster produces stunning creations influenced by the seasons: spring might see glazed parsley root with chicory and black-truffle shavings, onglet of beef with malted artichoke, cured halibut with oyster and apple emulsion, and sea-buckthorn mille-feuille with fig and goats-milk ice cream.

🍷 DRINKING & NIGHTLIFE

Old Thatch Tavern   Pub

(www.oldthatchtavernstratford.co.uk; Greenhill St; ⊙11.30am-11pm Mon-Sat, from noon Sun; 🛜) To truly appreciate Stratford's olde-worlde atmosphere, join the locals for a pint at the town's oldest pub. Built in 1470, this thatch-roofed treasure has great real ales and a gorgeous summertime courtyard.

Dirty Duck   Pub

(Black Swan; www.oldenglishinns.co.uk; Waterside; ⊙11am-11pm Mon-Sat, to 10.30pm Sun) Also called the 'Black Swan', this enchanting riverside alehouse is the only pub in

Old Thatch Tavern

ANDRIA PATINO / GETTY IMAGES ©

England to be licensed under two names. It's a favourite thespian watering hole, with a roll call of former regulars (Olivier, Attenborough et al) that reads like a who's who of actors.

Windmill Inn   Pub
(www.greeneking-pubs.co.uk; Church St; ⊙11am-11pm Sun-Thu, to midnight Fri & Sat; 🛜) Ale was already flowing at this low-ceilinged pub when rhyming couplets gushed from Shakespeare's quill. Flowers frame the whitewashed facade; there's a shaded rear beer garden.

❂ ENTERTAINMENT

Royal Shakespeare Company   Theatre
(RSC; ✏box office 01789-403493; www.rsc.org. uk; Waterside; tours adult £7-9, child £4.50-5, tower adult/child £2.50/1.25; ⊙tour times vary, tower 10am-5pm Sun-Fri, 10am-12.15pm & 2-5pm Sat mid-Mar–mid-Oct, 10am-4.30pm Sun-Fri, to 12.15pm Sat mid-Oct–mid-Mar) Stratford has two grand stages run by the world-renowned Royal Shakespeare Company – the **Royal Shakespeare Theatre** and the **Swan Theatre** on Waterside – as well as the smaller **Other Place** (✏box office 01789-403493; www.rsc.org.uk; 22 Southern Lane). The theatres have witnessed performances by such legends as Lawrence Olivier, Richard Burton, Judi Dench, Helen Mirren, Ian McKellan and Patrick Stewart. Various one-hour **guided tours** take you behind the scenes.

Zipping up the lift/elevator of the Royal Shakespeare Theatre's **tower** rewards with panoramic views over the town and River Avon. Spectacular views also unfold from its 3rd-floor **Rooftop Restaurant** (✏01789-403449; www.rsc.org.uk; 3rd fl, Royal Shakespeare Theatre, Waterside; mains £12.50-25.50; ⊙10.30am-9.30pm Mon-Thu, to 9.45pm

Stratford Literary Festival

A highlight of Stratford's cultural calendar is the week-long annual **Stratford Literary Festival** (✏01789-207100; www. stratfordliteraryfestival.co.uk; ⊙late Apr/early May), which has attracted literary big-hitters of the calibre of Robert Harris, PD James and Simon Armitage.

Sat, to 3.30pm Sun; 🛜👪), which opens to a terrace.

Contact the RSC for performance times, and book well ahead. There are often special deals for under-25s, students and seniors. A few tickets are held back for sale on the day of the performance but get snapped up fast.

❶ INFORMATION

Tourist Office (✏01789-264293; www. shakespeares-england.co.uk; Bridge Foot; ⊙9am-5.30pm Mon-Sat, 10am-4pm Sun) Just west of Clopton Bridge.

❶ GETTING AROUND

From 10am to 6pm April to October, a 1937-built, hand-wound chain ferry yo-yoes across the Avon between the **west bank** (one way 50p; ⊙10am-6pm Apr-Oct) and the **east bank** (one way 50p; ⊙10am-6pm Apr-Oct).

A bicycle is handy for getting out to the outlying Shakespeare properties. **Stratford Bike Hire** (✏07711-776340; www.stratfordbikehire. com; The Stratford Greenway, Seven Meadows Rd; bike hire per half-/full day from £10/15; ⊙9.30am-5pm) will deliver to your accommodation for free within a 6-mile radius of Stratford.

CAMBRIDGE

Cambridge at a Glance...

Bursting with exquisite architecture, exuding history and renowned for its quirky rituals, Cambridge is a university city extraordinaire. In this captivating seat of learning, cyclists loaded down with books negotiate cobbled passageways, students relax on manicured lawns and great minds debate life-changing research in historic pubs. Add first-rate museums and a lively cultural scene, and you have an enchanting city with masses of appeal.

Two Days in Cambridge

Orient yourself with a guided **tour** (p167), then follow up with more university sights: perhaps **King's College Chapel** (p164) or **St John's** (p164). Supper? Try the suitably collegiate **Chop House** (p169). On day two explore more colleges and their libraries: **Wren Library** (p164) at Trinity and **Pepys Library** (p165) at Magdalene, before plunging into the glorious **Botanic Garden** (p166). The **Pint Shop** (p169) is a hip place to dine.

Four Days in Cambridge

Day three is for fresh air – glide along in a chauffeur-driven **punt** (p167), or be bold and pilot your own, then punt, cycle or stroll to Grantchester's gorgeous tea **garden** (p167). You'll have earned dinner at **Smokeworks** (p169). On day four hit the big museums: first the **Fitz** (p166), refuel at **Hot Numbers** (p169), then the **Polar Museum** (p166). End your Cambridge visit with a gourmet treat at **Midsummer House** (p169).

Previous page: Bridge of Sighs, St John's College (p164)

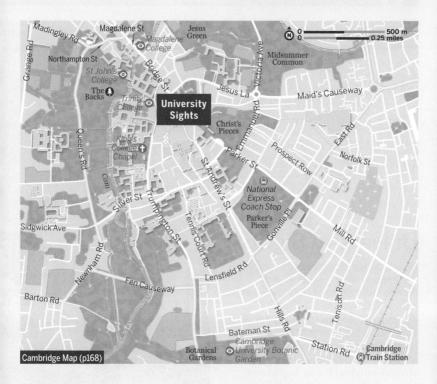

Cambridge Map (p168)

Arriving in Cambridge

Bus Direct National Express services include those to Gatwick (£41, 3¾ hours, seven daily), Heathrow (£31, 2¾ hours, hourly), London Victoria (£11, 2½ hours, two-hourly) and Oxford (£14, 3½ hours, hourly).

Train Direct services include those to London King's Cross (£25, one hour, two to four per hour) and Stansted Airport (£11, 35 minutes, every 30 minutes).

Where to Stay

Cambridge has varied and plentiful accommodation, but the city is hugely popular so booking ahead is advised. Options range from hostels, college halls and B&Bs to boutique spoils.

King's College Chapel (p164)

University Sights

In Cambridge, academic achievement permeates the very walls. August college buildings pack the core, while narrow alleyways twist between gracious chapels and timeless pubs. With a tangible air of tradition and innovation, this is the place where Newton refined his theory of gravity, Whipple invented the jet engine and Crick and Watson discovered DNA.

Great For...

❶ Need to Know

Colleges close at Christmas and from early April to mid-June. Opening hours can also vary; call ahead.

★ **Top Tip**

Cambridge has a jam-packed cultural schedule. For one-off events, check out the notices tied to railings all over the city centre, especially around St Mary's Church.

King's College Chapel

In a city crammed with showstopping buildings, this is the scene-stealer. Grandiose, 16th-century **King's College Chapel** (📞01223-331212; www.kings.cam.ac.uk; King's Pde; adult/child £9/6; ⏱9.30am-3.15pm Mon-Sat, 1.15-2.30pm Sun term time, 9.30am-4.30pm daily university holidays) is one of England's most extraordinary examples of Gothic architecture. Its inspirational, intricate, 80m-long, fan-vaulted ceiling is the world's largest and soars upward before exploding into a series of stone fireworks.

King's was begun in 1446 as an act of piety by Henry VI and was only finished by Henry VIII around 1516. The lofty stained-glass windows that flank the chapel's sides ensure it's remarkably light. The glass is original, a rare survivor of the excesses of the Civil War.

The antechapel and the choir are divided by a superbly carved wooden screen, designed and executed by Peter Stockton for Henry VIII. The screen bears his master's initials entwined with those of Anne Boleyn. Above is the magnificent bat-wing organ, originally constructed in 1686, though much altered since.

This hugely atmospheric space is a fitting stage for the chapel's world-famous choir; hear it during the magnificent, free, **evensong** (⏱term time only; 5.30pm Mon-Sat, 10.30am & 3.30pm Sun).

Trinity College

The largest of Cambridge's colleges, **Trinity** (📞01223-338400; www.trin.cam.ac.uk; Trinity St; adult/child £3/1; ⏱10am-4.30pm Jul-Oct, to 3.30pm Nov-Jun) offers an extraordinary Tudor gateway, an air of supreme elegance and a sweeping Great Court – the largest of its kind in the world. The college's vast hall has a dramatic hammer-beam roof and lantern;

> ✕ **Take a Break**
>
> Rest feet and boost sugar levels at Fitzbillies (p167), less a bakery, more an institution, thanks to its superb sweet treats.

beyond lie the dignified cloisters of Nevile's Court and the renowned and suitably musty **Wren Library** (⏱noon-2pm Mon-Fri year-round, plus 10.30am-12.30pm Sat term time) **FREE** which contains 55,000 books dated before 1820. Works include those by Shakespeare, St Jerome, Newton and Swift – and AA Milne's original *Winnie the Pooh;* both Milne and his son, Christopher Robin, were graduates. Other Trinity alumni include Sir Isaac Newton, Francis Bacon, Lord Byron, Tennyson, HRH Prince Charles, at least nine prime ministers and more than 30 Nobel Prize winners.

St John's College

Alma mater of six prime ministers, three saints and Douglas Adams (author of *The Hitchhiker's Guide to the Galaxy*), **St John's** (📞01223-33860; www.joh.cam.ac.uk; St John's St; adult/child £10/5; ⏱10am-5pm Mar-Oct, to

Punting on the River Cam before King's College Chapel

UNIVERSITY SIGHTS **165**

3.30pm Nov-Feb, closed mid-Jun) is superbly photogenic. It's also the second-biggest college after Trinity. Founded in 1511 by Henry VII's mother, Margaret Beaufort, it sprawls along both riverbanks, joined by the Bridge of Sighs, a masterpiece of stone tracery and focus for student pranks. Going into St John's or taking a punting tour are the only ways to get a clear view of the structure.

Magdalene College

The greatest asset of riverside **Magdalene College** (☎01223-332100; www.magd.cam. ac.uk; Magdalene St; ☺8am-6pm, closed early

☑ **Don't Miss**

The statue of Henry VIII at Trinity College's gates – his left hand holds a table leg, swapped with the original sceptre by prankster students.

Apr–mid-Jun) FREE – the college name is properly pronounced 'Maud-lyn' – is the **Pepys Library** (☺2-4pm Mon-Fri, 11.30am-12.30pm & 1.30-2.30pm Sat Easter-Aug, 2-4pm Mon-Sat Oct-Easter, closed Sep) FREE housing 3000 books bequeathed by the mid-17th-century diarist to his old college. This idiosyncratic collection of beautifully bound tomes is ordered by height, with treasures including vivid medieval manuscripts.

The Backs

Behind the Cambridge colleges' grandiose facades and stately courts, a series of gardens and parks line up beside the river. Collectively known as the **Backs**, the tranquil green spaces and shimmering waters offer picture-postcard snapshots of colleges, bridges and student life.

PREMIER PHOTO / SHUTTERSTOCK ©

◎ SIGHTS

Fitzwilliam Museum   Museum

(www.fitzmuseum.cam.ac.uk; Trumpington St; by donation; ⊘10am-5pm Tue-Sat, from noon Sun) **FREE** Fondly dubbed 'the Fitz' by locals, this colossal neoclassical pile was one of the first public art museums in Britain, built to house the fabulous treasures that the seventh Viscount Fitzwilliam bequeathed to his old university. Expect Roman and Egyptian grave goods, artworks by many of the great masters and some quirkier collections: banknotes, literary autographs, watches and armour.

Polar Museum   Museum

(☎01223-336540; www.spri.cam.ac.uk/museum; Lensfield Rd; ⊘10am-4pm Tue-Sat) **FREE** Tales of hostile environments, dogged determination and, sometimes, life-claiming mistakes are evoked powerfully at this compelling museum. Its focus

> *one of the first public art museums in Britain*

on polar exploration charts the feats of the likes of Roald Amundsen, Fridtjof Nansen, Ernest Shackleton and Captain Robert Falcon Scott. The affecting collections include paintings, photographs, clothing, equipment, maps, journals and last messages left for loved ones by Scott's polar crew.

Round Church   Church

(☎01223-311602; www.christianheritage.org.uk; Bridge St; £3.50; ⊘10am-5pm Tue-Sat, from 1.30pm Sun) Cambridge's intensely atmospheric Round Church is one of only four such structures in England. It was built by the mysterious Knights Templar in 1130 and shelters an unusual circular nave ringed by chunky Norman pillars. The carved stone faces crowning the pillars bring the 12th century vividly to life.

Cambridge University Botanic Garden   Gardens

(☎01223-336265; www.botanic.cam.ac.uk; 1 Brookside; adult/child £6/free; ⊘10am-6pm Apr-Sep, to 5pm Feb, Mar & Oct, to 4pm Nov-Jan) Founded by Charles Darwin's mentor,

Fitzwilliam Museum

ARIJEET BANNERJEE / SHUTTERSTOCK ©

Professor John Henslow, the beautiful Botanic Garden is home to 8000 plant species, a wonderful arboretum, glasshouses (containing both fierce carnivorous pitcher plants and the delicate slipper orchid), a winter garden and flamboyant herbaceous borders. Hour-long guided tours (free) are held at 2.30pm every Sunday from May through to September.

ACTIVITIES

Cambridge Chauffeur Punts   Boating
(📞01223-354164; www.punting-in-cambridge.co.uk; Silver St Bridge; chauffeured punts per hr adult/child £16/7, 6-person self-punt per hr £24; ⏰9am-8pm Jun & Aug, 10am-dusk Apr, May, Sept & Oct) Runs regular chauffeured punting tours and also offers self-hire.

Scudamore's Punting   Boating
(📞01223-359750; www.scudamores.com; Mill Lane; chauffeured punts per 45 min adult/child £20/10, 6-person self-punt per hr £30; ⏰9am-dusk) Rents punts, rowing boats, kayaks and canoes. Offers discounts if you book online.

TOURS

Walking Tours   Walking
(📞01223-791501; www.visitcambridge.org; Peas Hill; ⏰1-5 tours daily) The best **guided tours** of the city take in one of the colleges and the city's main sights. Options include the two-hour **Kings College & The Backs** tour (adult/child £20/10), and a 90-minute **Highlights** tour (adult/child £15/8), which often includes Pembroke College – the price covers college admission in both cases. They're popular – book ahead.

EATING

Urban Shed   Sandwiches £
(📞01223-324888; www.theurbanshed.com; 62 King St; sandwiches from £5; ⏰8.30am-5pm Mon-Fri, 9am-5.30pm Sat, 10am-5pm Sun; 📶) Unorthodox, retro Urban Shed has a personal-service ethos so strong that

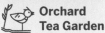
Orchard Tea Garden

After an idyllic punt, walk or cycle to Grantchester from Cambridge beside the Cam, flop into a deckchair under a leafy apple tree and wolf down calorific cakes or light lunches at the **Orchard Tea Garden** (📞01223-840230; www.theorchardteagarden.co.uk; 47 Mill Way; lunch mains £5-10, cakes £3; ⏰9am-6pm Apr-Oct, to 4pm Nov-Mar), a quintessentially English spot. This was the favourite haunt of the Bloomsbury Group who came to camp, picnic, swim and discuss their work. Book 24 hours ahead for the Orchard's famous cream teas (per person £20).

regular customers have a locker for their own mug. Old aeroplane seats perch beside cable-drum tables, their own-blend coffee is mellow and the choice of sandwiches is superb, with fillings including BBQ aubergine and Swiss cheese, coconut satay chicken, and grilled courgette with sunflower seeds.

Fitzbillies   Cafe £
(📞01223-352500; www.fitzbillies.com; 52 Trumpington St; mains £9-12; ⏰8am-6pm Mon-Fri, from 9am Sat, from 9.30am Sun) Cambridge's oldest bakery has a soft, doughy place in the hearts of generations of students, thanks to its ultrasticky Chelsea buns and other sweet treats. Pick up a bagful to take away or munch in comfort in the quaint cafe.

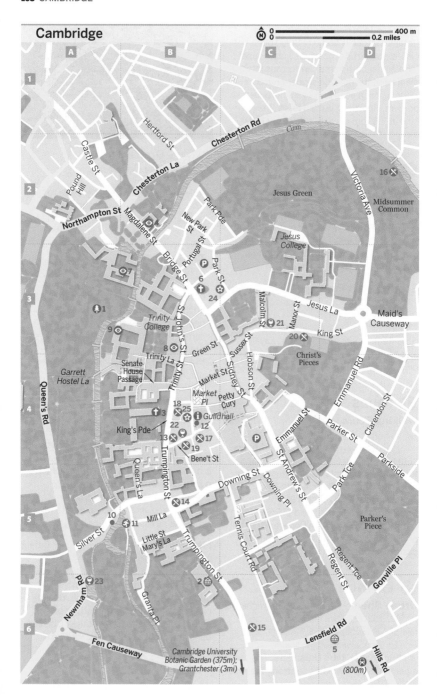

Cambridge

N 0 — 400 m
0 — 0.2 miles

A **B** **C** **D**

1

Castle St
Hertford St
Pound Hill
Chesterton La
Chesterton Rd
Cam
2
Northampton St
Magdalene St
Jesus Green
Victoria Ave
16
Midsummer Common
New Park St
Park Pde
Portugal St
Jesus College
Bridge St
Park St
6
24
Malcolm St
3
1
Trinity College
St John's St
Green St
Sussex St
Manor St
Jesus La
21
Maid's Causeway
9
8
Trinity La
Market St
Sidney St
Hobson St
20
King St
Christ's Pieces
Garrett Hostel La
Senate House Passage
Market Pl
Petty Cury
Emmanuel Rd
Queen's Rd
3
18
25
Guildhall
12
Emmanuel St
Parker St
Clarendon St
King's Pde
22
17
St Andrew's St
Parkside
13
19
Bene't St
Downing St
Downing Pl
Park Tce
Queen's La
Trumpington St
14
Emmanuel St
5
10
11
Mill La
Silver St
Little St Mary's La
Tennis Court Rd
Parker's Piece
Regent Tce
Regent St
Gonville Pl
Newnham Rd
23
Granta Pl
2
Trumpington St
5
15
Lensfield Rd
5
6
Fen Causeway
Cambridge University Botanic Garden (375m); Grantchester (3mi)
Hills Rd
(800m)

Cambridge

Hot Numbers — Cafe £

(www.hotnumberscoffee.co.uk; 4 Trumpington St; snacks £4-7; ⊙7am-7pm Mon-Fri, to 6pm Sat, 8am-6pm Sun; 🛜🍴) Hipster hang-out with bacon on sourdough toast for breakfast, single-origin bean coffee, cool tunes and a laid-back vibe.

Pint Shop — Modern British ££

(☑01223-352293; www.pintshop.co.uk; 10 Peas Hill; snacks from £5, mains £12-22; ⊙noon-10pm Mon-Fri, 11am-10.30pm Sat, 11am-10pm Sun) Popular Pint Shop's vision is to embrace eating and drinking equally. To this end, it's both a busy bar specialising in draught craft beer and a stylish dining room serving classy versions of traditional grub (dry-aged steaks, gin-cured sea trout, coal-baked fish and meat kebabs). All in all, hard to resist.

Cambridge Chop House — British ££

(☑01223-359506; www.cambscuisine.com/cambridge-chop-house; 1 King's Pde; mains £17-26; ⊙9am-11.30pm, noon-10.30pm Mon-Sat, to 9.30pm Sun) The window seats here deliver some of the best views in town – onto King's College's hallowed walls. The food is pure English establishment, too: hearty steaks and chops and chips, plus fish dishes and suet puddings. It's also open for breakfast (9-11.15am) and coffee and pastries (10-11.30am).

Smokeworks — Barbecue ££

(www.smokeworks.co.uk; 2 Free School Lane; mains £11-20; ⊙11.30am-10pm Mon-Thu, to 10.30pm Fri & Sat, to 9.30pm Sun; 🛜) This dark, industrial-themed dining spot draws discerning carnivores with its melt-in-your-mouth ribs, wings and wonderfully smoky pulled pork. The service is friendly and prompt, and the salted-caramel milkshakes come in a glass the size of your head.

Rainbow — Vegetarian ££

(☑01223-321551; www.rainbowcafe.co.uk; 9a King's Pde; mains £10-13; ⊙10am-10pm Tue-Sat, to 3pm Sun; 🍴) Quite a treat for non-meat eaters: a cheery basement bistro, tucked away at the end of an alley off King's Parade. In this warren of cosy rooms, rickety tables set the scene for an eclectic range of veg that's been transformed into a variety of bakes, roasts, pasta dishes and pies.

There are also tasty gluten-free options.

Midsummer House — Modern British £££

(☑01223-369299; www.midsummerhouse.co.uk; Midsummer Common; 5/8 courses £69/145; ⊙noon-1.30pm Wed-Sat, 7-9pm Tue-Sat; 🍴) At the region's top table, chef Daniel Clifford's double-Michelin-starred creations are distinguished by depth of flavour and immense technical skill. Savour

From left: Eagle; smoked salmon served at a Cambridge restaurant; Cambridge Arts Theatre

transformations of pumpkin (into velouté), mackerel (with Jack Daniels), quail, sea scallops and grouse, before a coriander–white chocolate dome, served with coconut, mango and jasmine rice.

🍸 DRINKING & NIGHTLIFE

Cambridge
Brew House   Microbrewery
(📞01223-855185; www.thecambridgebrewhouse.com; 1 King St; ⏱11am-11pm Sun-Thu, to midnight Fri & Sat) Pick a pint from the array on offer here and there's a fair chance it'll have been brewed in the gleaming vats beside the bar. Add a buzzy vibe, eclectic upcycled decor, dirty burgers and British tapas (mains £10 to £15) and you have the kind of pub you heartily wish was just down your road.

Eagle   Pub
(📞01223-505020; www.eagle-cambridge.co.uk; Bene't St; ⏱11am-11pm Sun-Thu, to midnight Fri & Sat; 🛜♿) Cambridge's most famous pub has loosened the tongues and pickled the grey cells of many an illustrious academic; among them Nobel Prize–winning

scientists Crick and Watson, who discussed their research into DNA here (note the blue plaque by the door). Fifteenth-century, wood-panelled and rambling, the Eagle's cosy rooms include one with WWII airmen's signatures on the ceiling.

Granta   Pub
(📞01223-505016; www.granta-cambridge.co.uk; 14 Newnham Rd; ⏱11am-11pm) If the exterior of this picturesque waterside pub, overhanging a pretty mill pond, looks strangely familiar, it could be because it is the darling of many a TV director. No wonder: with its snug deck, riverside terrace and punts moored up alongside, it's a highly atmospheric spot to sit, sup and watch the world drift by.

🎭 ENTERTAINMENT

ADC   Theatre
(📞01223-300085; www.adctheatre.com; Park St) This famous student-run theatre is home to the university's Footlights comedy troupe whose past members include Emma Thompson, Hugh Laurie and Stephen Fry.

Cambridge Arts Theatre Theatre

(01223-503333; www.cambridgeartstheatre. com; 6 St Edward's Passage) Cambridge's biggest bona-fide theatre puts on everything from highbrow drama and dance, to panto and shows fresh from London's West End.

ℹ INFORMATION

Tourist Office (📞01223-791500; www. visitcambridge.org; The Guildhall, Peas Hill; ⊘9.30am-5pm Mon-Sat Nov-Mar, plus 11am-3pm Sun Apr-Oct) Offers information plus a booking service for accommodation, walking and punting tours, events and tickets for King's College Chapel. Also sells maps, guides and souvenirs.

ℹ GETTING AROUND

Bicycle Cambridge is incredibly bike-friendly. **City Cycle Hire** (📞01223-365629; www. citycyclehire.com; 61 Newnham Rd; per half-day/day/week £9/12/25; ⊘9am-5.30pm Mon-Fri, plus 9am-5pm Sat Easter-Oct) is a mile southwest of the city centre. **Rutland Cycling** (📞01223-307655; www.rutlandcycling.com; Corn Exchange St; per 4hr/day £7/10; ⊘9am-6pm Mon-Fri, 10am-5pm Sun) is in the heart of town at the Grand Arcade shopping centre, with another branch just off Station Rd at the train station.

Bus Routes C1, C3 and C7 stop at the train station. A city Dayrider ticket (£4.30) provides 24 hours of unlimited bus travel around Cambridge.

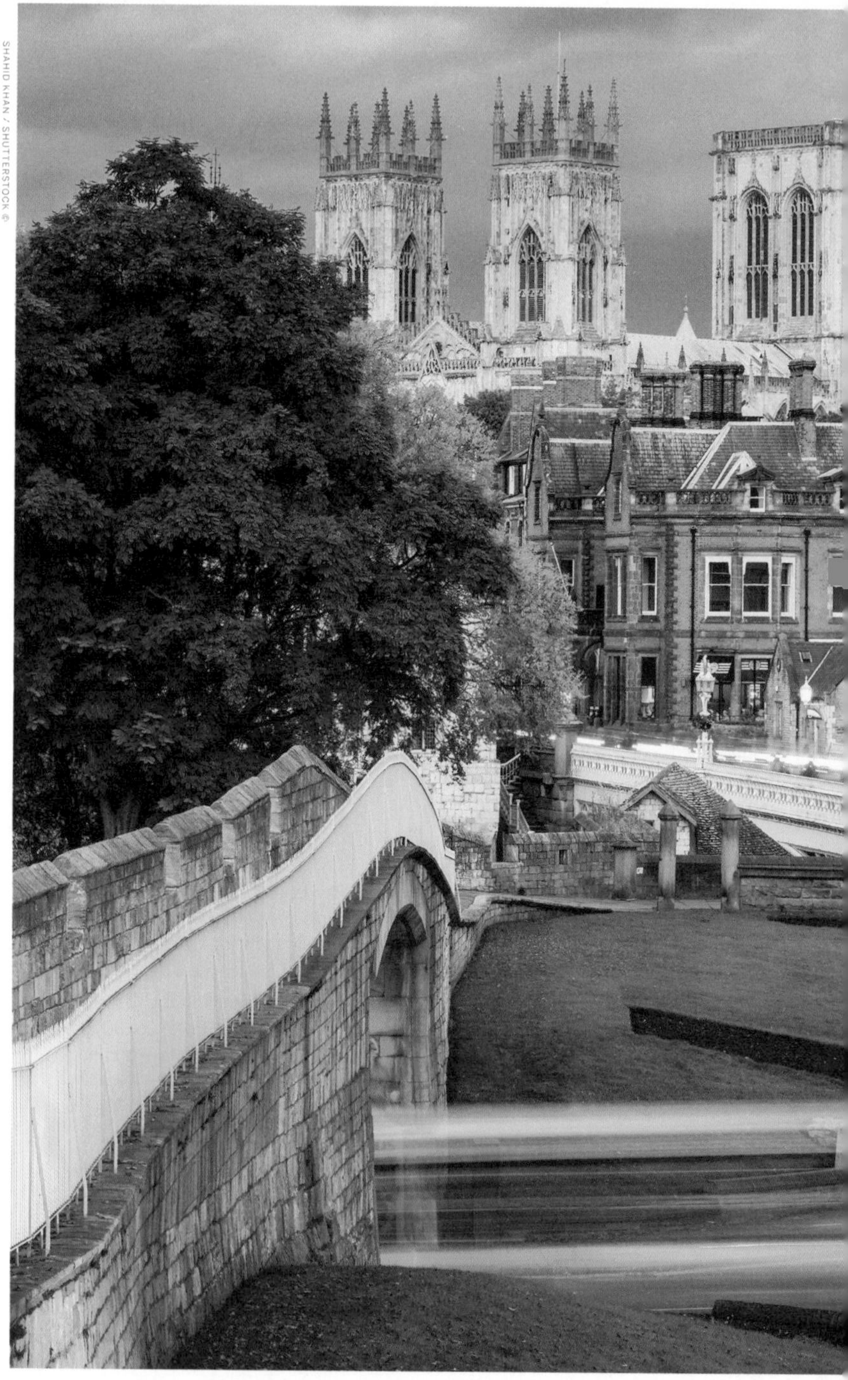

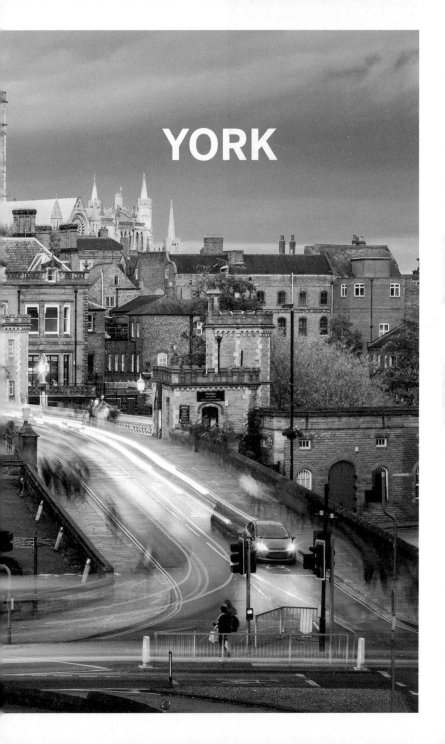

YORK

York at a Glance...

No other city in northern England says 'medieval' quite like York, where a magnificent circuit of 13th-century walls encloses a medieval spider's web of narrow streets. At its heart lies the immense, awe-inspiring York Minster, one of the most beautiful Gothic cathedrals in the world. On York's outskirts is Castle Howard, one of England's most impressive stately homes, and further out you can find the region's wild heart: the brooding Yorkshire dales and moors.

Two Days in York

Be awed by **York Minster** (p176) on day one, then tour the **city walls** (p183) to get your bearings and drink in the views. Quaff some craft beers at **Brew York** (p188), then make for **Mannion's** (p186) for foodie treats. On your second day, head straight for **Castle Howard** (p181), to marvel at the house, and join the peacocks in the grounds. After a detour to **Kirkham Priory** (p181), dine in fine style at **Cochon Aveugle** (p187).

Four Days in York

Get to know York better on day three: discover Vikings at **Jorvik** (p182), the **National Railway Museum** (p182), and ancient alleyways galore. Go **ghost hunting** (p185) in the evening, then recover with a stiff drink at the **Blue Bell** (p188). Day four, and it's time to experience Yorkshire's wild, wind-whipped beauty by hiking the moors or **dales** – you'll have earned that supper at **No 8 Bistro** (p186).

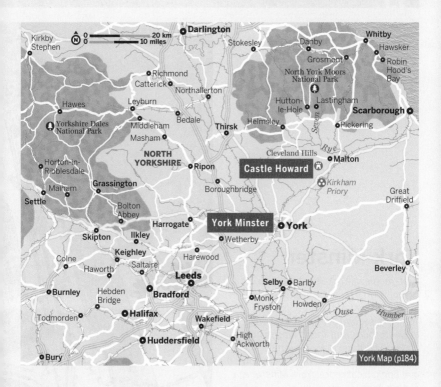

Arriving in York

Bus Buses are slower than trains, but cheaper – three services shuttle between York and London daily (from £36, 5½ hours).

Car Unless your hotel has parking, a car can be a pain in the city.

Train York is a major railway hub, with frequent, fast and direct services to many British cities – London King's Cross is only two hours away (£80, every half-hour).

Where to Stay

Beds can be hard to find in York in mid-summer. The tourist office's booking service charges £4, which can be money well spent. City-centre prices are higher, but there are plenty of decent B&Bs on the streets north and south of Bootham. Southwest of the centre, B&Bs are around Scarcroft, Southlands and Bishopthorpe Rds.

York Minster

Vast, medieval York Minster is one of the world's most beautiful Gothic buildings. Seat of the archbishop of York, it is second in importance only to Canterbury, and York's long history and rich heritage is woven into virtually every brick and beam. If you visit only one English cathedral, York Minster is a superb proposition.

Great For...

ℹ️ Need to Know

📞01904-557200; www.yorkminster.org; Deangate; adult/child £10/free, incl tower £15/5; 🕘9am-6pm Mon-Sat, 12.30-6pm Sun, last admission 4.30pm Mon-Sat, 3pm Sun

★ **Top Tip**

The YorkPass (one/three days £42/70) provides entry into 30 sights, including York Minster, Jorvik and Castle Howard.

Early History

The first church on this site was a wooden chapel built for the baptism of King Edwin of Northumbria on Easter Day 627. It was replaced with a stone church built on the site of a Roman basilica, parts of which can be seen in the foundations – as can fragments of the first 11th-century Norman minster.

Later History

The current minster, built mainly between 1220 and 1480, manages to encompass all the major stages of Gothic architectural development. The transepts (1220–55) were built in Early English style; the octagonal chapter house (1260–90) and nave (1291–1340) in the Decorated style; and the west towers, west front and central (or lantern) tower (1470–72) in Perpendicular style.

Nave

Entrance to the minster is via the west door, which leads into a tall, wide nave lined with the painted stone shields of nobles. Also note the dragon's head projecting from the gallery – it's a crane believed to have been used to lift a font cover. There are several fine windows dating from the early 14th century, but the most impressive is the Great West Window (1338) above the entrance, with its beautiful heart-shaped stone tracery

Transepts & Chapter House

The south transept is dominated by the exquisite Rose Window commemorating the union of the royal houses of Lancaster and York, through the marriage of Henry VII and Elizabeth of York, which ended the Wars of the Roses and began the Tudor dynasty.

The roof and stained-glass windows of Chapter House

Opposite, in the north transept, is the magnificent Five Sisters Window, with five lancets over 15m high. This is the minster's oldest complete window; most of its tangle of coloured glass dates from around 1250. Just beyond it to the right is the 13th-century chapter house, a fine example of the Decorated style. Sinuous and intricately carved stonework – there are more than 200 expressive carved heads and figures – surrounds an airy, uninterrupted space.

Choir Screen & East Window

Separating the choir from the nave is a superb 15th-century choir screen with 15 statues depicting the kings of England from William I to Henry VI. Behind the high altar is the huge Great East Window (1405). At 23.7m by 9.4m – roughly the size of a tennis court – it's the world's largest medieval stained-glass window and the cathedral's single most important treasure. Needless to say, its epic size matches the epic theme depicted within: the beginning and end of the world as described in Genesis and the Book of Revelations.

Undercroft

A set of stairs in the south transept leads down to the undercroft (open 10am to 4.15pm Monday to Saturday, 1pm to 3pm Sunday), the very bowels of the building. In 1967 the minster foundations were shored up when the central tower threatened to collapse; archaeologists uncovered Roman and Norman remains including a Roman culvert, still carrying water to the Ouse. An interactive exhibition here, *York Minster Revealed,* leads you through 2000 years of history on the site of the cathedral. The nearby treasury houses 11th-century artefacts including relics from the graves of medieval archbishops.

Crypt

The crypt, entered from the choir close to the altar, contains fragments from the Norman cathedral, including the font showing King Edwin's baptism, which also marks the site of the original wooden chapel. Look out for the Doomstone, a 12th-century carved stone showing a scene from the Last Judgement with demons casting doomed souls into Hell.

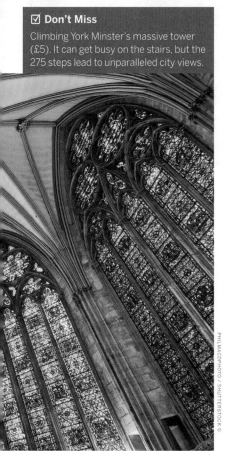

PHILMACDPHOTO / SHUTTERSTOCK ©

☑ Don't Miss

Climbing York Minster's massive tower (£5). It can get busy on the stairs, but the 275 steps lead to unparalleled city views.

✖ Take a Break

The laid-back, music-themed **Café Concerto** (☎01904-610478; www.cafeconcerto.biz; 21 High Petergate; lunch £6-9, dinner £10-17; ☺10.30am-9pm Tue-Fri, 10am-9.30pm Sat, 10am-5pm Sun, 10.30am-5pm Mon) is just a few paces away from York Minster, ready to feed you from breakfast through to dinner.

Castle Howard

Stately homes may be widespread in England, but you'll have to try pretty damn hard to find one as breathtakingly stately as Castle Howard, a work of theatrical grandeur and audacity set in the rolling Howardian Hills.

Welcome to one of the world's most beautiful buildings, instantly recognisable from its starring role in the 1980s TV series *Brideshead Revisited* and in the 2008 film of the same name. Both were based on Evelyn Waugh's 1945 novel of nostalgia for the English aristocracy.

The Beginnings

When the Earl of Carlisle hired his pal Sir John Vanbrugh to design his new home in 1699, he was hiring a man who had no formal training and was best known as a playwright. Luckily, Vanbrugh hired Nicholas Hawksmoor, who had worked as Christopher Wren's clerk of works – not only would Hawksmoor have a big part to play in the house's design, but he and Vanbrugh would later work wonders with Blenheim Palace.

Great For...

☑ **Don't Miss**

The Pre-Raphaelite stained glass in Castle Howard's ornate chapel.

KARL BLACKWELL / GETTY IMAGES ©

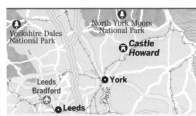

❶ Need to Know

🕿01653-648333; www.castlehoward.co.uk; adult/child house & grounds £18.95/9.95, grounds only £11.95/7.95; ⊗house 10am-4pm, grounds 10am-5pm, last admission 4pm; P

✗ Take a Break

Castle Howard has its own cafe, or head to the nearby Stone Trough Inn.

★ Top Tip

Try to visit on a weekday, when a quieter Castle Howard has even more atmosphere.

What's Nearby

Kirkham Priory   Ruins

(EH; www.english-heritage.org.uk; Kirkham; adult/child £4.50/2.70; ⊗10am-6pm Wed-Sun Apr-Jul & Sep, daily Aug, 10am-5pm Wed-Sun Oct; P) The picturesque ruins of Kirkham Priory rise gracefully above the banks of the River Derwent, sporting medieval floor tiles and an impressive 13th-century gatehouse (through which you'll enter) encrusted with heraldic symbols.

Stone Trough Inn   Pub Food ££

(🕿01653-618713; www.thestonetroughinn. com; Kirkham; mains £10-20; ⊗food served noon-9pm; P🛜🕯🐕) This lovely country inn is full of cosy nooks, with exposed stone walls, timber beams and open fires, and serves gourmet-style pub classics (eg fish and chips, steak pie with peas and gravy) with Yorkshire beers on tap. An added attraction is the outdoor terrace with views over the Derwent valley above Kirkham Priory. Three-course Sunday carvery lunch is £19.

The House & Grounds

What they created was a hedonistic mix of art, architecture, landscaping and natural beauty. The great baroque house with its magnificent central cupola is stuffed full of treasures, including the breathtaking Great Hall with its soaring Corinthian pilasters.

The entrance courtyard has a good cafe, a gift shop and a lovely farm shop.

As you wander around grounds patrolled by peacocks, views open up over Vanbrugh's playful Temple of the Four Winds, Hawksmoor's stately mausoleum and the distant hills.

Getting There & Away

Castle Howard is 15 miles northeast of York, off the A64. Ask at the tourist office (p189) about organised tours from York, or take bus 181 (£10 return, one hour, four daily Monday to Saturday year-round).

⊙ SIGHTS

Jorvik Viking Centre   Museum

([📞]ticket reservations 01904-615505; www.
jorvik-viking-centre.co.uk; Coppergate; adult/
child £11/8; ⊙10am-5pm Apr-Oct, to 4pm Nov-
Mar) Interactive multimedia exhibits aimed
at bringing history to life often achieve
exactly the opposite, but the much-hyped
Jorvik manages to pull it off with aplomb.
It's a smells-and-all reconstruction of the
Viking settlement unearthed here during
excavations in the late 1970s, experienced
via a 'time-car' monorail that transports
you through 9th-century Jorvik (the Viking
name for York). You can reduce time waiting
in line by booking timed-entry tickets
online; there is almost always a queue to
get in.

National Railway Museum   Museum

(www.nrm.org.uk; Leeman Rd; ⊙10am-6pm
Apr-Oct, to 5pm Nov-Mar; [P][♿]) **FREE** York's
National Railway Museum – the biggest
in the world, with more than 100 locomotives – is well-presented and crammed
with fascinating stuff. It is laid out on a vast
scale and is housed in a series of giant railway sheds – allow at least two hours to do
it justice. The museum also now includes
a high-tech simulator experience of riding
on the **Mallard** (£4), which set the world
speed record for a steam locomotive in
1938 (126mph).

Barley Hall   Historic Building

([📞]01904-615505; www.barleyhall.co.uk; 2 Coffee
Yard; adult/child £6/3; ⊙10am-5pm Apr-Oct,
to 4pm Nov-Mar) This restored medieval
townhouse, tucked down an alleyway,
includes a permanent exhibition of life in
the times of Henry VIII. It was once the
home of York's Lord Mayor. The centrepiece
is a double-height banquet hall decorated
with the Yorkshire rose – peek at it through
a window in the alleyway if you don't want
to pay to enter.

Yorkshire Museum   Museum

(www.yorkshiremuseum.org.uk; Museum St;
adult/child £7.50/free; ⊙10am-5pm) Most
of York's Roman archaeology is hidden
beneath the medieval city, so the superb
displays in the Yorkshire Museum are

National Railway Museum

KACA SKOKANOVA / SHUTTERSTOCK ©

invaluable if you want to get an idea of what Eboracum was like. There are maps and models of Roman York, funerary monuments, mosaic floors and wall paintings, and a 4th-century bust of Emperor Constantine. Kids will enjoy the dinosaur exhibit, centred around giant ichthyosaur fossils from Yorkshire's Jurassic coast.

The Shambles   Street
The Shambles takes its name from the Saxon word *shamel,* meaning 'slaughterhouse' – in 1862 there were 26 butcher shops on this street. Today the butchers are long gone, but this narrow cobbled lane, lined with 15th-century Tudor buildings that seem to meet above your head, is the most picturesque in Britain, and one of the most visited in Europe, often filled with visitors wielding cameras.

York Castle Museum   Museum
(www.yorkcastlemuseum.org.uk; Tower St; adult/ child £10/free; ⊙9.30am-5pm) This excellent museum has displays of everyday life through the centuries, with reconstructed domestic interiors, a Victorian street and a prison cell where you can try out a condemned man's bed – and it could be that of highwayman Dick Turpin (imprisoned here before being hanged in 1739). There's a bewildering array of evocative objects from the past 400 years, gathered together by a certain Dr Kirk from the 1920s onwards for fear the items would become obsolete and disappear completely.

Merchant Adventurers'
Hall   Historic Building
(☑01904-654818; www.merchantshallyork. org; Fossgate; adult/child £6.50/free; ⊙10am-4.30pm Sun-Fri, to 1.30pm Sat) York's most impressive semi-timbered building is still owned by the fraternity that built it almost 650 years ago and it is the oldest surviving guildhall of its kind in Britain. The owner was originally a religious fraternity and one of the hall's chambers is still a chapel. However, the building's name refers to the pioneering business exploits that made

 **York's
City Walls**

Don't miss the chance to walk York's City Walls (www.yorkwalls.org.uk), which follow the line of the original Roman walls and give a whole new perspective on the city. Allow 1½ to two hours for the full circuit of 4.5 miles.

Start and finish in the Museum Gardens or at **Bootham Bar** (on the site of a Roman gate), where an exhibit provides some historical context, and travel clockwise. Highlights include **Monk Bar**, which is the best-preserved medieval gate and still has a working portcullis, and **Walmgate Bar**, England's only city gate with an intact barbican.

the fraternity's fortunes while 'adventuring' its money in overseas markets at a time when York was an important international port.

TOURS

Brewtown   Beer Tour
(☑01904-636666; www.brewtowntours.co.uk; £60; ⊙11.30am-5pm) These craft-brewery minivan tours are a fuss-free way to get behind the scenes at Yorkshire's smaller breweries, some of which only open to the public for these tours. Owner Mark runs different routes (around York, Malton or Leeds) depending on the day of the week; each tour visits three breweries with tastings along the way, and sometimes even beer-pairing nibbles.

York

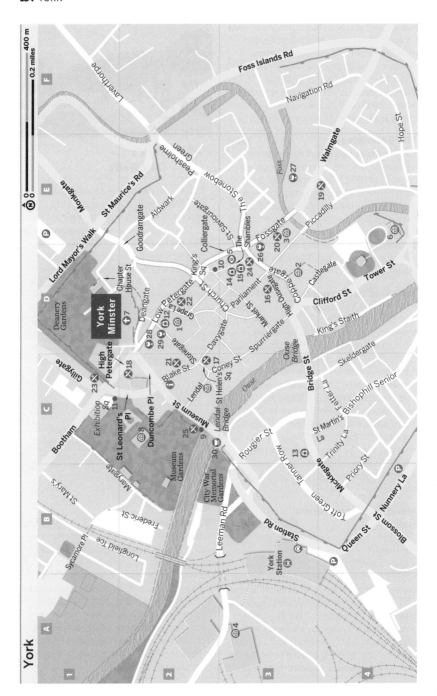

York

City Cruises York
Boating

(www.citycruisesyork.com; Lendal Bridge; adult/child from £9.50/5.50; ⊙tours 10.30am, noon, 1.30pm & 3pm; ⊕) These hour-long cruises on the River Ouse depart from King's Staith and, 10 minutes later, Lendal Bridge. Special lunch, afternoon tea and evening cruises are also offered. You can buy tickets on board or book at the office by Lendal Bridge.

York Citysightseeing
Bus

(www.city-sightseeing.com; day ticket adult/child £14/7; ⊙9am-5.30pm Easter-Nov, reduced service rest of year) Hop-on, hop-off route with 20 stops, calling at all the main sights. Buses leave every 12 to 30 minutes from Exhibition Sq near York Minster.

Ghost Hunt of York
Bus

(☏01904-608700; www.ghosthunt.co.uk; adult/child £6/4; ⊙tours 7.30pm) The kids will just love this award-winning and highly entertaining 75-minute tour laced with authentic ghost stories. It begins at the top end of the Shambles, whatever the weather (it's never cancelled), and there's no need to book – just turn up and wait till you hear the handbell ringing...

⊕ SHOPPING

Coney St, Davygate and the adjoining streets are the hub of York's city-centre shopping scene, but the real treats are the secondhand bookshops, and antique, bric-a-brac and independent shops to be found along Gillygate, Colliergate, Fossgate and Micklegate.

Antiques Centre
Antiques

(www.theantiquescentreyork.co.uk; 41 Stonegate; ⊙9.30am-5.30pm Mon-Sat, to 4pm Sun) A Georgian town house with a veritable maze of rooms and corridors, showcasing the wares of about 120 dealers selling everything from lapel pins and snuffboxes to oil paintings and longcase clocks. And the house is haunted as well...

Shambles Market
Food

(www.shamblesmarket.com; The Shambles; ⊙9am-5pm) Yorkshire cheeses, Whitby fish and local meat make good fodder for self-caterers at this anything-goes market behind the Shambles, which also touts arts, crafts and Yorkshire flat caps. The food-court section near where the Shambles joins Pavement is a good spot for cheap eats, coffee and ice-cream at picnic tables.

Yorkshire Afternoon Tea

For old-school afternoon tea, with white-aproned waiters, linen tablecloths and a teapot collection ranged along the walls, come to **Bettys** (☑01904-659142; www.bettys.co.uk; 6-8 St Helen's Sq; mains £6-14, afternoon tea £19.95; ☺9am-9pm Sun-Fri, 8.30am-9pm Sat; ⛄). The house speciality is the Yorkshire Fat Rascal, a huge fruit scone smothered in melted butter, while breakfast and lunch dishes, like bacon and raclette rösti, and Yorkshire rarebit, show off Betty's Swiss–Yorkshire heritage. No bookings, but be prepared to queue.

Minced pies at Bettys
ALASTAIR WALLACE / SHUTTERSTOCK ©

Ken Spelman Booksellers　Books

(www.kenspelman.com; 70 Micklegate; ☺9am-5.30pm Mon-Sat) This fascinating shop has been selling rare, antiquarian and secondhand books since 1947. With an open fire crackling in the grate in winter, it's a browser's paradise.

The Shop That Must Not Be Named　Gifts & Souvenirs

(30 The Shambles; ☺10am-6pm) Casting a spell over Harry Potter fans, this shop opened on the Shambles – the street said to be the inspiration for Diagon Alley – in 2017. Wands? Tick. Quidditch fan gear? Tick. Potions? Tick. Pure magic for muggles. There's now no less than three Potter shops on the Shambles, but this is the original and still the most convincing.

EATING

Eating well in York is not a problem – there are plenty of fine options throughout the city centre, from high-quality takeaway food to some of the most inventive cuisine in the country; most pubs also serve food.

Mannion & Co　Cafe, Bistro £

(☑01904-631030; www.mannionandco.co.uk; 1 Blake St; mains £7-12; ☺9am-5pm Mon-Sat, 10am-4.30pm Sun) Expect to queue for a table at this busy bistro (no reservations), with its convivial atmosphere and selection of delicious daily specials. Regulars on the menu include eggs Benedict for breakfast, a chunky Yorkshire rarebit (cheese on toast) made with home-baked bread, and lunch platters of cheese and charcuterie. Oh, and pavlova for pudding.

Shambles Kitchen　Fast Food £

(☑01904-674684; www.shambleskitchen.co.uk; 28 The Shambles; mains £4-7.50; ☺9am-4pm Mon-Fri, to 5pm Sat, 10am-4pm Sun; ☑) ✔ Fast food doesn't mean unhealthy at this hugely popular little takeaway (there are only three tables inside). The place is best known for its pulled-pork sandwiches on sourdough bread, but there are also yummy wraps, daily specials such as Goan curry and Korean chicken, and a choice of freshly made veg juices and smoothies. Food is served from 11am.

Hairy Fig　Cafe £

(☑01904-677074; www.thehairyfig.co.uk; 39 Fossgate; mains £5-12; ☺9am-4.30pm Mon-Sat) This cafe-deli is a standout in York. On the one side you've got the best of Yorkshire tripping over the best of Europe, with Italian white anchovies and truffle-infused olive oil stacked alongside York honey mead and baked pies; on the other you've got a Dickensian-style sweet store and backroom cafe serving dishes crafted from the deli.

No 8 Bistro　Bistro ££

(☑01904-653074; www.no8york.co.uk/bistro; 8 Gillygate; dinner mains £17-19; ☺noon-10pm Mon-Fri, 9am-10pm Sat & Sun; ☎⛄) ✔ A cool little place with modern artwork mimicking the Edwardian stained glass at the front, No 8 offers a day-long menu of top-notch bistro dishes using fresh local produce, such as Jerusalem artichoke risotto with fresh herbs, and Yorkshire lamb slow-cooked in hay and lavender. It also does breakfast (mains £6 to £9) and Sunday lunch. Booking recommended.

Mr P's Curious Tavern   British ££

(📞01904-521177; www.mrpscurioustavern.co.uk; 71 Low Petergate; dishes £5-14; ⊙noon-10pm Mon-Fri, 11am-11pm Sat, noon-6pm Sun) Mr P's specialises in imaginative small plates, deli meats and cheeses, with a quality wine list – not what you'd expect from its touristy location. It's housed inside a creaky (allegedly haunted) old house, and is part of the mini-empire from Michelin-starred Yorkshire chef Andrew Pern, of Star Inn fame.

Star Inn The City   British ££

(📞01904-619208; www.starinnthecity.co.uk; Lendal Engine House, Museum St; mains £14-28; ⊙9.30-11.30am, noon-9.30pm Mon-Sat, to 7.30pm Sun; 👪) Its riverside setting in a Grade II–listed engine house and quirky British menu make Andrew Pern's York outpost of the Star Inn (p187) an exceedingly pleasant place to while away the hours. Expect country-themed cosiness in winter, and dining out on the broad terrace in summer.

Ate O'Clock   Bistro ££

(📞01904-644080; www.ateoclock.co.uk; 13a High Ousegate; mains £6-18; ⊙noon-2pm & 6-9.30pm Tue-Fri, to 2.30pm & 5.30-9.30pm Sat; 🛜) 🍽 Heated outdoor seating in a cosy, covered alleyway makes this a popular choice. The menu is full of classic bistro dishes (sirloin steak, slow-roasted pork belly, pan-fried duck breast) and sandwiches made with fresh Yorkshire produce, or try one of the daily specials.

Cochon Aveugle   French £££

(📞01904-640222; www.lecochonaveugle.uk; 37 Walmgate; 4-course lunch £40, 8-course tasting menu £60; ⊙6-9pm Wed-Sat, noon-1.30pm Sat) 🍽 Black-pudding macaroon? Strawberry and elderflower sandwich? Blowtorched

A fruit and vegetable stall at Shambles Market (p185)

Yorkshire puddings stuffed with sausages and vegetables

mackerel with melon gazpacho? Fussy eaters beware – this small restaurant with huge ambition serves an ever-changing tasting menu (no à la carte) of infinite imagination and invention. You never know what will come next, except that it will be delicious. Bookings are essential.

🍷 DRINKING & NIGHTLIFE

The area around Ousegate and Micklegate can get a bit rowdy, especially at weekends. There are cocktail bars with outdoor seating on Swinegate Court (off Grape Lane).

Blue Bell   Pub

(☏01904-654904; 53 Fossgate; ⏰11am-11pm Mon-Thu, to midnight Fri & Sat, noon-10.30pm Sun; 📶) This is what a proper English pub looks like – a tiny, 200-year-old wood-panelled room with a smouldering fireplace, decor untouched since 1903, a pile of ancient board games in the corner, friendly and efficient bar staff, and weekly cask-ale specials chalked on a board. Bliss, with froth on top – if you can get in (it's often full). Cash only.

Guy Fawkes Inn   Pub

(☏01904-466674; www.guyfawkesinnyork.com; 25 High Petergate; ⏰11am-11pm Mon-Thu & Sun, to midnight Fri & Sat) The man who famously plotted to blow up the Houses of Parliament and inspired Bonfire Night in the UK was born on this site in 1570. Walk through the lovely Georgian wood-panelled pub to find Guy Fawkes' grandmother's cottage at the far end of the back patio, watched over by a giant wall mural.

The inn also has live music on Sunday nights (from 8.30pm), and 13 hotel rooms.

Brew York   Microbrewery

(☏01904-848448; www.brewyork.co.uk; Enterprise Complex, Walmgate; ⏰6-11pm Wed & Thu, from 4pm Fri, noon-11pm Sat, to 10pm Sun) Housed in a cavernous old warehouse, half the floor space in this craft brewery is occupied by giant brewing tanks while the rest is given over to simple wooden drinking benches and a bar with rotating keg and cask beers. At the far end of the brewery there's a small riverside terrace overlooking Rowntree Wharf.

House of Trembling Madness   Bar

(☏01904-640009; www.tremblingmadness.
co.uk; 48 Stonegate; ⊙10am-midnight Mon-Sat,
from 11am Sun) When a place describes
itself as a 'medieval drinking hall', it clearly
deserves investigation. The ground floor
and basement host an impressive shop
stacked with craft beers, gins, vodkas and
even absinthes; but head upstairs to the
first floor and you'll find the secret drinking
den – an ancient timber-framed room with
high ceilings, a bar and happy drinkers.

Perky Peacock   Cafe

(www.perkypeacockcoffee.co.uk; Lendal Bridge;
⊙7am-5pm Mon-Fri, from 9am Sat, to 4pm
Sun) One of York's charms is finding teeny
places like this cafe, shoe-horned into
historic buildings. In this case the host is a
14th-century, rotund watchtower crouched
by the riverbank. Sup an excellent coffee
under the ancient wood beams, or grab a
street-side table for a tasty pastry.

 INFORMATION

Post Office (22 Lendal; ⊙9am-5.30pm Mon-Fri,
to 4pm Sat)

York Tourist Office (☏01904-550099; www.
visityork.org; 1 Museum St; ⊙9am-5pm Mon-Sat,
10am-4pm Sun) Visitor and transport info for all
of Yorkshire, plus accommodation bookings (for
a small fee) and ticket sales.

 GETTING AROUND

Foot Central York is easy to get around on foot –
you're never more than 20 minutes' walk from
any of the major sights.

Bicycle You can rent bikes from **Cycle Heaven**
(☏01904-622701; www.cycle-heaven.co.uk;
York Railway Station, Station Rd; 2/24hr £10/20;
⊙8.30am-5.30pm Mon-Fri, 9am-5pm Sat year-

 Yorkshire's Moors & Dales

Yorkshire's varied landscape of wild
hills, tranquil valleys, high moors and
spectacular coastline offers plenty of
opportunities for outdoor activities.

For shorter walks and rambles, the
best area is the **Yorkshire Dales**, with a
great selection of walks through scenic
valleys or over wild hilltops, with a few
higher summits thrown in for good
measure. The East Riding's **Yorkshire
Wolds** hold hidden delights, while the
quiet valleys and dramatic, blustery
coast of the **North York Moors** also
offer sublime rambling opportunities.

Heather in bloom on the North York Moors
DANIEL J. RAO / SHUTTERSTOCK ©

round, 11am-4pm Sun May-Sep) at the train station for £20 per 24 hours. The tourist office has
a useful free map showing York's cycle routes, or
visit iTravel-York (www.itravelyork.info/cycling).
Castle Howard (15 miles northeast of York via
Haxby and Strensall) is an interesting destination, and there's also a section of the Trans-
Pennine Trail cycle path(www.transpennine
trail.org.uk) from Bishopthorpe in York to Selby
(15 miles) along the old railway line.

Taxi Station Taxis (☏01904-623332; www.
yorkstationtaxis.co.uk) has a kiosk outside the
train station.

THE LAKE
DISTRICT

The Lake District at a Glance...

The Lake District (or Lakeland, as it's commonly known around these parts) is the UK's most popular national park, with 15 million people pitching up annually. Indeed, ever since the Romantic poets arrived in the 19th century, this postcard panorama of craggy hills and glittering lakes has been stirring the imagination. The region is awash with historic hikes, including the awe-inspiring Hadrian's Wall, and literary links to William Wordsworth, Arthur Ransome, Beatrix Potter and other writers.

Two Days in the Lake District

Begin your literary Lakes odyssey with Wordsworth: his **birthplace** (p196) and **residence** (p196) will do for starters. By now you're in Grasmere, so head to the **Jumble Room** (p203) for a fun feed. Day two and onto the poet's family **home** (p196) for more intriguing insights, then hike Lakeland scenery at **Helm Crag** (p203) before dropping by to the suitably named **Traveller's Rest** (p203) for tea.

Four Days in the Lake District

On day three its time to switch writers. Beatrix Potter's **house** (p197) is bound to delight, then play at pirates by cruising (or sailing) **Coniston Water** (p197) – 'home' to Arthur Ransome's *Swallows and Amazons*. Day four sees you travelling back thousands of years as you head to **Housesteads** (p198) and **Vindolanda** (p199) to begin exploring the extraordinary Roman past at Hadrian's Wall.

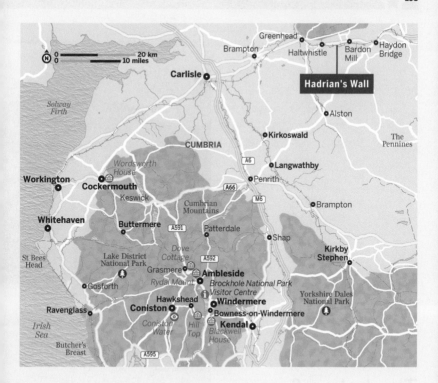

Arriving in the Lake District

Bus National Express coaches run direct from London Victoria and Glasgow to the key towns of Windermere and Kendal.

Car Windermere is 115 miles (2½ hours) northwest of York and 150 miles (three hours) south of Edinburgh.

Train To get to the Lake District via the main West Coast train line, change at Oxenholme for Windermere and Kendal.

Where to Stay

There's a huge range of places to stay in the Lake District: grand country hotels, country inns and boutique B&Bs – there's also a superb collection of hostels (both YHA and independent) and campsites.

Prices tend to be higher inside the national park's boundaries, however, and there are premiums in peak seasons such as Easter and over the summer school holidays.

Coniston Water (p197)

The Lakes & Literature

In terms of natural splendour, few English places can compare to the Lake District. Its beauty has inspired poets and painters for centuries. The legacy is a landscape rich in links to writers who created world-famous Romantic poetry and some of the nation's best-loved children's tales. What's more, the key sites are all within a curving, scenic 45-mile drive.

Great For...

ⓘ Need to Know

Brockhole National Park Visitor Centre (p202)

★ **Top Tip**

Several key sights operate by timed ticket; book early and aim for late-afternoons or weekdays.

William Wordsworth

Wordsworth House

The Romantic poet was born on 7 April 1770 at this handsome Georgian **house** (NT; ☏01900-824805; www.nationaltrust.org.uk/wordsworth-house; Main St; adult/child £7.90/3.95; ☺11am-5pm Sat-Thu Mar-Oct) in Cockermouth. Built around 1745, the house has been meticulously restored based on accounts from the Wordsworth archive: the kitchen, drawing room, study and bedrooms all look much as they would have to a young William. Costumed guides help bring things to life.

Dove Cottage

On the edge of Grasmere, around 30 miles southeast of Cockermouth, this tiny, creeper-clad **cottage** (☏015394-35544; www.wordsworth.org.uk; adult/child £8.95/free; ☺9.30am-5.30pm Mar-Oct, 10am-4.30pm Nov, Dec & Feb) was famously inhabited by Wordsworth between 1799 and 1808. Its cramped rooms are full of artefacts: try to spot the poet's passport, a pair of his spectacles and a portrait (a gift from Sir Walter Scott) of his favourite dog, Pepper. An informative guided tour is included.

Entry includes the next door **Wordsworth Museum & Art Gallery**, which has a significant Romantic-movement collection, including original manuscripts and creepy death masks of leading Romantic figures.

Rydal Mount

Wordsworth's most famous residence in the Lake District is undoubtedly Dove Cottage, but he actually spent a great deal more time at **Rydal Mount** (☏015394-33002; www.rydalmount.co.uk; adult/child £7.50/4, grounds only £5; ☺9.30am-5pm Mar-Oct, 11am-4pm Nov,

Coniston Water

Dec & Feb). This was the Wordsworth family's home from 1813 until the poet's death in 1850. You can wander around the library, dining room and drawing room (look out for William's pen, inkstand and picnic box in the cabinets). Upstairs are the family bedrooms and Wordsworth's attic study, containing his encyclopaedia and a sword belonging to his brother John, who was lost at sea.

Beatrix Potter

Hill Top

Just 9 miles south of Rydal Mount, the idyllic farmhouse known as **Hill Top** (NT; ☑015394-36269; www.nationaltrust.org.uk/hill-top; adult/child £10.90/5.45, admission to garden & shop free; ⊙10am-5.30pm Jun-Aug, to 4.30pm Sat-Thu Apr, May, Sep & Oct, weekends only Nov-Mar), purchased in 1905 by Beatrix Potter, was the inspiration for many of her tales: the house features in *Samuel Whiskers, Tom Kitten, Pigling Bland* and *Jemima Puddleduck,* and you might recognise the kitchen garden from *Peter Rabbit*.

Hill Top is in the tiny village of Near Sawrey. Entry is by timed ticket; it's very popular, so prepare to queue.

Beatrix Potter Gallery

Potter was also a talented botanical painter and amateur naturalist. This small **gallery** (NT; www.nationaltrust.org.uk/beatrix-potter-gallery; Red Lion Sq; adult/child £6.50/3.25; ⊙10.30am-5pm Sat-Thu mid-Mar–Oct) in Hawkshead, in what were once the offices of Potter's husband, solicitor William Heelis, has a collection of her watercolours of local flora and fauna (she was particularly fascinated by mushrooms). The gallery celebrated Beatrix Potter's 150th birthday in 2016 with a special exhibition featuring extracts from the author's coded journal.

Arthur Ransome

Coniston's gleaming 5-mile lake, **Coniston Water**, around 6 miles west of Hill Top and the third largest in the Lake District, inspired Ransome's classic children's tale *Swallows and Amazons*. Peel Island, toward the southern end of the lake, supposedly provided the model for Wild Cat Island.

Cruise boats ply the waters; hire dinghies, rowing boats, kayaks and motor boats from the **Coniston Boating Centre** (☑015394-41366; www.conistonboatingcentre.co.uk; Coniston Jetty).

☑ Don't Miss

Rowing your own boat, and playing at pirates, on the bewitching lake that inspired the *Swallows and Amazons* children's tales.

DAVID HUGHES / SHUTTERSTOCK ©

✖ Take a Break

Not too far from Dove Cottage, Jumble Room (p203) is a welcoming and imaginative dining choice in Grasmere.

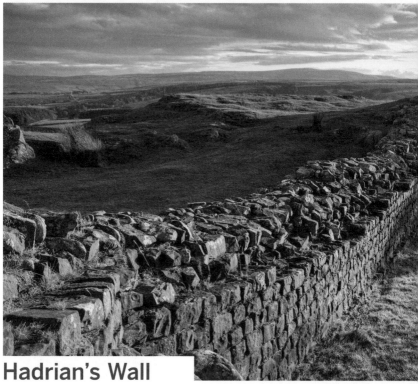

Hadrian's Wall

Named in honour of the emperor who ordered its construction, the 73-mile-long Hadrian's Wall was one of Rome's greatest engineering projects, built right across Britain's narrow neck between AD 122 and 128.

Designed to separate Romans and Scottish Picts, the remaining awe-inspiring sections of Hadrian's Wall are testament to Roman ambition and tenacity.

Housesteads Roman Fort & Museum

The most dramatic site of Hadrian's Wall, and the best-preserved **Roman fort** (EH; ☎01434-344363; www.english-heritage.org.uk; Haydon Bridge; adult/child £7.80/4.70; ⊙10am-6pm Apr-Sep, to 5pm Oct, to 4pm Nov-Mar) in the whole country, is at Housesteads 7 miles northeast of Haltwhistle. From here, high on a ridge and covering 5 acres, you can survey the snaking wall, with a sense of awe at the landscape and the Roman lookouts.

Remains here include an impressive hospital, granaries and spectacularly situated communal flushable latrines.

Great For...

☑ Don't Miss

The evocative Roman writing tablets on display at Vindolanda fort.

ⓘ Need to Know

Hadrian's Wall Country (http://hadrians wallcountry.co.uk) is the official portal for the entire area.

✕ Take a Break

All of the sites featured have cafes for mid-sightseeing stops.

★ Top Tip

Make savings with a joint ticket for Vindolanda Fort and the Roman Army Museum.

Vindolanda Roman Fort & Museum

Handily near Housesteads Roman Fort & Museum, the sweeping site of **Vindolanda** (☏01434-344277; www.vindolanda.com; Bardon Mill; adult/child £7.90/4.75, with Roman Army Museum £11.60/6.80; ⊙10am-6pm Apr-Sep, to 5pm early Feb-Mar & Oct, to 4pm Nov-early Feb) offers a fascinating glimpse into the daily life of a Roman garrison town. It's a large, extensively excavated site, which includes impressive parts of the fort and town and reconstructed turrets and temple.

Vindolanda is 5.8 miles northeast of Haltwhistle.

Roman Army Museum

On the site of the Carvoran Roman Fort a mile northeast of Greenhead, this revamped **museum** (☏01697-747485; www.  vindolanda.com/roman-army-museum; Greenhead; adult/child £6.60/3.75 with Vindolanda £11.60/6.80; ⊙10am-6pm Apr-Sep, to 5pm mid-Feb–Mar & Oct) has three new galleries covering the Roman army and the empire; the wall (with a 3D film comparing what the wall was like nearly 2000 years ago and today); and colourful background detail to Hadrian's Wall life.

Birdoswald Roman Fort

Technically in Cumbria, the remains of this once-formidable **fort** (EH; ☏01697-747602; www.english-heritage.org.uk; Gilsland, Greenhead; adult/child £8.30/5; ⊙10am-6pm Apr-Sep, 10am-5pm Oct, 10am-4pm Sat & Sun Nov–mid-Feb, 10am-4pm Wed-Sun mid-Feb–Mar) on an escarpment overlooking the beautiful Irthing Gorge are on a minor road off the B6318, about 3 miles west of Greenhead. The longest intact stretch of wall extends from here to Harrow's Scar Milecastle. A 4m-high gatehouse leads to interactive, kid-friendly exhibits, which were revamped in 2018.

Hadrian's Wall

ROME'S FINAL FRONTIER

Of all Britain's Roman ruins, Emperor Hadrian's 2nd-century wall, cutting across northern England from the Irish Sea to the North Sea, is by far the most spectacular; Unesco awarded it World Heritage status in 1987.

We've picked out the highlights, one of which is the prime remaining Roman fort on the wall, Housesteads, which we've reconstructed here.

Housesteads' Granaries
Nothing like the clever underground ventilation system, which kept vital supplies of grain dry in Northumberland's damp and drizzly climate, would be seen again in these parts for 1500 years.

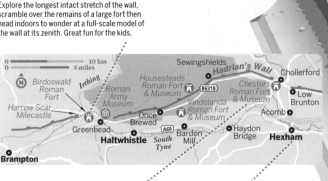

Milecastle

North Gate

Interval Tower

Birdoswald Roman Fort
Explore the longest intact stretch of the wall, scramble over the remains of a large fort then head indoors to wonder at a full-scale model of the wall at its zenith. Great fun for the kids.

[Map]

0 — 10 km
0 — 5 miles

Birdoswald Roman Fort · Irthing · Roman Army Museum · Sewingshields · Housesteads Roman Fort & Museum · Hadrian's Wall · B6318 · Chollerford · Chesters Roman Fort & Museum · Low Brunton · Harrow Scar Milecastle · Greenhead · Haltwhistle · Once Brewed · A69 · Vindolanda Roman Fort & Museum · South Tyne · Bardon Mill · Acomb · Haydon Bridge · Hexham · Brampton

Chesters Roman Fort
Built to keep watch over a bridge spanning the River North Tyne, Britain's best-preserved Roman cavalry fort has a terrific bathhouse, essential if you have months of nippy northern winter ahead.

Hexham Abbey
This may be the finest non-Roman sight near Hadrian's Wall, but the 7th-century parts of this magnificent church were built with stone quarried by the Romans for use in their forts.

Housesteads' Hospital
Operations performed at the hospital would have been surprisingly effective, even without anaesthetics; religious rituals and prayers to Aesculapius, the Roman god of healing, were possibly less helpful for a hernia or appendicitis.

Housesteads' Latrines
Communal toilets were the norm in Roman times and Housesteads' are remarkably well preserved – fortunately no traces remain of the vinegar-soaked sponges that were used instead of toilet paper.

QUICK WALL FACTS & FIGURES

Latin name Vallum Aelium

Length 73.5 miles (80 Roman miles)

Construction date AD 122–128

Manpower for construction
Three legions (around 16,000 men)

Features At least 16 forts, 80 milecastles, 160 turrets

Did you know Hadrian's wasn't the only Roman wall in Britain – the Antonine Wall was built across what is now central Scotland in the AD 140s, but it was abandoned soon after.

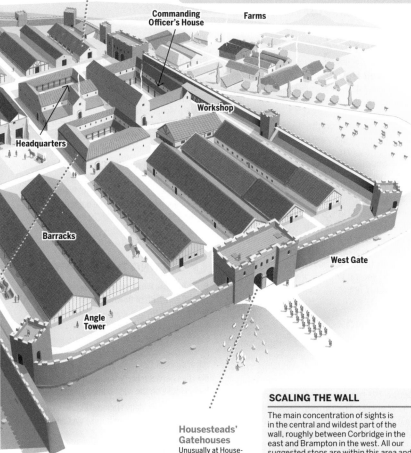

Commanding Officer's House

Farms

Workshop

Headquarters

Barracks

West Gate

Angle Tower

Housesteads' Gatehouses
Unusually at Housesteads neither of the gates faces the enemy, as was the norm at Roman forts; builders aligned them east–west. Ruts worn by cart wheels are still visible in the stone.

FREE GUIDES

At some sites, knowledgeable volunteer heritage guides are on hand to answer questions and put meat on the wall's stony bones.

SCALING THE WALL

The main concentration of sights is in the central and wildest part of the wall, roughly between Corbridge in the east and Brampton in the west. All our suggested stops are within this area and follow an east–west route. The easiest way to travel is by car, scooting along the B6318, but special bus AD122 will also get you there. Hiking along the designated Hadrian's Wall Path (84 miles) allows you to appreciate the achievement up close.

Windermere

Stretching for 10.5 miles between Ambleside and Newby Bridge, Windermere isn't just the queen of Lake District lakes – it's also the largest body of water anywhere in England, closer in scale to a Scottish loch.

Confusingly, the town of Windermere is split in two: Windermere Town is actually 1.5 miles from the lake, at the top of a steep hill, while touristy, overdeveloped Bowness-on-Windermere (usually shortened just to Bowness) sits on the lake's eastern shore.

◎ SIGHTS

Blackwell House   Historic Building
(☎015394-46139; www.blackwell.org.uk; adult/child under 16yr £8/free; ⊙10.30am-5pm Apr-Oct, to 4pm Feb, Mar, Nov & Dec) Two miles south of Bowness on the B5360, Blackwell House is a glorious example of the 19th-century Arts and Crafts movement, which championed handmade goods and craftsmanship over the mass-produced mentality of the Industrial Revolution. Designed by Mackay Hugh Baillie Scott for Sir Edward Holt, a wealthy brewer, the house shimmers with Arts and Crafts details: light, airy rooms, bespoke craftwork, wood panelling, stained glass and delft tiles. The mock-medieval Great Hall and serene White Drawing Room are particularly fine.

✖ EATING

Mason's Arms   Pub Food ££
(☎015395-68486; www.masonsarmsstrawberry bank.co.uk; Winster; mains £12.95-18.95) Three miles east of Crosthwaite, near Bowlands Bridge, the marvellous Mason's Arms is a local secret. The rafters, flagstones and cast-iron range haven't changed in centuries, and the patio has to-die-for views across fields and fells. The food is hearty – Cumbrian stewpot, slow-roasted Cartmel lamb – and there are lovely rooms and cottages for rent (£175 to £350). In short, a cracker.

◉ DRINKING & NIGHTLIFE

Crafty Baa   Craft Beer
(☎015394-88002; 21 Victoria St, Windermere Town; ⊙11am-11pm) The clue's in the name – the craft-beer revolution comes to Windermere, with a vast selection of brews: Czech pilsners, weissbiers, smoked lagers, even mango, gooseberry and coconut beers, chalked up on a wall of slates and served (if you wish) with snack platters. The space (a former house) is tiny, but plans are afoot to expand next door.

❶ INFORMATION

Brockhole National Park Visitor Centre
(☎015394-46601; www.brockhole.co.uk; ⊙10am-5pm) In a 19th-century mansion 3 miles north of Windermere on the A591, this is the Lake District's flagship visitor centre. It also has a cafe, an adventure playground, gardens and kid-friendly activities such as archery, minigolf, treetop nets and the new 'Brave the Cave' attraction.

Windermere Information Centre (☎015394-46499; www.windermereinfo.co.uk; Victoria St, Windermere Town; ⊙8.30am-5.30pm) Windermere's visitor centre is now run by the outdoor-activity provider **Mountain Goat** (☎015394-45161; www.mountain-goat.com; Victoria St, Windermere Town).

❶ GETTING THERE & AWAY

Boat To cross Windermere by car, bike or on foot, head south of Bowness to the **Windermere Ferry** (www.cumbria.gov.uk/roads-transport/highways-pavements/windermereferry.asp; car/bicycle/pedestrian £4.40/£1/50p; ⊙every 20 min 6.50am-9.50pm Mon-Fri, 9.10am-9.50pm Sat & Sun Mar-Oct, to 8.50pm Nov-Feb), which shuttles between Ferry Nab on the east bank to Ferry House on the west bank.

Bus There's one daily National Express coach from London (£46, eight hours) via Lancaster and Kendal.

Train Windermere is the only town inside the national park accessible by train. It's on the branch line to Kendal and Oxenholme, with onward connections to Edinburgh, Manchester and London Piccadilly.

Grasmere

Huddled at the edge of an island-studded lake surrounded by woods, pastures and slate-coloured hills, it's most famous as the former home of the grand old daddy of the Romantics himself, poet William Wordsworth, who set up home at nearby Dove Cottage in 1799, and spent much of the rest of his life here.

🚴 ACTIVITIES

Helm Crag — Hiking

If you only do one fell walk in Grasmere, make it Helm Crag. Sometimes referred to as 'the Lion and the Lamb', after the twin crags atop its summit, it's a rewarding two-hour climb, but it's dauntingly steep in places, with around 335m of elevation gain. The trail starts on Easedale Rd and is fairly well signposted.

🛍 SHOPPING

Sarah Nelson's Gingerbread Shop — Food

(☏015394-35428; www.grasmeregingerbread.co.uk; Church Cottage; ⏱9.15am-5.30pm Mon-Sat, 12.30-5pm Sun) In business since 1854, this famous sweet shop next to the village church makes Grasmere's essential souvenir: traditional gingerbread with a half-biscuity, half-cakey texture (six/12 pieces for £3.50/6.70), cooked using the original top-secret recipe. Friendly service is provided by ladies dressed in frilly pinafores and starched bonnets.

🍴 EATING

Jumble Room — Modern British ££

(☏015394-35188; www.thejumbleroom.co.uk; Langdale Rd; dinner mains £14.50-23; ⏱5.30-9.30pm Wed-Mon) Husband-and-wife team Andy and Crissy Hill have turned this village bistro into a much-loved dining landmark. It's a really fun and friendly place to eat. Spotty crockery, cow murals and primary colours set the boho tone, matched by a magpie menu that borrows flavours and ingredients from a global cookbook – Malaysian seafood curry one week, Persian lamb the next.

Windermere Lake Cruises

Since the launch of the first passenger ferry in 1845, taking a **cruise** (☏015394-43360; www.windermere-lakecruises.co.uk; tickets from £2.70) has been an essential part of every Windermere itinerary. The most popular route is the Islands Cruise (adult/child/family £8.60/4.30/23), a 45-minute circular cruise around Windermere's shoreline and islands. From April to October, rowing boats (£16 per hour) and cute cabin motorboats (from £30 for two adults per hour; children under 16 free) can be hired from the pier at Bowness.

JULIUSKIELAITIS / SHUTTERSTOCK ©

🍺 DRINKING & NIGHTLIFE

Traveller's Rest — Pub

(☏015394-35604; www.lakedistrictinns.co.uk/travellers-rest; A591; ⏱10am-11pm) With its sputtering fires and inglenook bar, this 16th-century coaching inn on the A591 makes a fine place for a pint and a simple pie supper.

ℹ GETTING THERE & AWAY

Bus 555 (at least hourly, including Sundays) runs regularly from Windermere to Grasmere (15 minutes) via Ambleside, Rydal Church and Dove Cottage, then travels onwards to Keswick.

The open-top 599 (two or three per hour in summer) runs from Grasmere via Ambleside, Troutbeck Bridge, Windermere and Bowness.

On both buses, Grasmere to Ambleside is £4.70, to Bowness and Windermere is £7.20.

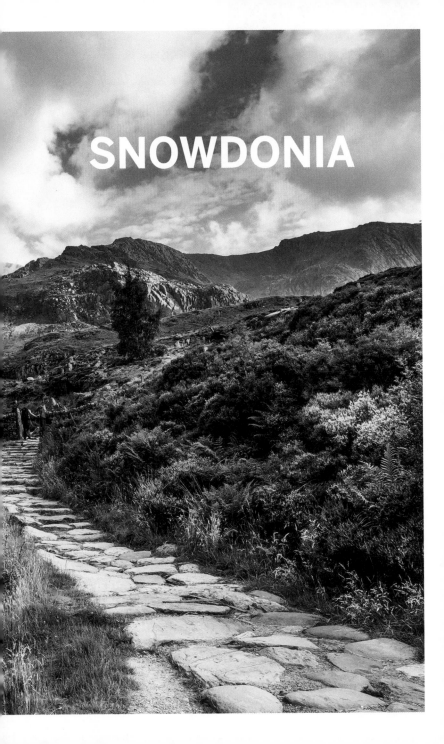

SNOWDONIA

Snowdonia at a Glance...

Wales is crowned with Snowdonia – a range of rocky peaks, glacier-hewn valleys and bird-filled estuaries stretching across the north of the country. This is Wales' best-known and most-visited slice of nature, and every year more than 400,000 people walk, climb or take the train to the 1085m summit of Snowdon. Alongside Wales' biggest natural lake, Snowdonia National Park's 823 sq miles are also home to a breathtaking array of adrenaline pursuits that will make your heart pound.

Two Days in Snowdonia

Check the weather, then go for the big one on your first day: climbing **Snowdon** (p210) – or riding the train to the top. Celebrate with supper at the **Tŷ Gwyn Hotel** (p213). The following day, ride the rapids – on a raft or kayak, it's up to you – at the **National White Water Centre** (p209), then hang ten with the dudes at **Surf Snowdonia** (p209).

Four Days in Snowdonia

Take it (relatively) easy on day three – zip-lining through subterranean **slate mines** (p208) and bouncing on giant trampolines at **Zip World Slate Caverns** (p209). Dinner? A cosy one at **Bistro Betws-y-Coed** (p212). Start day four by gazing at Wales' highest **waterfalls** (p213) before hiking through **Gwydyr Forest** (p212). End your Snowdonia adventures with music at the **Stables Bar** (p213).

Previous page: A cobbled path near Capel Curig

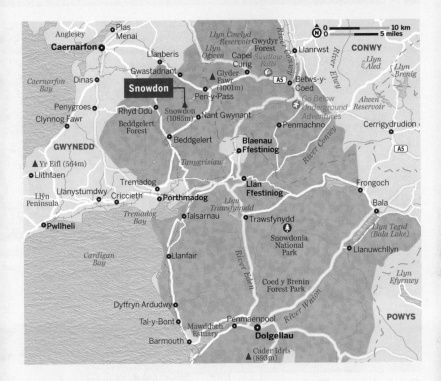

Arriving in Snowdonia

Bus Bus services are extensive, reaching towns such as Betws-y-Coed, Llanberis, Dolgellau and Bala.

Car The A5, A494, A470 and A487 are the principal roads into the park.

Train There are three major rail routes into and around the park: the Cambrian, North Wales Coast and Conwy Valley lines.

Where to Stay

Accommodation is not a problem in well-peopled Snowdonia. Hotels and B&Bs cluster around the towns, especially Betws, and there are numerous hostels, self-catering cottages and campgrounds. Some can close seasonally or be overrun in school holidays.

Outdoor Thrills

Snowdonia is not only a superb place for hiking, it also boasts the kind of adventurous activities that make heroes of everyday folk and adrenaline junkies grin.

Great For...

☑ **Don't Miss**

White-knuckle, white-water rafting or kayaking on the foaming waters of the River Trywery.

Climbing & Mountaineering

At the western edge of the village of Capel Curig, the **Plas y Brenin National Mountain Sports Centre** (☑01690-720214; www.pyb.co.uk; A4086) has excellent facilities and a huge array of year-round courses, from basic rock climbing and mountaineering, to kayaking, canoeing and abseiling.

Adrenaline Activities

Head into the depths of an old slate mine and try your hand zip-lining across lakes and abseiling down shafts with **Go Below Underground Adventures** (☑01690-710108; www.go-below.co.uk; adventures from £49; ⊘9am-5pm). You don't need caving experience, or to squeeze through tiny spaces, but claustrophobes may demur.

Rafting with the National White Water Centre

D. PIMBOROUGH / SHUTTERSTOCK ©

❶ Need to Know

Snowdonia National Park Information Centre (p213) is an invaluable source of information about walking trails, mountain conditions and more.

✕ Take a Break

Pete's Eats (☏01286-870117; www.petes-eats.co.uk; 40 High St; mains £5-6; ✿8am-8pm; 📶) in Llanberis is a legendary adventurists' cafe.

★ Top Tip

Book activities well in advance and allow some flexibility in case conditions force a reschedule.

1 uplift £5, day pass from £31; ✿10am-4pm Thu-Mon), which boasts six blue, red, black and double-black mountain-bike runs down the mountainside near Blaenau Ffestiniog's slate caverns.

White-Water Activities

On the River Tryweryn's reliable white water, rafting, kayaking and canoeing is possible around 200 days per year. Trips with the **National White Water Centre** (Canolfan Dŵr Gwyn Genedlaethol; ☏01678-521083; www.ukrafting.co.uk; Frongoch; 1/2hr trip £35/66; ✿9am-4.30pm Mon-Fri) traverse a 1.5-mile stretch through abundant Class III white water and Class IV sections.

Surfing

Lying just outside the national park's eastern border, in the lush Conwy Valley, **Surf Snowdonia** (☏01492-353123; www.surfsnowdonia.co.uk; Conway Rd, Dolgarrog; ✿8am-11pm; 📶) is an unexpected slice of Maui: an adventure park with a vast artificial wave pool (open 10am until sunset). If learning to surf (adult/child £55/45) doesn't excite, there are lagoon 'crash and splash' sessions (£25 per hour), kayaking and walking.

The booking office is at Conwy Falls, on the A5 south of Betws at the Penmachno turn-off.

If you'd rather try trampolining in a slate mine, **Zip World Slate Caverns** (☏01248-601444; www.zipworld.co.uk; Llechwedd Slate Caverns; ✿booking office 8am-6.30pm; 📶) offers Bounce Below, a 'cathedral-sized' cavern with bouncy nets, walkways, tunnels and slides (one hour adult/child £25/20). It also offers Titan, 8000m of zip wires over deep open pits (£50 per two hours), and zip wires through the caverns (£65).

Mountain Biking

If you don't know the meaning of fear, check out **Antur Stiniog** (☏01766-238007; www.anturstiniog.com; Llechwedd Slate Caverns;

Snowdon

No Snowdonia experience is complete without coming face-to-face with Snowdon (1085m), one of Britain's most awe-inspiring mountains. You can climb it on foot or let the train take the strain.

Welcome to Wales' highest mountain. 'Yr Wyddfa' in Welsh (pronounced (uhr-with-vuh, meaning 'The Tomb'), it's the mythical resting place of the giant Rhita Gawr, who demanded King Arthur's beard for his cloak, and was killed for his temerity. On a clear day the views stretch to Ireland and the Isle of Man.

Climbing Snowdon

The most straightforward route to the summit is the **Llanberis Path** (9 miles return) running beside the train line. The two paths starting from Pen-y-Pass require the least amount of ascent, but are nevertheless tougher walks: the **Miner's Track** (8 miles return) starts off wide and gentle but gets steep beyond Llyn Llydaw; and the more interesting **Pyg Track** (7 miles return) is more rugged still.

Great For...

☑ **Don't Miss**

The views over jagged ridges and deep lakes. Even on gloomy days you could be above the clouds.

Hiker on Snowdon

DILCHASPIYAN / SHUTTERSTOCK ©

❶ Need to Know

Hafod Eryri (https://snowdonrailway.co.uk; ⏱10am-20min before last train departure Easter-Oct; ☎) is Snowdon's information centre.

✖ Take a Break

The Hafod Eryri centre on Snowdon's summit has a decent cafe.

★ Top Tip

Arrive early or use public transport – the Pen-y-Pas car park can fill up by 8am.

Two tracks start from the Caernarfon–Beddgelert road (A4085): the **Snowdon Ranger Path** (8 miles return) is the safest route in winter, while the **Rhyd Ddu Path** (8 miles return) is the least-used route and boasts spectacular views. The most challenging route is the **Watkin Path** (8 miles return), involving an ascent of more than 1000m on its southerly approach from Nantgwynant, and finishing with a scramble across a steep-sided scree-covered slope.

The classic **Snowdon Horseshoe** (7.5 miles return) branches off from the Pyg Track to follow the precipitous ridge of **Crib Goch** (one of the most dangerous routes on the mountains and only recommended for the very experienced) with a descent over the peak of Y Lliwedd and a final section down the Miner's Track.

Snowdon Mountain Railway

If you can't, or would rather not, climb Snowdon, there is an alternative. Opened in 1896, the **Snowdon Mountain Railway** (☎01286-870223; www.snowdonrailway.co.uk; adult/child return diesel £29/20, steam £37/27; ⏱9am-5pm mid-Mar–Oct) is the UK's highest rack-and-pinion railway. Vintage steam and modern diesel locomotives haul carriages from Llanberis up to Snowdon's summit in an hour. Book tickets well in advance.

Getting To Snowdon

All the trailheads are accessible by Snowdon Sherpa bus services S1, S2, S4 or S97 (single/day ticket £2/5).

The **Welsh Highland Railway** (☎01766-516000; www.festrail.co.uk; ⏱Easter-Oct, limited service winter) stops at the trailhead of the Rhyd Ddu Path, and there is a request stop (Snowdon Ranger Halt) where you can alight for the Snowdon Ranger Path.

Betws-y-Coed

Betws-y-Coed (bet-us-ee-coyd) sits at the junction of three river valleys (the Llugwy, the Conwy and the Lledr) and on the verge of the Gwydyr Forest. With outdoor-gear shops appearing to outnumber pubs, walking trails leaving right from the centre and guesthouses occupying a fair proportion of its slate Victorian buildings, it's the perfect base for exploring Snowdonia.

◎ SIGHTS

Gwydyr Forest   Forest

The 28-sq-mile Gwydyr Forest, planted since the 1920s with oak, beech and larch, encircles Betws-y-Coed and is scattered with the remnants of lead and zinc mine workings. Named for a more ancient forest in the same location, it's ideal for a day's walking, though it gets very muddy in wet weather. *Walks Around Betws-y-Coed* (£5),

the perfect base for exploring Snowdonia

Dawn over the Gwydyr Forest

available from the National Park Information Centre (p213), details several circular forest walks.

The northern section of the park is home to the Gwydyr Bach and Gwydyr Mawr Mountain Bike Trail, a challenging 16-mile circuit starting immediately southwest of Llanrwst, 3.5 miles north of Betws. A map and pamphlet detailing the route can be downloaded for free at www.mbwales.com.

⊗ EATING

Bistro Betws-y-Coed   Welsh ££

(☏01690-710328; www.bistrobetws-y-coed. co.uk; Holyhead Rd; lunch £8-9, dinner £15-18; ⊘noon-2.30pm & 6.30-9pm Jun-Sep, shorter hours rest of year) Perhaps the best place to eat in town, Bistro Betws offers some interesting adaptations of national staples, such as haddock with Welsh-rarebit crumb. Watch out for possible shot pellets in the sautéed breast of wild pheasant with black-pudding potato cake and whisky sauce, and book in summer as it gets absolutely packed.

Bwyd i Fynd · Cafe £

(Food to Go; ☏01690-710006; www.bwydifynd.
co.uk; Station Approach; Welsh cakes 70p;
☺9am-10pm, shorter hours Oct-Mar) This
pint-sized spot serves Welsh cakes straight
from the griddle, from traditional fare to
unusually flavoured sweet and savoury
ones; all are made with organic Welsh eggs
and butter. Pies, homemade cakes and
good coffee are also available: all ideal
picnic fodder.

Tŷ Gwyn Hotel · European ££

(☏01690-710383; www.tygwynhotel.co.uk; A5;
mains £15-19; ☺noon-2pm & 6-9pm; 🅿) This
400-year-old coaching inn oozes character
from every one of its numerous exposed
beams. The menu is full of delicious-
sounding local ingredients (Pen Loyn
Farm lamb loin, whole lake trout from Llyn
Brenig) and a decent number of veggie
options (the wild-mushroom and pine-nut
stroganoff is good), but the real appeal is
the quirky old building itself.

🍷 DRINKING & NIGHTLIFE

Stables Bar · Pub

(☏016907-10219; www.stables-bistro.co.uk;
A5; ☺11.30am-11pm; 🛜) Attached to the
grander Royal Oak, and doing a roaring
trade in lasagne, curries and pints for
weary walkers, the Stables (Y Stablau) is
the only pub per se in Betwys. It's a long,
low-ceilinged, tile-floored barn of a place,
but very welcoming. There's also music,
including Dixieland, blues and Welsh
male choirs.

ℹ INFORMATION

Snowdonia National Park Information
Centre (☏01690-710426; www.eryri-npa.
gov.uk; Royal Oak Stables; ☺9.30am-5.30pm
Easter-Oct, to 4pm rest of year) More than just a

Swallow Falls

Betws-y-Coed's main natural tourist
draw are these **falls** (Rhaeadr Ewynnol;
adult/child £1.50/50p), located 2 miles
west of town, alongside the A5 on the
River Llugwy. It's a beautiful spot, with
the 42m torrent, Wales' highest, weav-
ing through the rocks into a green pool
below. Outside seasonal opening hours,
bring coins for the turnstile (no change
is available).

PHIL KIERAN / SHUTTERSTOCK ©

repository of books, maps and local craft, this
office is an invaluable source of information
about walking trails, mountain conditions
and more.

🚍 GETTING THERE & AROUND

Betws-y-Coed is on the Conwy Valley Line
(www.conwyvalleyrailway.co.uk), with up to
five trains every day to Llandudno (£6.60,
50 minutes) and Blaenau Ffestiniog (£5.40,
34 minutes).

Snowdon Sherpa bus service S2 heads to
Swallow Falls (seven minutes), Capel Curig
(12 minutes), Pen-y-Pass (25 minutes), Llanberis
(35 minutes) and Bangor (route S6, in summer,
one hour); all trips are £2.

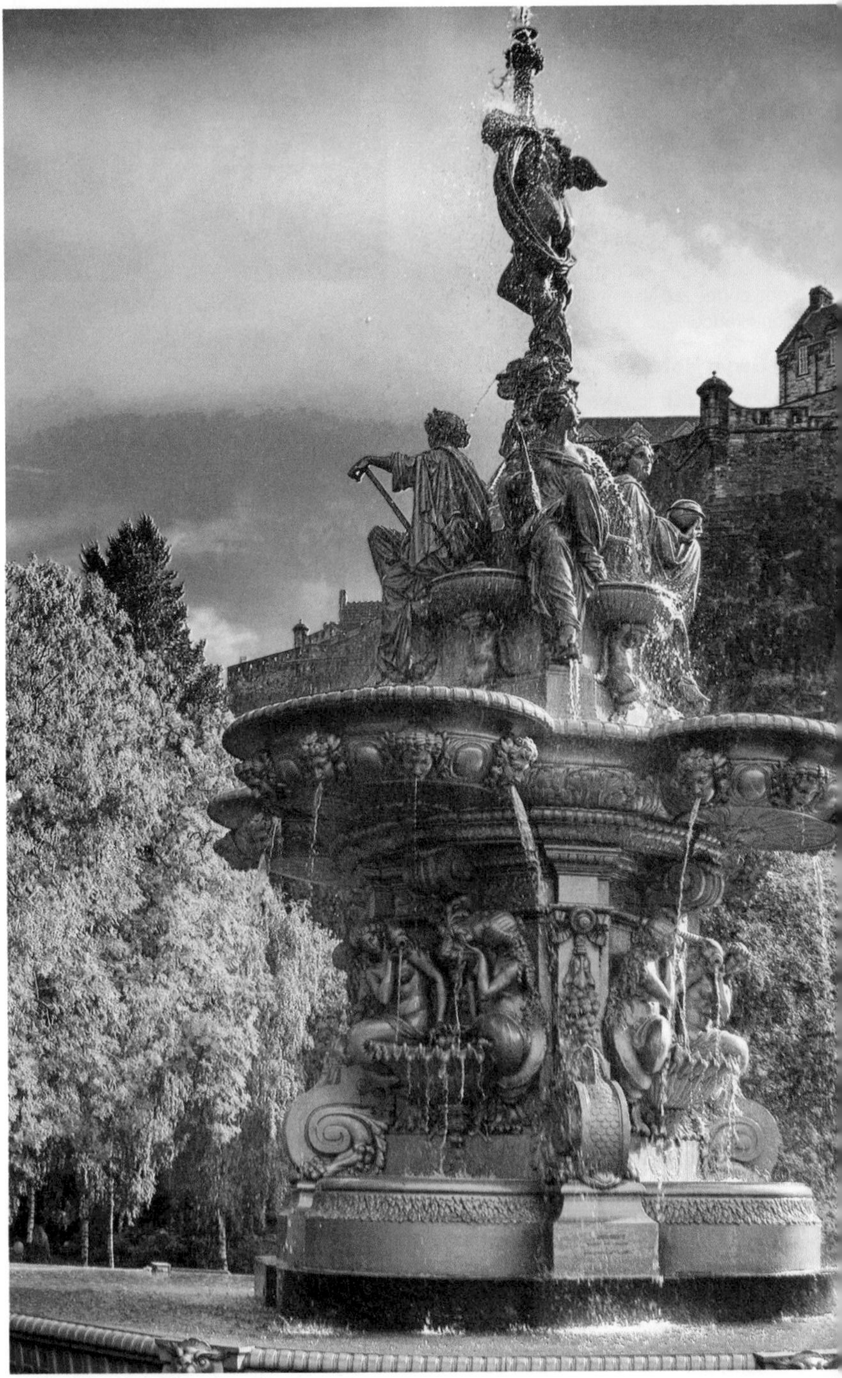

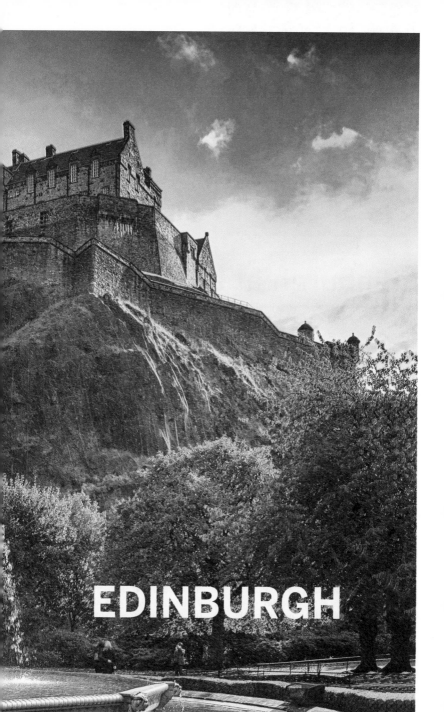

EDINBURGH

In This Chapter

Edinburgh at a Glance...

Draped across a series of rocky hills overlooking the sea, Edinburgh is one of Europe's most beguiling cities. It is here that each summer the world's biggest arts festival rises, phoenix-like, from the ashes of last year's rave reviews and broken box-office records to produce yet another string of superlatives. Deeply cultured but also intrinsically down-to-earth, Edinburgh is a city of loud, crowded pubs, decadent restaurants, beer-fuelled poets and foul-mouthed comedians.

Two Days in Edinburgh

First up, **Edinburgh Castle** (p219), then a stroll down the **Royal Mile** (p228), via **Real Mary King's Close** (p231). Scare yourself silly on a churchyard **ghost tour** (p239), then recover at cosily romantic **Ondine** (p241). On day two, soak up the culture at the **National Museum of Scotland** (p236) before cracking the code at the **Rosslyn Chapel** (p225). Head to **Contini** (p241) for dinner.

Four Days in Edinburgh

Get active on day three with a hike up to **Arthur's Seat** (p236), then slow it down at the **Scotch Whisky Experience** (p237). Weave your way to **Grain Store** (p241) for dinner, followed by a **bar crawl** (p244) of the city's whisky bars. On day four, after swanning around the **Royal Yacht Britannia** (p237), explore the Old Town's **alleyways** (p234). Hungry? Stop by excellent **Timberyard** (p241).

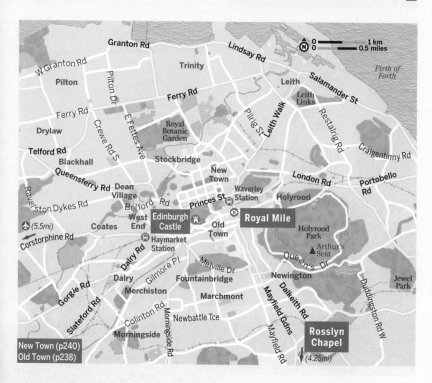

Arriving in Edinburgh

Edinburgh Airport Bus 100 shuttles to Waverley Bridge (£4.50, 30 minutes, every 10 minutes), outside the main train station, via Haymarket and the West End. Trams to the city centre (£6, 33 minutes, every six to eight minutes) run from 6am to midnight. Taxis to the city centre cost £20.

Edinburgh Waverley Train Station The main, central train station. Trains for the west also stop at Edinburgh Haymarket.

Where to Stay

Edinburgh offers a wide range of accommodation options, from moderately priced guest houses set in lovely Victorian villas and Georgian townhouses to expensive and stylish boutique hotels. There are also plenty of international chain hotels, and a few truly exceptional hotels housed in magnificent historic buildings. At the budget end, the youth hostels and independent backpacker hostels often have twins and doubles.

ANNA KUCHEROVA / SHUTTERSTOCK ©

Edinburgh Castle

Edinburgh Castle has played a pivotal role in Scottish history, both as a royal residence and as a military stronghold. King Malcolm Canmore (r 1058–93) and Queen Margaret first made their home in Edinburgh Castle in the 11th century. The castle last saw military action in 1745. Today it's one of Scotland's most atmospheric tourist attractions.

Great For...

☑ Don't Miss

The graffiti of American and French prisoners carved into the doors of the Castle Vaults.

Entrance Gateway

The Entrance Gateway, flanked by statues of Robert the Bruce and William Wallace, opens to a cobbled lane that leads up beneath the 16th-century Portcullis Gate to the cannons ranged along the Argyle and Mills Mount Batteries. The battlements here have great views over the New Town to the Firth of Forth.

One O'Clock Gun

At the far end of Mills Mount Battery is the famous One O'Clock Gun, where crowds gather to watch a gleaming WWII 25-pounder fire an ear-splitting time signal at exactly 1pm (every day except Sundays, Good Friday and Christmas Day).

St Margaret's Chapel

South of Mills Mount, the road curls up leftwards to the highest part of Castle Rock,

A stained-glass window in St Margaret's Chapel

ⓘ Need to Know

Map p238; ☑0131-225 9846; www.edinburgh
castle.gov.uk; Castle Esplanade; adult/child
£18.50/11.50, audio guide £3.50/£1.50;
⏱9.30am-6pm Apr-Sep, to 5pm Oct-Mar, last
entry 1hr before closing; 🚌23, 27, 41, 42, 67

✕ Take a Break

The **Tea Rooms at Edinburgh Castle**
(Map p238; www.edinburghcastle.scot/
shop-eat/cafes; Crown Sq; mains £9-15;
⏱9.30am-5pm Apr-Oct, 10.30am-4pm
Nov-Mar; 👶; 🚌23, 27, 41, 42) serves good
lunches.

★ Top Tip

Visit at lunchtime for the deafening
One O'Clock Gun.

crowned by tiny, Romanesque St Margaret's
Chapel, the oldest building in Edinburgh. It
was probably built by David I or Alexander I
in memory of their mother, Queen Margaret,
around 1130. Beside the chapel stands
Mons Meg, a giant 15th-century siege gun.

Crown Square

The main group of buildings on the summit
of Castle Rock sits around Crown Sq, dominated by the shrine of the Scottish National
War Memorial. Opposite is the Great Hall,
built for James IV (r 1488–1513) and the
meeting place for the Scottish parliament
until 1639. Its most remarkable feature is the
original 16th-century hammer-beam roof.

Castle Vaults

The Castle Vaults beneath the Great Hall
were used variously as storerooms, bakeries
and a prison. They've been renovated to resemble 18th-century prisons, where graffiti
carved by French and American inmates can
be seen on the ancient wooden doors.

The Royal Palace

On the eastern side of the square is the
Royal Palace, built during the 15th and 16th
centuries. it contains the castle's highlight:
the Honours of Scotland (the Scottish
crown jewels), among the oldest crown jewels in Europe. Locked away in a chest after
the Act of Union in 1707, the crown (made
in 1540 from the gold of Robert the Bruce's
14th-century coronet), sword and sceptre
lay forgotten until they were unearthed at
the instigation of the novelist Sir Walter
Scott in 1818. Also here is the legendary
Stone of Destiny, stolen from Scone Abbey
near Perth by Edward I of England in 1296
and returned to Edinburgh Castle in 1996.

Edinburgh Military Tattoo (p223)

Edinburgh's Festivals

Get set for culture galore – Edinburgh hosts an amazing number of festivals throughout the year. August in particular sees a frenzy of events, with several world-class festivals running at the same time, notably the Edinburgh International Festival, the Festival Fringe and the Military Tattoo. Hogmanay, Scotland's New Year's celebrations, is also peak party time.

Great For...

ⓘ Need to Know

Find listings for all of Edinburgh's festivals on the umbrella website www.edinburghfestivalcity.com.

★ **Top Tip**

Book as early as possible; the Fringe Office (p222) for the Fringe, The Hub (p223) for the International Festival.

The program for the Edinburgh International Festival is usually published at the beginning of April; the Festival Fringe program comes out in early June.

Edinburgh Festival Fringe

When the first Edinburgh Festival was held in 1947, there were eight theatre companies that didn't make it onto the main program. Undeterred, they grouped together and held their own minifestival – on the fringe – and an Edinburgh institution was born. Today the **Edinburgh Festival Fringe** (☎0131-226 0026; www.edfringe.com; ⊘Aug) is the biggest festival of the performing arts in the world.

Since 1990 the Fringe has been dominated by stand-up comedy, but the sheer variety of shows on offer is staggering – everything from chainsaw juggling to performance poetry to Tibetan yak-milk gargling.

So how do you decide what to see? There are daily reviews in the *Scotsman* – one good review and a show sells out in hours – but the best recommendation is word of mouth.

The big names play at megavenues organised by big agencies such as Assembly (www.assemblyfestival.com) and the Gilded Balloon (www.gildedballoon.co.uk), and charge megaprices (some up to and over £30), but there are plenty of good shows in the £5-to-£20 range and, best of all, lots of free stuff.

The Fringe takes place over 3½ weeks, the last two weeks overlapping with the first two of the Edinburgh International Festival.

For bookings and information, head to the **Edinburgh Festival Fringe Office** (☎0131-226 0026; www.edfringe.com; 180 High St; ⊘noon-3pm Mon-Sat mid-Jun–mid-Jul, 10am-6pm daily mid-Jul–1 Aug, 9am-9pm daily Aug; ☐all South Bridge buses).

A street performer on the Royal Mile (p228)

Edinburgh International Festival

First held in 1947 to mark a return to peace after the ordeal of WWII, the **Edinburgh International Festival** (☏0131-473 2000; www.eif.co.uk; ⊙Aug-Sep) is festooned with superlatives – the oldest, the biggest, the most famous, the best in the world. The original was a modest affair, but today hundreds of the world's top musicians and performers congregate in Edinburgh for three weeks of diverse and inspirational music, opera, theatre and dance.

The festival takes place over the three weeks ending on the first Saturday in

---

☑ Don't Miss

Edinburgh Festival Fringe's 'Fringe Sunday'. Usually the second Sunday, it's a smorgasbord of free performances, staged in the Meadows park.

GEORGECLERK / GETTY IMAGES ©

September. Tickets for popular events, especially music and opera, sell out quickly, so it's best to book as far in advance as possible. You can buy tickets in person at the **Hub** (☏0131-473 2015; www.thehub-edinburgh.com; Castlehill; ⊙ticket centre 10am-5pm Mon-Fri; ☏; 🚌23, 27, 41, 42), or by phone or internet.

Edinburgh Military Tattoo

August in Edinburgh kicks off with the **Edinburgh Military Tattoo** (☏0131-225 1188; www.edintattoo.co.uk; ⊙Aug), a spectacular display of military marching bands, massed pipes and drums, acrobats, cheerleaders and motorcycle display teams, all played out in front of the magnificent backdrop of the floodlit castle. Each show traditionally finishes with a lone piper, dramatically lit, playing a lament on the battlements. The Tattoo takes place over the first three weeks of August (from a Friday to a Saturday); there's one show at 9pm Monday to Friday and two (at 7.30pm and 10.30pm) on Saturday, but no performance on Sunday.

Edinburgh International Book Festival

Held in a little village of marquees in the middle of Charlotte Sq, the **Edinburgh International Book Festival** (☏0845 373 5888; www.edbookfest.co.uk; ⊙Aug) is a fun fortnight of talks, readings, debates, lectures, book signings and meet-the-author events, with a cafe-bar and tented bookshop thrown in. The festival lasts for two weeks (usually the first two weeks of the Edinburgh International Festival).

✕ Take a Break

Just steps away from the Edinburgh Festival Fringe Office are tasty Italian dishes at cheery **Gordon's Trattoria** (Map p238; ☏0131-225 7992; www.gordonstrattoria.com; 231 High St; mains £12-23; ⊙noon-11pm Sun-Thu, to midnight Fri & Sat; ♿; 🚌all South Bridge buses).

224 TOP EXPERIENCE

Rosslyn Chapel

The success of Dan Brown's novel The Da Vinci Code *and the subsequent Hollywood film has prompted a flood of visitors to this, Scotland's most beautiful and enigmatic church.*

Rosslyn Chapel was built in the mid-15th century for William St Clair, third earl of Orkney, and the ornately carved interior – at odds with the architectural fashion of its time – is a monument to the mason's art, rich in symbolic imagery and shrouded in mystery.

Famous highlights include the Apprentice Pillar; Lucifer, the Fallen Angel; and the Green Man. Alongside these notables, there's plenty more symbolism to explore.

The chapel is owned by the Episcopal Church of Scotland and services are still held here on Sunday mornings.

Rosslyn's Symbolism

As well as flowers, vines, angels and biblical figures, the carved stones include many examples of the pagan 'Green Man'; other

Great For...

☑ **Don't Miss**

The Apprentice Pillar with its intricate curved stonework and accompanying murderous back story.

ⓘ Need to Know

Collegiate Church of St Matthew; ☎0131-440 2159; www.rosslynchapel.com; Chapel Loan, Roslin; adult/child £9/free; ⏲9.30am-6pm Mon-Sat Jun-Aug, to 5pm Sep-May, noon-4.45pm Sun year-round; Ⓟ; 🚌37 ✏

✕ Take a Break

Rosslyn's visitor-centre **coffee shop** (Chapel Loan, Roslin; mains £4-9; ⏲9.30am-6pm Mon-Sat Jun-Aug, to 5pm Sep-May, noon-4.45pm Sun year-round; 🚌37) **has views over Roslin Glen.**

> ### ★ Top Tip
> Hourly talks by qualified guides are included in admission.

figures are associated with Freemasonry and the Knights Templar. Intriguingly, there are also carvings of plants from the Americas that predate Columbus' voyage of discovery. The symbolism of these images has led some researchers to conclude that Rosslyn is some kind of secret Templar repository, and it has been claimed that hidden vaults beneath the chapel could conceal anything from the Holy Grail or the head of John the Baptist to the body of Christ himself.

The Ceiling

The spectacular ceiling vault is decorated with engraved roses, lilies and stars: can you spot the sun and the moon?

Explore Some More

After visiting the chapel, head downhill to see the spectacularly sited ruins of Roslin Castle, then take a walk along leafy Roslin Glen.

How to Get There

Rosslyn Chapel is on the eastern edge of the village of Roslin, 7 miles south of Edinburgh's centre. Lothian Bus 37 to Penicuik Deanburn links Edinburgh to the village of Roslin. (Bus 37 to Bush does not go via Roslin.)

Rosslyn Chapel

DECIPHERING ROSSLYN

Rosslyn Chapel is a small building, but the density of decoration inside can be overwhelming. It's well worth buying the official guidebook by the Earl of Rosslyn first; find a bench in the gardens and have a skim through before going into the chapel – the background information will make your visit all the more interesting. The book also offers a useful self-guided tour of the chapel, and explains the legend of the Master Mason and the Apprentice.

Entrance is through the ❶ **north door**. Take a pew and sit for a while to allow your eyes to adjust to the dim interior; then look up at the ceiling vault, decorated with engraved roses, lilies and stars, (Can you spot the sun and the moon?). Walk left along the north aisle to reach the Lady Chapel, separated from the rest of the church by the ❷ **Mason's Pillar** and the ❸ **Apprentice Pillar**. Here you'll find carvings of ❹ **Lucifer**, the Fallen Angel, and the ❺ **Green Man**. Nearby are ❻ **carvings** that appear to resemble Indian corn (maize). Finally, go to the western end and look up at the wall – in the left corner is the head of the ❼ **Apprentice**; to the right is the (rather worn) head of the ❽ **Master Mason**.

ROSSLYN CHAPEL & THE DA VINCI CODE

Dan Brown was referencing Rosslyn Chapel's alleged links to the Knights Templar and the Freemasons – unusual symbols found among the carvings, and the fact that a descendant of its founder, William St Clair, was a Grand Master Mason – when he chose it as the setting for his novel's denouement. Rosslyn is indeed a coded work, written in stone, but its meaning depends on your point of view. See The Rosslyn Hoax? by Robert LD Cooper for an alternative interpretation of the chapel's symbolism.

E&E IMAGE LIBRARY / AGE FOTOSTOCK ©

Lucifer, the Fallen Angel
At head height, to the left of the second window from the left, is an upside-down angel bound with rope, a symbol often associated with Freemasonry. The arch above is decorated with the Dance of Death.

EXPLORE SOME MORE

After visiting the chapel, head downhill to see the spectacularly sited ruins of Roslin Castle, then take a walk along leafy Roslin Glen.

The Apprentice
High in the corner, beneath an empty statue niche, is the head of the murdered Apprentice, with a deep wound in his forehead above the right eye. Legend says the Apprentice was murdered in a jealous rage by the Master Mason. The worn head on the side wall to the left of the Apprentice is that of his mother.

RM

North Door

The Master Mason
❽

Baptistry

PRACTICAL TIPS

Local guides give hourly talks throughout the day, which are included in the admission price. No photography is allowed inside the chapel.

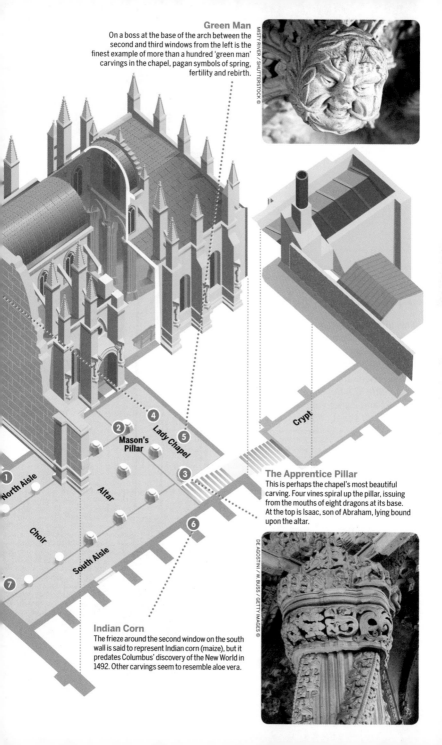

Green Man
On a boss at the base of the arch between the second and third windows from the left is the finest example of more than a hundred 'green man' carvings in the chapel, pagan symbols of spring, fertility and rebirth.

MISTY RIVER / SHUTTERSTOCK ©

Crypt

2 Mason's Pillar
4
5 Lady Chapel
3

1 North Aisle

Altar

Choir

6

South Aisle

7

The Apprentice Pillar
This is perhaps the chapel's most beautiful carving. Four vines spiral up the pillar, issuing from the mouths of eight dragons at its base. At the top is Isaac, son of Abraham, lying bound upon the altar.

DE AGOSTINI / W. BUSS / GETTY IMAGES ©

Indian Corn
The frieze around the second window on the south wall is said to represent Indian corn (maize), but it predates Columbus' discovery of the New World in 1492. Other carvings seem to resemble aloe vera.

The Royal Mile

This infinitely appealing mile-long street earned its nickname in the 16th century when the king used it to travel between the castle and the Palace of Holyroodhouse. There are five sections: Castle Esplanade, Castlehill, Lawnmarket, High St and Canongate. Twisting wynds (alleyways) shoot off alongside.

Great For...

ⓘ **Need to Know**

Leave enough time to enjoy the sights; a full day ensures you're not rushed.

★ **Top Tip**

Head to the Outlook Tower in the Camera Obscura for knockout city views.

From big-name attractions along the main streets to tempting detours into the maze of hidden alleyways, the Royal Mile is an irresistible place to explore.

Camera Obscura

This curious 19th-century **device** (Map p238; www.camera-obscura.co.uk; Castlehill; adult/child £15.50/11.50; ⊙9am-10pm Jul & Aug, 9.30am-8pm Apr-Jun, Sep & Oct, 10am-7pm Nov-Mar; ☒23, 27, 41, 42, 67) uses lenses and mirrors to throw a live image of the city onto a large horizontal screen.

Gladstone's Land

One of Edinburgh's most prominent 17th-century merchants was Thomas Gledstanes, who in 1617 purchased the tenement later known as **Gladstone's Land** (NTS; Map p238; ☎0131-226 5856; www. nts.org.uk/visit/places/gladstones-land; 477 Lawnmarket; adult/child £10/5; ⊙by prebooked guided tour; ☒23, 27, 41, 42, 67). It contains fine painted ceilings, walls and beams, and some splendid furniture from the 17th and 18th centuries.

St Giles Cathedral

The great grey bulk of **St Giles Cathedral** (Map p238; www.stgilescathedral.org.uk; High St; ⊙9am-7pm Mon-Fri, to 5pm Sat, 1-5pm Sun Apr-Oct, 9am-5pm Mon-Sat, 1-5pm Sun Nov-Mar; ☒23, 27, 41, 42) FREE dates largely from the 15th century, but much of it was restored in the 19th century. One of the most interesting corners of the kirk is the Thistle Chapel, built in 1911 for the Knights of the Most Ancient and Most Noble Order of the Thistle. The elaborately carved Gothic-style stalls have canopies topped with the helms

St Giles Cathedral

and arms of the 16 knights – look out for the bagpipe-playing angel amid the vaulting.

Monuments include the tombs of James Graham, Marquis of Montrose, who led Charles I's forces in Scotland and was hanged in 1650 at the Mercat Cross, and his Covenanter opponent Archibald Campbell, Marquis of Argyll, who was decapitated in 1661 after the Restoration of Charles II.

Real Mary King's Close

Edinburgh's 18th-century City Chambers were built over the sealed-off remains of Mary King's Close, and the lower levels of this

medieval Old Town **alley** (Map p238; ☎0131-225 0672; www.realmarykingsclose.com; 2 Warriston's Close; adult/child £15.50/9.50; ☺10am-9pm Apr-Oct, 9am-5.30pm Mon-Thu, 9.30am-9pm Fri & Sat, to 6.30pm Sun Nov, 10am-5pm Sun-Thu, to 9pm Fri & Sat Dec-Mar; ☐23, 27, 41, 42) have survived almost unchanged amid the foundations for 250 years. Now open to the public, this spooky, subterranean labyrinth gives a fascinating insight into the everyday life of 17th-century Edinburgh. Costumed characters lead tours through a 16th-century townhouse and the plague-stricken home of a 17th-century gravedigger; there's something about the crumbling 17th-century tenement room that makes the hairs rise on the back of your neck, with the ghost of a pattern on the walls, and the ancient smell of stone and dust thick in your nostrils.

In one of the former bedrooms off the close, a psychic once claimed to have been approached by the ghost of a little girl called Annie. It's hard to tell what's more frightening – the story of the ghostly child, or the bizarre heap of tiny dolls and teddies left in a corner by sympathetic visitors.

Advance booking is recommended.

Scottish Parliament Building

The **Scottish Parliament Building** (Map p238; ☎0131-348 5200; www.parliament.scot; Horse Wynd; ☺9am-6.30pm Tue-Thu, 10am-5pm Mon, Fri & Sat in session, 10am-5pm Tue-Thu in recess; ♿; ☐6, 300) **FREE**, on the site of a former brewery, was officially opened by HM the Queen in October 2004. Designed by Catalan architect Enric Miralles (1955–2000), the ground plan of the parliament complex represents a 'flower of democracy rooted in Scottish soil' (best seen looking down from Salisbury Crags).

MAREMAGNUM / GETTY IMAGES ©

Royal Mile

A GRAND DAY OUT

Planning your own procession along the Royal Mile involves some tough decisions – it would be impossible to see everything in a single day, so it's wise to decide in advance what you don't want to miss and shape your visit around that. Remember to leave time for lunch, for exploring some of the Mile's countless side alleys and, during festival time, for enjoying the street theatre that is bound to be happening in High St.

The most pleasant way to reach the Castle Esplanade at the start of the Royal Mile is to hike up the zigzag path from the footbridge behind the Ross Bandstand in Princes St Gardens (in springtime you'll be knee-deep in daffodils). Starting at ❶ **Edinburgh Castle** means that the rest of your walk is downhill. For a superb view up and down the length of the Mile, climb the ❷ **Camera Obscura's Outlook Tower** before visiting ❸ **Gladstone's Land** and ❹ **St Giles Cathedral**.

CLAUDIO DIVIZIA / SHUTTERSTOCK ©

Edinburgh Castle
If you're pushed for time, visit the Great Hall, the Honours of Scotland and the Prisons of War exhibit. Head for the Half Moon Battery for a photo looking down the length of the Royal Mile.

ROYAL VISITS TO THE ROYAL MILE

1561: Mary, Queen of Scots arrives from France and holds an audience with John Knox.
1745: Bonnie Prince Charlie fails to capture Edinburgh Castle, and instead sets up court in Holyroodhouse.
2004: Queen Elizabeth II officially opens the Scottish Parliament building.

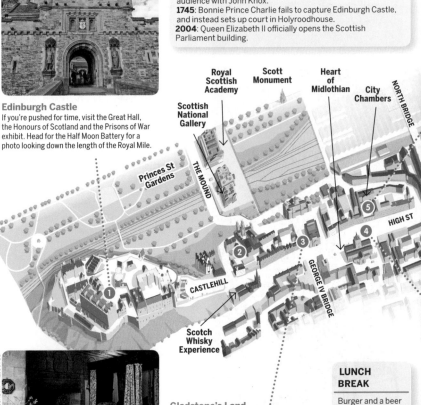

DE AGOSTINI / W BUSS / GETTY IMAGES ©

Gladstone's Land
The 1st floor houses a faithful recreation of how a wealthy Edinburgh merchant lived in the 17th century. Check out the beautiful Painted Bedchamber, with its ornately decorated walls and wooden ceilings.

LUNCH BREAK

Burger and a beer at **Holyrood 9A**; steak and chips at **Maxie's Bistro**; slap-up seafood at **Ondine**.

If history's your thing, you'll want to add **⑤ Real Mary King's Close**, **⑥ John Knox House** and the **⑦ Museum of Edinburgh** to your must-see list.

At the foot of the mile, choose between modern and ancient seats of power – the **⑧ Scottish Parliament** or the **⑨ Palace of Holyroodhouse**. Round off the day with an evening ascent of Arthur's Seat or, slightly less strenuously, Calton Hill. Both make great sunset viewpoints.

TAKING YOUR TIME

Minimum time needed for each attraction:

Edinburgh Castle two hours
Gladstone's Land 45 minutes
St Giles Cathedral 30 minutes
Real Mary King's Close one hour (tour)
Scottish Parliament one hour (tour)
Palace of Holyroodhouse one hour

Real Mary King's Close
The guided tour is heavy on ghost stories, but a highlight is standing in an original 17th-century room with tufts of horsehair poking from the crumbling plaster, and breathing in the ancient scent of stone, dust and history.

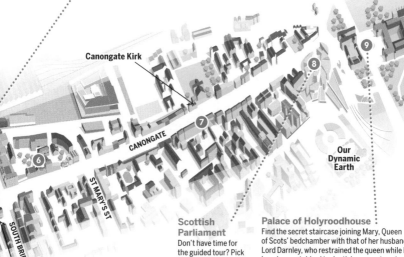

Canongate Kirk

CANONGATE

ST MARY'S ST

SOUTH BRIDGE

Tron Kirk

Our Dynamic Earth

Scottish Parliament
Don't have time for the guided tour? Pick up a 'Discover the Scottish Parliament Building' leaflet from reception and take a self-guided tour of the exterior, then hike up to Salisbury Crags for a great view of the complex.

Palace of Holyroodhouse
Find the secret staircase joining Mary, Queen of Scots' bedchamber with that of her husband, Lord Darnley, who restrained the queen while his henchmen stabbed to death her secretary (and possible lover), David Rizzio.

St Giles Cathedral
Look out for the Burne-Jones stained-glass window (1873) at the west end, showing the crossing of the River Jordan, and the bronze memorial to Robert Louis Stevenson in the Moray Aisle.

PHOTOPROF30 / SHUTTERSTOCK ©

HEARTLAND ARTS / SHUTTERSTOCK ©

DAVID IONUT / SHUTTERSTOCK ©

Edinburgh Walking Tour

Edinburgh's winding, ancient alleyways (or wynds) are a big part of the city's appeal. This walk leads you up steep steps and along cobbled streets awash with history and atmosphere. And into a pub, too.

Start Castle Esplanade
Distance 1 mile
Duration Two hours

Classic Photo The statue of John Knox framed by the towers of New College.

4 At **New College** visit a courtyard containing a statue of John Knox, a firebrand preacher who led the Protestant Reformation in Scotland.

3 Ramsay Garden is one of Edinburgh's most desirable addresses – where late 19th-century apartments were built around the octagonal Ramsay Lodge.

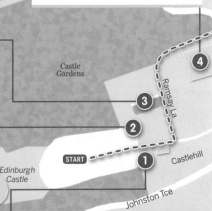

Castle Gardens

Ramsay La

Edinburgh Castle

START

Castlehill

Johnston Tce

2 On a west-facing wall of this low building, spot the **Witches Well** fountain, commemorating the 4000 people (mostly women), executed on suspicion of sorcery.

King's Stables Rd

1 At Castle Esplanade head to the 17th-century **Cannonball House** to spot the iron ball lodged in the wall between the two largest windows facing the castle.

Take a Break Stop by **Maxie's Bistro** (☎0131-226 7770; www.maxiesbistro.com; 5b Johnston Tce; ☉noon-11pm; mains £11-25), a cosy eatery with a terrace overlooking Victoria St.

W Port

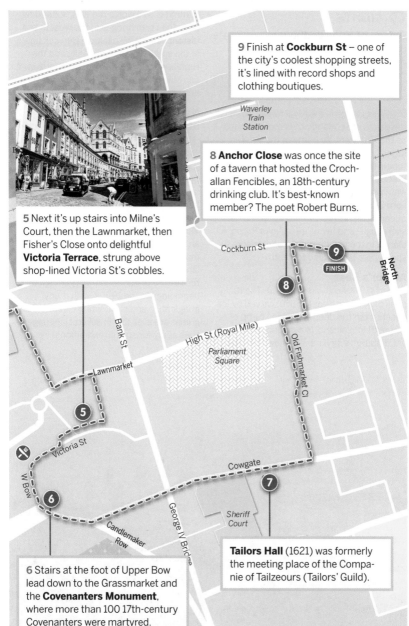

9 Finish at **Cockburn St** – one of the city's coolest shopping streets, it's lined with record shops and clothing boutiques.

Waverley Train Station

8 Anchor Close was once the site of a tavern that hosted the Crochallan Fencibles, an 18th-century drinking club. It's best-known member? The poet Robert Burns.

5 Next it's up stairs into Milne's Court, then the Lawnmarket, then Fisher's Close onto delightful **Victoria Terrace**, strung above shop-lined Victoria St's cobbles.

Cockburn St

9 FINISH

8

North Bridge

Bank St

High St (Royal Mile)

Parliament Square

Old Fishmarket Cl

Lawnmarket

5

Victoria St

Cowgate

W Bow

6

7

Candlemaker Row

George IV Bridge

Sheriff Court

6 Stairs at the foot of Upper Bow lead down to the Grassmarket and the **Covenanters Monument**, where more than 100 17th-century Covenanters were martyred.

Tailors Hall (1621) was formerly the meeting place of the Companie of Tailzeours (Tailors' Guild).

N 0 ——— 200 m
   0 ——— 0.1 miles

2 CLAUDIO DIVIZIA © 4 PETE SPIRO / SHUTTERSTOCK © 5 BLESKY / SHUTTERSTOCK ©

◎ SIGHTS

Palace of Holyroodhouse   Palace

(Map p238; ☑0303-123 7306; www.royal
collection.org.uk/visit/palace-of-holyroodhouse;
Canongate, Royal Mile; adult/child incl audio guide
£14/8.10; ⊙9.30am-6pm, last entry 4.30pm Apr-
Oct, to 4.30pm, last entry 3.15pm Nov-Mar; ⊒6,
300) This palace is the royal family's official
residence in Scotland but is more famous
as the 16th-century home of the ill-fated
Mary, Queen of Scots. The highlight of the
tour is **Mary's Bedchamber**, home to the
unfortunate queen from 1561 to 1567. It
was here that her jealous second husband,
Lord Darnley, restrained the pregnant
queen while his henchmen murdered her
secretary – and favourite – David Rizzio. A
plaque in the neighbouring room marks the
spot where Rizzio bled to death.

Arthur's Seat   Viewpoint

(Map p238; Holyrood Park; ⊒6, 300) The rocky
peak of Arthur's Seat (251m), carved by ice
sheets from the deeply eroded stump of a
long-extinct volcano, is a distinctive feature
of Edinburgh's skyline. The view from the
summit is well worth the walk, extending
from the Forth bridges in the west to the
distant conical hill of North Berwick Law
in the east, with the Ochil Hills and the
Highlands on the northwestern horizon. You
can hike from Holyrood to the summit in
around 45 minutes.

National Museum
of Scotland   Museum

(Map p238; ☑0300-123 6789; www.nms.ac.uk/
national-museum-of-scotland; Chambers St;
⊙10am-5pm; ⊕; ⊒45, 300) **FREE** Elegant
Chambers St is dominated by the long
facade of the National Museum of Scotland. Its extensive collections are spread
between two buildings: one modern, one
Victorian – the golden stone and striking
architecture of the new building (1998)
make it one of the city's most distinctive
landmarks. The museum's five floors trace
the history of Scotland from geological
beginnings to the 1990s, with many
imaginative and stimulating exhibits. Audio
guides are available in several languages.
Fees apply for special exhibitions.

View of Edinburgh from Arthur's Seat

BRENDAN HOWARD / SHUTTERSTOCK ©

Scottish National Portrait Gallery — Gallery

(Map p240; ☎0131-624 6200; www.national galleries.org; 1 Queen St; ☉10am-5pm; 👬; 🚌all York Pl buses, 🚇St Andrew Sq) **FREE** The Venetian Gothic palace of the Scottish National Portrait Gallery is one of the city's top attractions. Its galleries illustrate Scottish history through paintings, photographs and sculptures, putting faces to famous names from Scotland's past and present, from Robert Burns, Mary, Queen of Scots, and Bonnie Prince Charlie to actor Sean Connery, comedian Billy Connolly and poet Jackie Kay. There's an admission fee for special exhibitions.

Royal Yacht Britannia — Ship

(www.royalyachtbritannia.co.uk; Ocean Terminal; adult/child incl audio guide £16/8.50; ☉9.30am-6pm Apr-Sep, to 5.30pm Oct, 10am-5pm Nov-Mar, last entry 1½hr before closing; 🅿; 🚌11, 22, 34, 36, 200, 300) Built on Clydeside, the former Royal Yacht Britannia was the British Royal Family's floating holiday home during their foreign travels from the time of her launch in 1953 until her decommissioning in 1997, and is now permanently moored in front of **Ocean Terminal** (☎0131-555 8888; www.oceanterminal.com; Ocean Dr; ☉10am-8pm Mon-Fri, to 7pm Sat, 11am-6pm Sun; 📶; 🚌11, 22, 34, 36, 200, 300). The tour, which you take at your own pace with an audio guide (available in 30 languages), lifts the curtain on the everyday lives of the royals, and gives an intriguing insight into the Queen's private tastes.

Scotch Whisky Experience — Museum

(Map p238; www.scotchwhiskyexperience.co.uk; 354 Castlehill; adult/child from £15.50/7.50; ☉10am-6pm Apr-Jul, to 5pm Aug-Mar; 🚌23, 27, 41, 42) A former school houses this multimedia centre that takes you through the making of whisky, from barley to bottle, in a series of exhibits, demonstrations and talks that combine sight, sound and smell, including the world's largest collection of malt whiskies (3384 bottles!). The pricier tours include extensive whisky tastings and samples of Scottish cuisine. There's also a

Edinburgh Shopping

Edinburgh's shopping experience extends far beyond the big-name department stores of Princes St. Classic north-of-the-border buys include cashmere, Harris tweed, tartan goods, Celtic jewellery, smoked salmon and Scotch whisky.

Kilberry Bagpipes (Map p238; ☎0131-556 9607; www.kilberrybagpipes.com; 27 St Mary's St; ☉8.30am-4.30pm Mon-Fri, 10am-2pm Sat; 🚌6, 300) A maker and retailer of traditional Highland bagpipes, Kilberry also sells piping accessories, snare drums, books, CDs and learning materials.

Valvona & Crolla (Map p240; ☎0131-556 6066; www.valvonacrolla.co.uk; 19 Elm Row; ☉8.30am-6pm Mon-Thu, 8am-8pm Fri & Sat, 10am-5pm Sun; 🚌all Leith Walk buses) The queen of Edinburgh delicatessens, established during the 1930s, Valvona & Crolla is packed with Mediterranean goodies, including an excellent choice of fine wines. It also has a good cafe.

21st Century Kilts (Map p240; http://21stcenturykilts.com; 48 Thistle St; ☉10am-6pm Tue & Thu-Sat; 🚌23, 27) With celebrity customers including Alan Cummings, Robbie Williams and Vin Diesel, 21st Century Kilts offers modern fashion kilts in a variety of fabrics, both off-the-peg and made to measure.

Jenners (Map p240; ☎0131-225 2442; www.houseoffraser.co.uk; 48 Princes St; ☉9.30am-6.30pm Mon-Wed, to 8pm Thu, to 7pm Fri, 9am-7pm Sat, 11am-6pm Sun; 🚌Princes St) Founded in 1838, and acquired by House of Fraser in 2005, Jenners is the grande dame of Scottish department stores.

Bagpipes

Old Town

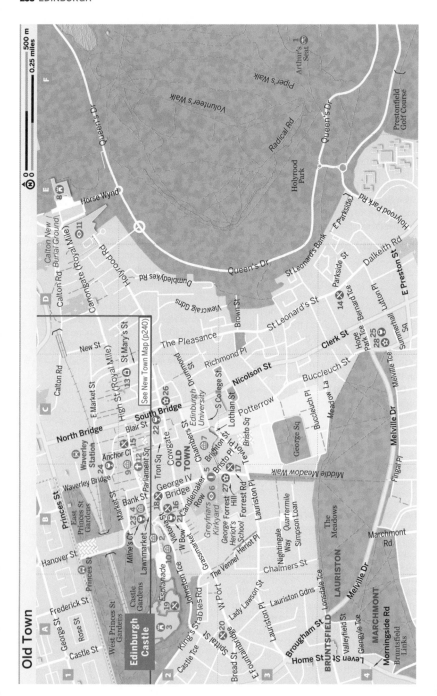

Old Town

restaurant (Map p238; ☑0131-477 8477; www.scotchwhiskyexperience.co.uk/restaurant; mains £12-25; ☺noon-8.30pm Sun-Thu, to 9pm Fri & Sat; 🛜👪) that serves traditional Scottish dishes with, where possible, a dash of whisky thrown in.

Greyfriars Bobby Statue　Monument

(Map p238; cnr George IV Bridge & Candle-maker Row; 🚍23, 27, 41, 42, 45, 67) Probably the most popular photo opportunity in Edinburgh, the life-size statue of Grey-friars Bobby, a Skye terrier who captured the hearts of the British public in the late 19th century, stands outside **Greyfriars Kirkyard** (Map p238; www.greyfriarskirk.com; Candlemaker Row; ☺24hr; 🚍2, 23, 27, 41, 42, 67). From 1858 to 1872 the wee dog maintained a vigil over the grave of his master, an Edinburgh police officer. The story was immortalised in a novel by Eleanor Atkinson in 1912, and in 1961 was made into a movie by – who else? – Walt Disney.

 TOURS

Edinburgh Literary Pub Tour　Walking

(www.edinburghliterarypubtour.co.uk; adult/student £14/10; ☺7.30pm daily May-Sep, limited days Oct-Apr) An enlightening two-hour trawl through Edinburgh's literary history – and its associated *howffs* (pubs) – in the entertaining company of Messrs Clart and McBrain. One of the city's best walking tours.

City of the Dead Tours　Walking

(www.cityofthedeadtours.com; adult/concession £11/9; ☺9pm Easter-Oct, 8.30pm Nov-Easter) This nightly tour of Greyfriars Kirkyard is probably the scariest of Edinburgh's 'ghost' tours. Many people have reported encounters with the 'Mackenzie Poltergeist', the ghost of a 17th-century judge who persecuted the Covenanters and now haunts their former prison in a corner of the kirkyard. Not suitable for children under 12.

Majestic Tour　Boating

(https://edinburghtour.com; adult/child £15/7.50; ☺daily year-round except 25 Dec) Hop-on, hop-off tour departing every 15 to 20 minutes from Waverley Bridge to the Royal Yacht Britannia at Ocean Terminal via the New Town, the Royal Botanic Garden and Newhaven, returning via Leith Walk, Holyrood and the Royal Mile.

 EATING

Edinburgh has more restaurants per capita than any other UK city, including a handful of places with Michelin stars.

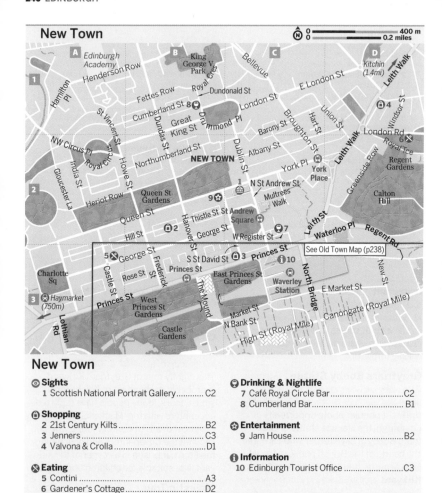

New Town

⦿ Sights
1 Scottish National Portrait Gallery C2

🛍 Shopping
2 21st Century Kilts B2
3 Jenners C3
4 Valvona & Crolla D1

✕ Eating
5 Contini A3
6 Gardener's Cottage D2

⦿ Drinking & Nightlife
7 Café Royal Circle Bar C2
8 Cumberland Bar B1

✪ Entertainment
9 Jam House B2

ⓘ Information
10 Edinburgh Tourist Office C3

Mums Cafe £

(Map p238; ☑0131-260 9806; www.monstermash cafe.co.uk; 4a Forrest Rd; mains £9-12; ⊘9am-10pm Mon-Sat, 10am-10pm Sun; 🛜🧇; 🚌2, 23, 27, 41, 42, 300) 🍴 This nostalgia-fuelled cafe serves up classic British comfort food that wouldn't look out of place on a 1950s menu – bacon and eggs, bangers and mash, shepherd's pie, fish and chips. But there's a twist – the food is all top-quality nosh freshly prepared from local produce. There's also a good selection of bottled craft beers and Scottish-brewed cider.

Gardener's Cottage Scottish ££

(Map p240; ☑0131-558 1221; www.thegardeners cottage.co; 1 Royal Terrace Gardens, London Rd; 4-course lunch £21, 7-course dinner £50; ⊘noon-2pm & 5-10pm Mon-Fri, 10am-2pm & 5-10pm Sat & Sun; 🚌all London Rd buses) 🍴 This country cottage in the heart of the city, bedecked with flowers and fairy lights, offers one of Edinburgh's most interesting dining experiences – two tiny rooms with communal tables made of salvaged timber, and a set menu based on fresh local produce (most of the vegetables and fruit are from its own organic garden). Bookings essential; brunch served at weekends.

Aizle
Scottish ££

(Map p238; ☑0131-662 9349; http://aizle.co.uk; 107-109 St Leonard's St; 5-course dinner £55; ⊙5-9pm Wed-Sat; 🛜; ☐14) If you tend to have trouble deciding what to eat, Aizle (the name is an old Scots word for 'spark' or 'ember') will do the job for you. There's no menu here, just a five-course dinner conjured from a monthly 'harvest' of the finest and freshest local produce (listed on a blackboard), and presented beautifully – art on a plate.

Contini
Italian ££

(Map p240; ☑0131-225 1550; www.contini.com/contini-george-street; 103 George St; mains £14-18; ⊙8am-10pm Mon-Fri, 10am-10.30pm Sat, 11am-8pm Sun; 🛜🏃♿; ☐all Princes St buses) A palatial Georgian banking hall enlivened by fuchsia-pink banners and lampshades is home to this lively, family-friendly Italian bar and restaurant, where the emphasis is on fresh, authentic ingredients (produce imported weekly from Milan; homemade bread and pasta) and the uncomplicated enjoyment of food.

Timberyard
Scottish £££

(Map p238; ☑0131-221 1222; www.timberyard.co; 10 Lady Lawson St; 4-course lunch or dinner £55; ⊙noon-2pm & 5.30-9.30pm Tue-Sat; 🛜♿; ☐2, 300) 🍴 Ancient, worn floorboards, cast-iron pillars, exposed joists, and tables made from slabs of old mahogany create a rustic, retro atmosphere in this slow-food restaurant where the accent is on locally sourced produce from artisan growers and foragers. Typical dishes include seared scallop with leek, fennel and cured egg yolk, and roast quail with salsify and thyme.

Ondine
Seafood £££

(Map p238; ☑0131-226 1888; www.ondine restaurant.co.uk; 2 George IV Bridge; mains £18-38, 2-/3-course lunch £19/24; ⊙noon-3pm & 5.30-10pm Mon-Sat; 🛜; ☐23, 27, 41, 42) Ondine is one of Edinburgh's finest seafood restaurants, with a menu based on sustainably sourced fish. Take a seat at the curved Oyster Bar and tuck into oysters Kilpatrick, smoked-haddock chowder, lobster thermi-

dor, a roast-shellfish platter or just good old haddock and chips (with minted pea purée, just to keep things posh).

Kitchin
Scottish £££

(☑0131-555 1755; http://thekitchin.com; 78 Commercial Quay; 3-course lunch/dinner £33/75; ⊙noon-2.30pm & 6-10pm Tue-Sat; 🏃; ☐16, 22, 36, 300) Fresh, seasonal, locally sourced Scottish produce is the philosophy that has won a Michelin star for this elegant but unpretentious restaurant. The menu moves with the seasons, of course, so expect fresh salads in summer and game in winter, and shellfish dishes such as baked scallops with white wine, vermouth and herb sauce when there's an 'r' in the month.

Grain Store
Scottish £££

(Map p238; ☑0131-225 7635; www.grainstore-restaurant.co.uk; 30 Victoria St; mains £18-32; ⊙noon-2.30pm & 6-9.45pm Mon-Sat, noon-2.30pm & 6-9.30pm Sun; ☐2, 23, 27, 41, 42) An atmospheric upstairs dining room on picturesque Victoria St, the Grain Store has a well-earned reputation for serving the finest Scottish produce, perfectly prepared in dishes such as Orkney scallops with pumpkin, chestnut and pancetta, and braised venison shoulder with brambles, salsify and kale. The three-course lunch for £16 is good value.

🍸 DRINKING & NIGHTLIFE

Edinburgh has more than 700 pubs – more per square mile than any other UK city – and they are as varied and full of character as the people who drink in them.

Bow Bar
Pub

(Map p238; www.thebowbar.co.uk; 80 West Bow; ⊙noon-midnight Mon-Sat, to 11.30pm Sun; ☐2, 23, 27, 41, 42) One of the city's best traditional-style pubs (it's not as old as it looks), serving a range of excellent real ales, Scottish craft gins and a vast selection of malt whiskies, the Bow Bar often has standing-room only on Friday and Saturday evenings.

Café Royal Circle Bar
Pub

(Map p240; ☑0131-556 1884; www.caferoyal edinburgh.co.uk; 17 W Register St; ⊙11am-11pm Mon-Wed, to midnight Thu, to 1am Fri & Sat, to

10pm Sun; ☎; 🚌Princes St) Perhaps *the* classic Edinburgh pub, the Café Royal's main claims to fame are its magnificent oval bar and its Doulton tile portraits of famous Victorian inventors. Sit at the bar or claim one of the cosy leather booths beneath the stained-glass windows, and choose from the seven real ales on tap.

Royal Dick
Microbrewery

(Map p238; ☎0131-560 1572; www.summerhall. co.uk/the-royal-dick; 1 Summerhall; ⊘noon-1am Mon-Sat, 12.30pm-midnight Sun; ☎; 🚌41, 42, 67) The decor at the Royal Dick alludes to its past as the home of Edinburgh University's veterinary school: there are shelves of laboratory glassware and walls covered with animal bones, even an old operating table. But rather than being creepy, it's a warm, welcoming place for a drink, serving artisan ales and craft gins produced by its own microbrewery and distillery.

Cabaret Voltaire
Club

(Map p238; www.thecabaretvoltaire.com; 36-38 Blair St; ⊘5pm-3am Tue-Sat, 8pm-1am Sun; ☎; 🚌all South Bridge buses) An atmospheric warren of stone-lined vaults houses this

self-consciously 'alternative' club, which eschews huge dance floors and egotistical DJ worship in favour of a 'creative crucible' hosting an eclectic mix of DJs, live acts, comedy, theatre, visual arts and the spoken word. Well worth a look.

✪ ENTERTAINMENT

Sandy Bell's
Traditional Music

(Map p238; www.sandybellsedinburgh.co.uk; 25 Forrest Rd; ⊘noon-1am Mon-Sat, 12.30pm-midnight Sun; 🚌2, 23, 27, 41, 42, 45) This unassuming pub has been a stalwart of the traditional-music scene since the 1960s (the founder's wife sang with the Corries). There's music every weekday evening at 9pm, and from 2pm Saturday and 4pm Sunday, plus lots of impromptu sessions.

Summerhall
Theatre

(Map p238; ☎0131-560 1580; www.summerhall. co.uk; 1 Summerhall; ⊘box office 10am-6pm; 🚌41, 42, 67) Formerly Edinburgh University's veterinary school, the Summerhall complex is a major cultural centre and entertainment venue, with old halls and lecture theatres (including an original

From left: Bow Bar (p241); Royal Dick; Café Royal Circle Bar (p241)

anatomy lecture theatre) now serving as venues for drama, dance, cinema and comedy performances. It's also one of the main venues for Edinburgh Festival (p223) events.

Caves
Live Music

(Map p238; https://unusualvenuesedinburgh. com/venues/the-caves-venue-edinburgh; 8-12 Niddry St S; ☐300) A spectacular subterranean venue set in the ancient stone vaults beneath the South Bridge, the Caves stages a series of one-off club nights and live-music gigs, as well as *ceilidh* (traditional music) nights during the Edinburgh Festival. Check the What's On link on the website for upcoming events.

Jam House
Live Music

(Map p240; ☎0131-220 2321; www.thejamhouse. com; 5 Queen St; from £4; ☉6pm-3am Fri & Sat; ☐St Andrew Sq) The brainchild of rhythm-and-blues pianist and TV personality Jools Holland, the Jam House is set in a former BBC TV studio and offers a combination of fine dining and live jazz and blues performances. Admission is for over-21s only, and there's a smart-casual dress code.

ⓘ INFORMATION

DANGERS & ANNOYANCES

Lothian Rd, Dalry Rd, Rose St and the western end of Princes St, at the junction with Shandwick Pl and Queensferry St, can get a bit rowdy late on Friday and Saturday nights after pub-closing time. Calton Hill offers good views during the day but is best avoided at night.

Be aware that the area between Salamander St and Leith Links in Leith is a red-light district – lone women here at any time of day might be approached by kerb crawlers.

USEFUL WEBSITES

Edinburgh Festival Guide (www.edinburgh festivalcity.com) Everything you need to know about Edinburgh's many festivals.

Lonely Planet (www.lonelyplanet.com/ edinburgh) Destination information, hotel bookings, traveller forum and more.

VisitScotland Edinburgh (www.visitscotland. com/edinburgh) Official Scottish-tourist-board site.

The List (www.list.co.uk) Local listings and reviews for restaurants, bars, clubs and theatres.

Edinburgh's Best Whisky Bars

Bow Bar (p241) Busy Grassmarket-area pub with huge selection of malt whiskies.

Malt Shovel (Map p238; ☎0131-225 6843; www.maltshovelinn-edinburgh.co.uk; 11-15 Cockburn St; ⏰11am-11pm Mon-Wed, to midnight Thu & Sun, to 1am Fri & Sat; 🖥🍴; 🚌6) Old-school pub with more than 100 single malts behind the bar.

Cumberland Bar (Map p240; ☎0131-558 3134; www.cumberlandbar.co.uk; 1-3 Cumberland St; ⏰noon-midnight Mon-Wed, to 1am Thu-Sat, 11am-11pm Sun; 🖥; 🚌23, 27) Good summer choice; enjoy your malt while sitting in the garden.

Malt Shovel
LOU ARMOR / SHUTTERSTOCK ©

TOURIST INFORMATION

Edinburgh Tourist Office (Edinburgh iCentre; Map p240; ☎0131-473 3868; www.visitscotland.com/info/services/edinburgh-icentre-p234441; Waverley Mall, 3 Princes St; ⏰9am-7pm Mon-Sat, 10am-7pm Sun Jul & Aug, to 6pm Jun, to 5pm Sep-May; 🖥; 🚇St Andrew Sq) Accommodation booking service, currency exchange, gift shop and bookshop, internet access, and counters selling tickets for Edinburgh city tours and Scottish Citylink bus services.

Edinburgh Airport Tourist Office (☎0131-473 3690; www.visitscotland.com; East Terminal, Edinburgh Airport; ⏰7.30am-7.30pm Mon-Fri, to 7pm Sat & Sun) VisitScotland Information Centre in the airport's terminal extension.

ℹ GETTING THERE & AWAY

Edinburgh lies in east-central Scotland, and is well served by air, road and rail.

Air Eight miles west of the city, **Edinburgh Airport** (EDI; ☎0844 448 8833; www.edinburghairport.com), has numerous flights to other parts of Scotland and the UK, Ireland and mainland Europe. Flight time from London is around one hour.

Car Driving times are around one hour from Glasgow, two hours from Newcastle, and four to five hours from York. The drive from London can take anything from eight hours upwards and is not recommended.

Train The main rail terminus in Edinburgh is Waverley train station, located in the heart of the city. Trains arriving from, and departing for, the west also stop at Haymarket station, which is more convenient for the West End.

ℹ GETTING AROUND

CAR

Though useful for day trips beyond the city, a car in central Edinburgh is more of a liability than a convenience. There is restricted access on Princes St, George St and Charlotte Sq, many streets are one way, and finding a parking place in the city centre is like striking gold. Queen's Dr around Holyrood Park is closed to motorised traffic on Sunday.

PUBLIC TRANSPORT

For timetable information, contact **Traveline** (☎0871 200 22 33; www.travelinescotland.com).

Bus Reasonably priced; extensive network. The main bus operators are Lothian Buses and First (www.firstgroup.com).

Tram The tram line runs from the airport via Haymarket and Princes St to York Pl at the east end of the city centre and is operated by Edinburgh Trams (www.edinburghtrams.com).

Taxi Local operators include **Central Taxis** (☎0131-229 2468; www.taxis-edinburgh.co.uk), **City Cabs** (☎0131-228 1211; www.citycabs.co.uk) and **ComCab** (☎0131-272 8001; www.comcab-edinburgh.co.uk).

Where to Stay

Fittingly for a city of so much character, Edinburgh has a fabulous range of places to sleep. Book ahead, especially in the summer and at New Year.

Neighbourhood	Atmosphere
Holyrood & Arthur's Seat	Mostly quiet and peaceful. Holyrood Park on your doorstep for morning and evening walks. Not too many bars or restaurants. Poor public transport; a hike to the nearest bus stop.
Leith	Lots of bars and restaurants. Handy for Royal Yacht Britannia. Good bus service. Few sights in the neighbourhoods, and a bus ride away from the main city-centre sights.
New Town	Central, with good transport connections and a vast choice of eating places. Close to main train stations. Accommodation can be expensive but still gets booked out well in advance.
Old Town	Right in the thick of things, walking distance to the castle and Royal Mile. Can be noisy; gets crowded in high season. Steep walk uphill from train and bus stations.
South Edinburgh	Spacious rooms in Victorian villas and terraces, often on quiet backstreets. Good choice of restaurants and bars. Few attractions in the immediate area, and a bit of a hike from the city centre.
Stockbridge	Pleasant village atmosphere. Good local shops, cafes and restaurants. No nightlife apart from pubs. A steep walk uphill to the city centre.
West End & Dean Village	Close to the city centre, Haymarket train station and tram line. Hotels and B&Bs in attractive Georgian town houses. Can be expensive. Limited choice of restaurants and bars in immediate vicinity.

THE SCOTTISH HIGHLANDS

The Scottish Highlands at a Glance...

With its sweeping lochs and brooding glens, the Highlands are a magnet for outdoors enthusiasts. Glen Coe and Fort William draw hikers and skiers; Royal Deeside offers a home to the Queen and magnificent castles; Inverness, the Highland capital, provides urban rest and relaxation; while nearby Loch Ness and its elusive monster add a hint of mystery. And then from Fort William the roads lead to the sea, where – waiting just offshore – lies the wildlife-rich Isle of Mull.

Two Days in the Scottish Highlands

Cruise Royal Deeside on day one, taking in the Queen's estate, **Balmoral** (p251), and nearby **Braemar Castle** (p251). The **Bothy** (p260) is a characterful place to refuel. On day two it's time to go Loch Ness Monster–hunting on a **boat trip** (p254). Next up, tour iconic **Urquhart Castle** (p254), before exploring the loch's quieter eastern shore. The **Dores Inn** (p255) is an idyllic spot to dine.

Four Days in the Scottish Highlands

On day three, head southwest to Fort William to dip into the **West Highland Museum** (p260), ride a **steam train** (p260) and tour a **distillery** (p260). Feast on superb Scottish fare at **Lime Tree** (p260). On day four, travel to the Isle of Mull, and head out on a **whale-watching tour** (p258). Stop by **Duart Castle** (p259) and stroll **Calgary Beach** (p259). Fill up on seafood at **Café Fish** (p259).

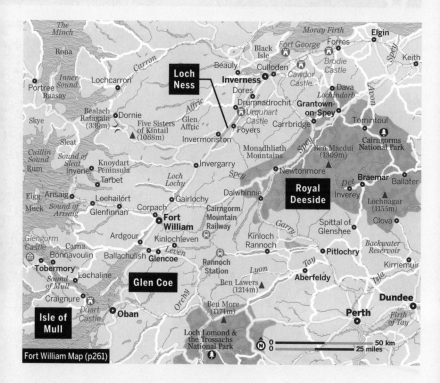

Fort William Map (p261)

Arriving in the Scottish Highlands

Bus Scottish Citylink (www.citylink.co.uk) runs buses connecting Inverness to Fort William along the Great Glen.

Car Braemar is around 100 miles (2½ hours) north of Edinburgh by car; Fort William is around a three-hour drive (150 miles) from Edinburgh.

Train Trains run roughly every two hours from Edinburgh to Inverness (£40, 3½ hours).

Where to Stay

Inverness and Fort William have the most options; in between, the Great Glen also has a wide range of possibilities (especially hikers' hostels). The Isle of Mull boasts everything from campsites to swish hotels, while Royal Deeside is rich with hotels and B&Bs. For all areas, and all price ranges, it pays to book ahead in spring and summer.

Ballater

Royal Deeside

The picturesque upper valley of the River Dee takes in the settlements of Ballater and Braemar. Made famous by its long associations with the monarchy, the region is known as Royal Deeside.

Great For...

☑ Don't Miss

The hike to Balmoral Castle's Prince Albert's Cairn, erected by a heart-broken Queen Victoria.

Ballater

The attractive little village of Ballater owes its 18th-century origins to the curative waters of nearby Pannanich Springs (now bottled commercially as Deeside Natural Mineral Water), and its proximity to nearby Balmoral Castle.

In the village, look out for the crests on the shop fronts along the main street proclaiming 'By Royal Appointment' – evidence that the village is a major supplier of provisions to Balmoral Castle.

Pleasant walks in the surrounding area include the steep one-hour woodland hike up Craigendarroch.

You can hire bikes from **CycleHighlands** (☏ 01339-755864; www.cyclehighlands.com; The Pavilion, Victoria Rd; bicycle hire per half-/full day £15/20; ⊙ 9am-6pm) and **Bike Station** (☏ 01339-754004; www.bikestationballater.

PITSCH27 / SHUTTERSTOCK ©

ℹ️ Need to Know

In winter Braemar is one of the coldest places in the country – temperatures as low as -29°C have been recorded – and during spells of severe cold, hungry deer wander the streets looking for a bite to eat.

✕ Take a Break

Stop by the Bothy (p260) in Braemar for lunchtime treats.

★ Top Tip

Take outdoor kit for a visit to Balmoral Castle; the audio tour is largely outside.

co.uk; Station Sq; bicycle hire per 3hr/day £12/18; ☉9am-6pm), both of which also offer guided bike rides and advice on local trails.

Balmoral Castle

Built for Queen Victoria in 1855 as a private residence for the royal family, **Balmoral** (☏01339-742534; www.balmoralcastle.com; Crathie; adult/child £11.50/6; ☉10am-5pm Apr-Jul, last admission 4.30pm; P) kicked off the revival of the Scottish Baronial style of architecture that characterises so many of Scotland's 19th-century country houses. The admission fee includes an interesting and well thought-out audioguide, but the tour is very much an outdoor one through garden and grounds.

As for the castle itself, only the ballroom, which displays a collection of Landseer paintings and royal silver, is open to the public (don't expect to see the Queen's private quarters).

You can buy a booklet that details several way-marked walks within Balmoral Estate; the best is the climb to Prince Albert's Cairn, a huge granite pyramid that bears the inscription, 'To the beloved memory of Albert the great and good, Prince Consort. Erected by his broken hearted widow Victoria R. 21st August 1862'.

Braemar Castle

Just nine miles west of Balmoral, turreted **Braemar Castle** (www.braemarcastle.co.uk; adult/child £8/4; ☉10am-5pm Jul & Aug, Wed-Sun Apr-Jun, Sep & Oct; P) dates from 1628 and served as a government garrison after the 1745 Jacobite rebellion. It was taken over by the local community in 2007, which now offers guided tours of the historic castle apartments. There's a short walk from the car park to the castle.

Loch Ness

Deep, dark and narrow, the bitterly cold waters of Loch Ness have long drawn waves of people hunting Nessie, the elusive Loch Ness Monster. Despite the crowds, it's still possible to find tranquillity and gorgeous views. Add a highly photogenic castle and some superb hiking and you have a loch with bags of appeal.

Great For...

ⓘ Need to Know

A complete circuit of the loch is about 70 miles; travel anticlockwise for the best views.

Tales of the Loch Ness Monster truly took off in the 1930s, when reported sightings led to a press furore and a string of high-profile photographs. Reports have tailed off recently, but the bizarre mini-industry that's grown up around Nessie is a spectacle in itself.

Drumnadrochit

Seized by monster madness, its gift shops bulging with Nessie cuddly toys, Drumnadrochit is a hotbed of beastie fever, with Nessie attractions battling it out for the tourist dollar.

The **Loch Ness Centre & Exhibition** (☎01456-450573; www.lochness.com; adult/child £7.95/4.95; ☺9.30am-6pm Jul & Aug, to 5pm Easter-Jun, Sep & Oct, 10am-4pm Nov-Easter; P ♿) adopts a scientific approach that allows you to weigh the evidence for

yourself. Exhibits include those on hoaxes and optical illusions and some original equipment – sonar survey vessels, miniature submarines, cameras and sediment coring tools – used in various monster hunts, as well as original photographs and film footage of reported sightings.

To head out yourself, **Nessie Hunter** (☎01456-450395; www.lochness-cruises.com; adult/child £16/10; ☺Easter-Oct) offers one-hour monster-hunting cruises, complete with sonar and underwater cameras. Cruises depart from Drumnadrochit hourly (except 1pm) from 10am to 6pm daily.

Urquhart Castle

Commanding a superb location 1.5 miles east of Drumnadrochit, with outstanding views, **Urquhart Castle** (HES; ☎01456-450551; adult/child £9/5.40; ☺9.30am-8pm

Urquhart Castle

Jun-Aug, to 6pm Apr, May & Sep, to 5pm Oct, to 4.30pm Nov-Mar; P) is a popular Nessie-hunting hot spot. A huge visitor centre (most of which is beneath ground level) includes a video theatre and displays of medieval items discovered in the castle.

The castle has been repeatedly sacked and rebuilt over the centuries; in 1692 it was blown up to prevent the Jacobites from using it. The five-storey tower house at the northern point is the most impressive remaining fragment and offers fine views across the water.

☑ Don't Miss

Climbing to the battlements of the iconic tower of Urquhart Castle, for grandstand views from the rocky head-land, up and down Loch Ness.

BOTOND HORVATH / SHUTTERSTOCK ©

Loch Ness' East Side

While tour coaches pour down the west side of Loch Ness to the hot spots of Drumnadrochit and Urquhart Castle, the narrow B862 road along the eastern shore is relatively peaceful. It leads to the village of Foyers, where you can enjoy a pleasant hike to the Falls of Foyers.

It's also worth making the trip just for the **Dores Inn** (✆01463-751203; www.thedoresinn.co.uk; Dores; mains £10-27; ☺pub 10am-11pm, food served noon-2pm & 6-9pm; P ☎), a beautifully restored country pub adorned with recycled furniture, local landscape paintings and fresh flowers. The menu specialises in quality Scottish produce, from haggis, turnips and *tatties* (potatoes), and haddock and chips, to steaks, scallops and seafood platters. The pub garden has stunning Loch Ness views and a dedicated monster-spotting vantage point.

Hiking at Loch Ness

The South Loch Ness Trail (www.visit invernesslochness.com) links a series of footpaths and minor roads along the less-frequented southern side of the loch. The 28 miles from Loch Tarff near Fort Augustus to Torbreck on the fringes of Inverness can be done on foot, by bike or on horseback.

The climb to the summit of Meall-fuarvonie (699m), on the northwestern shore of Loch Ness, makes an excellent short hill walk: the views along the Great Glen from the top are superb. It's a 6-mile round trip, so allow about three hours. Start from the car park at the end of the minor road leading south from Drum-nadrochit to Bunloit.

✗ Take a Break

On the southern edge of Drumnadro-chit, the **Loch Ness Inn** (✆01456-450991; www.staylochness.co.uk; Lewiston; mains £10-20; P ☎) is a good place for lunch or dinner.

Glen Coe

Scotland's most famous glen is also one of its grandest. It was written into history in 1692 when the resident MacDonalds were murdered by Campbell soldiers in a notorious massacre.

The events of that one night in 1692 still seem to echo around Glen Coe. Soldiers largely from Campbell clan territory, on government orders, turned on their MacDonald hosts killing 38; another 40 MacDonalds perished having fled into snow-covered hills.

Arriving in Glen Coe

The approach to the glen from the east is guarded by the rocky pyramid of Buachaille Etive Mor and the lonely Kings House Hotel. The road leads over the Pass of Glencoe and into the narrow upper glen. The southern side is dominated by three massive, brooding spurs, known as the Three Sisters, while the northern side is enclosed by the continuous steep wall of the knife-edged Aonach Eagach ridge. The road threads its way past deep gorges and

---

Great For...

☑ **Don't Miss**

The cracking views from the Glencoe Mountain Resort. Ski lift provided.

Hiking at Sron na Lairig, Glen Coe

WESTEND61 / GETTY IMAGES ©

ℹ️ **Need to Know**

Glencoe Visitor Centre (NTS; 📞01855-811307; www.nts.org.uk; adult/child £6.50/5; ⏰9.30am-5.30pm Mar-Oct, 10am-4pm Nov-Feb; 🅿️) 🧭

✕ **Take a Break**

Take a load off at the friendly **Glencoe Cafe** (📞01855-811168; www.glencoecafe. co.uk; Glencoe village; mains £4-8; ⏰10am-4pm, to 5pm May-Sep, closed Nov; 🅿️📶).

★ **Top Tip**

Learn all about Glen Coe's past at the visitor centre on the way into the village.

crashing waterfalls to the more pastoral lower reaches of the glen around Loch Achtriochtan and the only settlement here: Glencoe village.

Hiking at Glen Coe

There are several short, pleasant walks around Glencoe Lochan, near the village. To get there, turn left off the minor road to the youth hostel, just beyond the bridge over the River Coe. There are three walks (40 minutes to an hour), all detailed on a signboard at the car park.

The Lost Valley is a magical mountain sanctuary still rumoured to be haunted by the ghosts of MacDonalds who died here. It's only 2.5 miles round trip, but allow three hours. A rough path from the car park at Allt na Reigh (on the A82, 6 miles east of Glencoe village) bears left down to

a footbridge over the river, then climbs up the wooded valley between Beinn Fhada and Gearr Aonach. The route leads steeply up through a maze of giant, jumbled, moss-coated boulders before emerging unexpectedly into a broad, open valley with a flat, 800m-long meadow.

The summits of Glen Coe's mountains are for experienced mountaineers only. Cicerone's *Ben Nevis & Glen Coe*, by Ronald Turnbull, details everything from short easy walks to challenging mountain climbs.

Other Activities

Scotland's oldest ski area, **Glencoe Mountain Resort** (📞01855-851226; www. glencoemountain.com; Kingshouse; chairlift adult/child £12/6; ⏰9am-4.30pm), is also one of the best, with grand views across the wild expanse of Rannoch Moor. The chairlift continues to operate in summer providing access to mountain-biking trails.

Glengorm Castle

The Isle of Mull

With black basalt crags, blinding white sand and emerald waters, Mull has some of Scotland's finest scenery. A lovely waterfront 'capital', impressive castles and superb wildlife-watching ensure it's an irresistible island escape.

Mull's main town, Tobermory, is a picturesque fishing port with brightly painted houses arranged around a sheltered quay.

Bird & Wildlife Watching

An all-day whale-watching trip (£80) with **Sea Life Surveys** (☏01688-302916; www.sealifesurveys.com; Ledaig) has a 95% success rate for sightings. The four-hour Whalewatch cruise (adult/child £60/30) is better for families.

Nature Scotland (☏07743 956380; www.naturescotland.com) offers excellent wildlife tours, including afternoon trips that can link to ferries (adult/child £30/25, four hours), evening otter-spotting trips (£40/35, three to four hours), all-day walking trips and winter stargazing excursions.

Britain's largest bird of prey, the white-tailed eagle, has been successfully

Great For...

☑ Don't Miss

Heading out to sea on a whale-watching trip, fingers crossed, with Sea Life Surveys.

STEFANO_VALERI / SHUTTERSTOCK ©

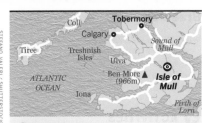

❶ Need to Know

Explore Mull (📞01688-302875; www.isle-of-mull.net; Ledaig; ⏱9am-5pm Easter-Jun & Sep–mid-Oct, to 7pm Jul & Aug; 📶) has local info, books all manner of island tours, and hires out bikes.

✕ Take a Break

Café Fish (📞01688-301253; www.thecafefish.com; The Pier; mains £15-26; ⏱noon-3pm & 5.30-11pm mid-Mar–Oct; 📶) 🖋 in Tobermory is superb.

★ Top Tip

Three CalMac car ferries link Mull with the mainland; check sailings at www.calmac.co.uk.

reintroduced here. **Mull Eagle Watch** (📞01680-812556; www.mulleaglewatch.com; adult/child £8/4; ⏱Apr-Sep) has guided raptor experiences.

North Mull

A long, single-track road leads north for 4 miles from Tobermory to majestic **Glengorm Castle** (📞01688-302321; www.glengormcastle.co.uk; Glengorm; ⏱buildings 10am-5pm Easter-Oct) **FREE**, with views across the sea to Ardnamurchan, Rum and the Outer Hebrides. The castle outbuildings house a nature centre, a farm shop and an excellent cafe. The castle isn't open to the public, but it houses an upmarket B&B and you can explore the beautiful grounds.

About 12 miles west of Tobermory, silver-sand **Calgary Beach**, Mull's best (and busiest), is flanked by cliffs and boasts views out to Coll and Tiree.

Duart Castle

The ancestral seat of the Maclean clan, **Duart Castle** (📞01680-812309; www.duartcastle.com; adult/child £7/3.50; ⏱10.30am-5pm daily May–mid-Oct, 11am-4pm Sun-Thu Apr) enjoys a spectacular position on a rocky outcrop overlooking the Sound of Mull. Built in the 13th century, it was abandoned for 160 years before a 1912 restoration. Along with dungeons, courtyard and battlements, there's a lot of clan history, including the villainous Lachlan Cattanach, who took his wife out to an island in the strait, then left her to drown when the tide came in.

Walking on Mull

Stand-out walking includes the popular climb of Ben More and the spectacular trip to Carsaig Arches.

Braemar

Braemar is a pretty little village with a grand location on a broad plain ringed by mountains where the Dee valley and Glen Clunie meet. It's an excellent base for hill walking, and there's also skiing at nearby Glenshee.

⊕ ACTIVITIES

An easy walk from Braemar is up Creag Choinnich (538m), a hill to the east of the village above the A93. The 1-mile route is waymarked and takes about 1½ hours return. For a longer walk (4 miles; about three hours return) and superb views of the Cairngorms, head for the summit of Morrone (859m), southwest of Braemar. Ask at the tourist office (p260) for details of these and other walks.

You can rent bikes at **Braemar Mountain Sports** (☑01339-741242; www.braemarmountainsports.com; 5 Invercauld Rd; bike hire per 4hr/day £15/20; ⊙9am-6pm).

⊗ EATING

Bothy   Cafe £

(Invercauld Rd; mains £4-7; ⊙9am-5.30pm Sun-Thu, to 6pm Fri & Sat; 🛜) An appealing little cafe tucked behind the Mountain Sports (p260) shop, with a sunny terrace out front and a balcony at the back overhanging the river.

⊕ INFORMATION

Braemar Tourist Office (☑01399-741600; The Mews, Mar Rd; ⊙9am-6pm Aug, to 5pm Jun, Jul, Sep & Oct, reduced hours Nov-May) Opposite the Fife Arms Hotel; has lots of useful info on walks in the area.

⊕ GETTING THERE & AWAY

From Edinburgh, Braemar is a 2½ hour (100 mile) drive.

Fort William

Basking on Loch Linnhe's shores amid magnificent mountain scenery, Fort William has one of the most enviable settings in all of Scotland. It's an excellent base for exploring the surrounding mountains and glens.

⊚ SIGHTS

Jacobite Steam Train   Heritage Railway

(☑0844 850 4685; www.westcoastrailways.co.uk; day return adult/child from £35/20; ⊙daily mid-Jun–Aug, Mon-Fri mid-May–mid-Jun, Sep & Oct) The Jacobite Steam Train, hauled by a former LNER K1 or LMS Class 5MT locomotive, travels the scenic two-hour run between Fort William and Mallaig. Classed as one of the great railway journeys of the world, the route crosses the historic Glenfinnan Viaduct, made famous in the Harry Potter films – the Jacobite's owners supplied the steam locomotive and rolling stock used in the film.

West Highland Museum   Museum

(☑01397-702169; www.westhighlandmuseum.org.uk; Cameron Sq; ⊙10am-5pm Mon-Sat May-Sep, to 4pm Oct-Apr, 11am-3pm Sun Jul & Aug) FREE This small but fascinating museum is packed with all manner of Highland memorabilia. Look out for the secret portrait of Bonnie Prince Charlie – after the Jacobite rebellions, all things Highland were banned, including pictures of the exiled leader, and this tiny painting looks like nothing more than a smear of paint until viewed in a cylindrical mirror, which reflects a credible likeness of the prince.

Ben Nevis Distillery   Distillery

(☑01397-702476; www.bennevisdistillery.com; Lochy Bridge; guided tour from £5; ⊙9am-5pm Mon-Fri year-round, 10am-4pm Sat Easter-Oct, noon-4pm Sun Jul & Aug; ℗) A tour of this distillery makes for a warming rainy day alternative to exploring the hills.

⊕ ACTIVITIES

Crannog Cruises   Wildlife

(☑01397-700714; www.crannog.net/cruises; adult/child £15/7.50; ⊙11am, 1pm & 3pm Easter-Oct) Operates 1½-hour wildlife cruises on Loch Linnhe, visiting a seal colony and a salmon farm.

⊗ EATING

Lime Tree   Scottish ££

(☑01397-701806; www.limetreefortwilliam.co.uk; Achintore Rd; mains £16-20; ⊙6.30-9.30pm; ℗🛜) 🍴 Fort William is not over-endowed with great places to eat, but the restaurant at this small hotel and art gallery has put

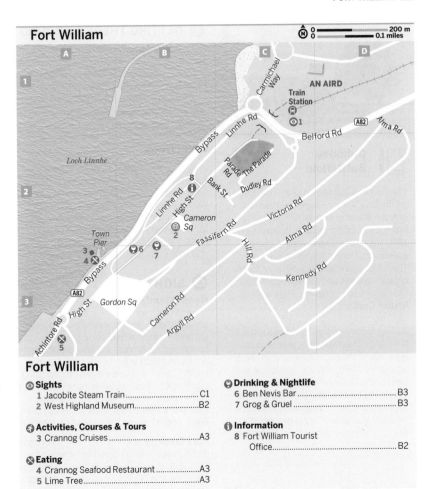

Fort William

⦿ Sights
1 Jacobite Steam Train C1
2 West Highland Museum B2

⊕ Activities, Courses & Tours
3 Crannog Cruises A3

⊗ Eating
4 Crannog Seafood Restaurant A3
5 Lime Tree A3

⊖ Drinking & Nightlife
6 Ben Nevis Bar B3
7 Grog & Gruel B3

ℹ Information
8 Fort William Tourist
   Office B2

the UK's Outdoor Capital on the gastronomic map. The chef turns out delicious dishes built around fresh Scottish produce, ranging from Loch Fyne oysters to Loch Awe trout and Ardnamurchan venison.

Crannog Seafood Restaurant
Seafood ££

(☏01397-705589; www.crannog.net; Town Pier; mains £15-24; ⊙noon-2.30pm & 6-9pm) ✐ The Crannog wins the prize for the best location in town – perched on the Town Pier, giving window-table diners an uninterrupted view down Loch Linnhe. Informal and unfussy,

it specialises in fresh local fish – there are three or four daily fish specials plus the main menu – though there are lamb, venison and vegetarian dishes, too. Two-/three-course lunch costs £16/19.

⊖ DRINKING & NIGHTLIFE

Grog & Gruel
Pub

(☏01397-705078; www.grogandgruel.co.uk; 66 High St; ⊙noon-midnight; 🛜) The Grog & Gruel is a traditional-style, wood-panelled pub with an excellent range of cask ales from regional Scottish and English microbreweries.

 Culloden Battlefield

The Battle of Culloden in 1746 – the last pitched battle ever fought on British soil – saw the defeat of Bonnie Prince Charlie and the end of the Jacobite dream when 1200 Highlanders were slaughtered by government forces in a 68-minute rout. The battle sounded the death knell for the old clan system, and the horrors of the Clearances soon followed. The excellent **Visitor Centre** (NTS; www.nts.org.uk/culloden; adult/child £11/9.50; ☺9am-7pm Jun-Aug, to 6pm Mar-May, Sep & Oct, 10am-4pm Nov-Feb; P) has everything you need to know about the battle, including the lead-up and the aftermath, with perspectives from both sides. An innovative film puts you on the battlefield in the middle of the mayhem and an audio guide in included for a self-guided tour of the battlefield itself. Culloden is 6 miles east of Inverness.

Traditional house on the Culloden Battlefield
MATTHI / SHUTTERSTOCK ©

Ben Nevis Bar   Pub
(☏01397-702295; www.thebennevisbarfortwilliam.co.uk; 105 High St; ☺11am-11pm Mon-Fri, to 11.30pm Sat, to 10.30pm Sun; 🛜) The lounge here enjoys a good view over the loch, and the bar exudes a relaxed, jovial atmosphere where climbers and tourists can work off leftover energy jigging to live music (Friday and Saturday nights).

ⓘ INFORMATION
Fort William Tourist Office (☏01397-701801; www.visithighlands.com; 15 High St; internet per 20min £1; ☺9am-5pm Mon-Sat, 10am-3pm Sun, longer hours Jun-Aug; 🛜) Internet access.

ⓘ GETTING THERE & AROUND
Fort William is 146 miles from Edinburgh, 104 miles from Glasgow and 66 miles from Inverness. Buses run regularly along the Great Glen between Fort William and Inverness.

A Zone 2 Dayrider ticket (£9.10) gives unlimited travel for one day on Stagecoach bus services as far as Glencoe and Fort Augustus.

Inverness

Inverness has a great location astride the River Ness at the northern end of the Great Glen. In summer it overflows with visitors intent on monster hunting at nearby Loch Ness, but it's worth a visit in its own right for a stroll along the picturesque River Ness, a cruise on Loch Ness, and a meal in one of the city's excellent restaurants.

◉ SIGHTS
Ness Islands   Park
The main attraction in Inverness is a leisurely stroll along the river to the Ness Islands. Planted with mature Scots pine, fir, beech and sycamore, and linked to the river banks and each other by elegant Victorian footbridges, the islands make an appealing picnic spot. They're a 20-minute walk south of the castle – head upstream on either side of the river (the start of the Great Glen Way), and return on the opposite bank.

Fort George   Fortress
(HES; 01667-462777; www.historicenvironment.scot; adult/child £9/5.40; ☺9.30am-5.30pm Apr-Sep, 10am-4pm Oct-Mar; P) One of the finest artillery fortifications in Europe, Fort George was established in 1748 in the aftermath of the Battle of Culloden, as a base for George II's army of occupation in the Highlands. By the time of its completion in 1769 it had cost the equivalent of around £1 billion in today's money. It still functions as a military barracks; public areas have exhibitions on 18th-century soldiery, and the mile-plus walk around the ramparts offers fine views.

Cawdor Castle   Castle
(☏01667-404615; www.cawdorcastle.com; Cawdor; adult/child £11.50/7.20; ☺10am-5.30pm May-Sep; P) This castle, 5 miles southwest of Nairn, was once the seat of the Thane of Cawdor, one of the titles bestowed on

MATTHÄUS ROJEK / GETTY IMAGES ©

Ness Islands

Shakespeare's *Macbeth*. The real Macbeth – an ancient Scottish king – couldn't have lived here though, since he died in 1057, 300 years before the castle was begun. Nevertheless the tour gives a fascinating insight into the lives of the Scottish aristocracy.

Brodie Castle   Castle

(NTS; ☑01309-641371; www.nts.org.uk; Brodie; adult/child £11/6.50; ⊙10am-5pm Mar-Oct, 11am-3pm Nov & Dec; P) Set in 70 hectares of parkland, Brodie Castle has a library with more than 6000 peeling, dusty volumes, wonderful clocks, a huge Victorian kitchen and a 17th-century dining room with wildly extravagant moulded plaster ceilings depicting mythological scenes. The Brodies have been living here since 1160, but the present structure dates mostly from 1567, with many additions over the years. The castle is 4 miles west of Forres.

✖ EATING

Café 1   Bistro ££

(☑01463-226200; www.cafe1.net; 75 Castle St; mains £12-28; ⊙noon-2.30pm & 5-9.30pm Mon-Fri, 12.30-3pm & 6-9.30pm Sat; 📝👶) 🍴 Café 1 is a friendly, appealing bistro with candlelit tables amid elegant blonde-wood and wrought-iron decor. There's an international menu based on quality Scottish produce, from Aberdeen Angus steaks to crisp pan-fried sea bass and meltingly tender pork belly. There's a separate vegan menu.

Cawdor Tavern   Pub Food ££

(www.cawdortavern.co.uk; mains £12-25; ⊙food served noon-9pm Mon-Sat, 12.30-9pm Sun; P 📶👶) Cawdor Tavern, in the village close to Cawdor Castle (p262), is worth a visit, though it can be difficult deciding what to drink as it stocks more than 100 varieties of whisky. There's also excellent pub food, with tempting daily specials.

ⓘ INFORMATION

Inverness Tourist Office (☑01463-252401; www.visithighlands.com; 36 High St; ⊙9am-5pm Mon & Wed-Sat, from 10am Tue, 10am-3pm Sun, longer hours Mar-Oct; 📶) Accommodation booking service; also sells tickets for tours and cruises.

ⓘ GETTING THERE & AWAY

Inverness is connected by train to Edinburgh (£40, 3½ hours, eight daily) and by bus to Fort William (£12.20, two hours, six daily).

SKYE

Skye at a Glance...

In a country famous for stunning scenery, the Isle of Skye takes top prize. From the craggy peaks of the Cuillins and the bizarre pinnacles of the Old Man of Storr and the Quiraing to spectacular sea cliffs, there's a photo opportunity at almost every turn. Walkers, sea-kayakers and climbers share this wilderness with red deer and golden eagles, and can refuel at the end of the day in convivial pubs and top seafood restaurants.

Two Days in Skye

On day one, tour the **Trotternish Peninsula** (p269), marvelling at extraordinary rock formations and exploring fairy glens. Peel off to **Dunvegan Castle** (p275), then dine in style at **Three Chimneys** (p274). Day two, and it's time to hike. Depending on the weather, and your capabilities, it might be to **Coire Lagan or Loch Coruisk** (p269) – it's spectacular either way. Hungry now? Feast on Skye produce at **Dulse & Brose** (p273).

Four Days in Skye

Day three: hills done, water next – **Whitewave Outdoor Centre** (p271) can get you eking out inaccessible coves. Keep it aquatic with dinner at **Sea Breezes** (p273) and shellfish straight from the boat. Relax on day four with a voyage aboard **MV Stardust** (p272), a trip to **Talisker Distillery** (p273) and then souvenir-shopping at **Skye Batiks** (p272). End your island adventure in style at cosy **Scorrybreac** (p273).

Arriving in Skye

Bus There are buses from Glasgow to Portree (£44, seven hours, three daily), and Uig (£44, 7½ hours, two daily) via Crianlarich, Fort William and Kyle of Lochalsh, plus a service from Inverness to Portree (£26.40, 3¼ hours, three daily).

Car The Skye Bridge opened in 1995, linking the island to the mainland by road; the crossing is now free.

Where to Stay

Skye is one of Scotland's most popular tourist areas, and offers a wide range of accommodation from basic campsites and hostels to luxury hotels. The latest trend is glamping (luxurious camping) and in the last few years many places have installed distinctive timber camping 'pods'. The island's popularity means that it's always best to book ahead.

Cuillin Hills over Loch Coruisk

Exploring Skye's Wild Side

With its spectacular scenery, Skye offers some of the finest – and, in places, most challenging – outdoor experiences in Scotland. From splashing through streams or kayaking hidden coves to sleeping under the stars, this is a place to test your outdoor mettle.

Great For...

☑ **Don't Miss**

The impressive landslides, pointed rocks and eroding cliffs at Staffin Bay.

Skye's main town, Portree, is an ideal place to orientate yourself before exploring the island's wild spaces.

Trotternish Peninsula

The Trotternish Peninsula to the north of Portree has some of Skye's most beautiful – and bizarre – scenery. A loop road allows a circular driving tour of the peninsula from Portree, passing on return through the village of Uig.

The 50m-high, pot-bellied pinnacle of crumbling basalt known as the **Old Man of Storr** (P) is prominent above the road 6 miles north of Portree. Walk up to its foot from the car park at the northern end of Loch Leathan (2 miles round-trip). This seemingly unclimbable pinnacle was first scaled in 1955 by English mountaineer Don

Old Man of Storr

❶ Need to Know

Portree Tourist Office (p274)

★ Top Tip

Skye's hills can be challenging; don't attempt the longer walks in bad weather or in winter.

✕ Take a Break

Single Track (p275), on the Trotternish Peninsula, sells seriously good coffee and cakes.

Whillans, a feat that has been repeated only a handful of times since.

The peninsula's Staffin Bay is dominated by the dramatic basalt escarpment of the **Quiraing**: its impressive land-slipped cliffs and pinnacles constitute one of Skye's most remarkable landscapes. From a parking area at the highest point of the minor road between Staffin and Uig you can walk north to the Quiraing in half an hour.

Just south of Uig, a minor road (signposted 'Sheader and Balnaknock') leads in a mile or so to the **Fairy Glen**, a strange and enchanting natural landscape of miniature conical hills, rocky towers, ruined cottages and a tiny roadside lochan.

Cuillin Hills

The Cuillin Hills are Britain's most spectacular mountain range (the name comes from the Old Norse *kjöllen,* meaning 'keel-shaped'). Though small in stature – Sgurr Alasdair, the highest summit, is only 993m – the peaks are near-alpine in character, with knife-edge ridges, jagged pinnacles, scree-filled gullies and hectares of naked rock. While they are a paradise for experienced mountaineers, the higher reaches of the Cuillin are off limits to the majority of walkers.

The good news is that there are also plenty of fantastic low-level hikes within the ability of most walkers. One of the best (on a fine day) is the steep climb from Glenbrittle campsite to **Coire Lagan** (6 miles round-trip, allow at least three hours). The impressive upper corrie contains a lochan for bathing (for the hardy!), and the surrounding cliffs are a playground for rock climbers – bring your binoculars.

Even more spectacular, but much harder to reach on foot, is **Loch Coruisk** (from the Gaelic Coir'Uisg, the Water Corrie), a remote loch ringed by the highest peaks of the Cuillin. Accessible by **boat trip** (☏0800 731 3089; www.bellajane.co.uk; Elgol Pier; adult/ child £28/16; ☾Apr-Oct) from Elgol, or via an arduous 5.5-mile hike from Kilmarie, Coruisk was popularised by Sir Walter Scott in his 1815 poem *Lord of the Isles*. Crowds of Victorian tourists and landscape artists followed in Scott's footsteps, including JMW Turner, whose watercolours were used to illustrate Scott's works.

There are two main bases for exploring the Cuillin – Sligachan to the north (on the Kyle of Lochalsh–Portree bus route), and Glenbrittle to the south (no public transport).

Kilmarie to Coruisk

The walk from Kilmarie to Coruisk and back via Camasunary and the 'Bad Step' is superb, but shouldn't be underestimated (11 miles round-trip, allow at least six hours). The Bad Step is a rocky slab poised above the sea that you have to scramble across; it's easy in fine, dry weather, but some walkers find it intimidating.

Duirinish & Waternish

The sparsely populated Duirinish peninsula is dominated by the distinctive flat-topped peaks of Helabhal Mhor (469m) and Helabhal Bheag (488m), known locally as **MacLeod's Tables**. There are some fine walks from Orbost, including the summit of **Helabhal Bheag** (allow 3½ hours return) and the 5-mile trail from Orbost to **MacLeod's Maidens**, a series of pointed sea stacks at the southern tip of the peninsula.

It's worth making the long drive beyond Dunvegan to the western side of the Duirinish peninsula to see the spectacular sea cliffs of **Waterstein Head** and to walk down to **Neist Point lighthouse** with its views to the Outer Hebrides.

Loch Coruisk (p269)

Walking Tours

Skye Wilderness Safaris (☎01470-552292; www.skye-wilderness-safaris.com; per person £95-120; ☺May-Sep) runs one-day guided hiking trips for small groups (four to six people) through the Cuillin Hills, into the Quiraing or along the Trotternish ridge; transport to/from Portree is included.

Sea Kayaking

The sheltered coves and sea lochs around the coast of Skye provide enthusiasts with magnificent sea-kayaking opportunities.

★ Top Tip

Come prepared for changeable weather: when it's fine it's very fine indeed, but all too often it isn't.

Whitewave Outdoor Centre (☎01470-542414; www.white-wave.co.uk; 19 Linicro, Kilmuir; half-day kayak session per person £40-50; ☺Mar-Oct) offers sea-kayaking instruction and guiding for both beginners and experts; prices include equipment hire. Other activities include mountain-boarding, bushcraft and rock climbing.

Climbing

The Cuillin Hills are a playground for rock climbers, and the two-day traverse of the Cuillin Ridge is the finest mountaineering expedition in the British Isles. There are several mountain guides in the area who can provide instruction and safely intro-duce inexperienced climbers to the more difficult routes.

Skye Guides (☎01471-822116; www.skyeguides.co.uk) offers a one-day intro-duction to rock-climbing course at around £260; a private mountain guide can be hired for £280 a day (both rates are for two clients).

Maps & Books

Detailed guidebooks include a series of four walking guides by Charles Rhodes, avail-able from the Aros Centre (p272) and the tourist office (p274) in Portree. You'll need Ordnance Survey (OS) 1:50,000 maps 23 and 32, or Harvey's 1:25,000 *Superwalker – The Cuillin*.

✕ Take a Break

There are quite a few places to eat in the Duirinish Peninsula (p274), including some of the best restaurants and cafes on the island.

Portree

Portree is Skye's largest and liveliest town. It has a pretty harbour lined with brightly painted houses, and there are great views of the surrounding hills.

◎ SIGHTS

Aros Centre   Cultural Centre
(☑01478-613750; www.aros.co.uk; Viewfield Rd; exhibition £5; ⊙9am-5pm; P ♿) FREE On the southern edge of Portree, the Aros Centre is a combined visitor centre, book and gift shop, restaurant, theatre and cinema. The St Kilda Exhibition details the history and culture of these remote rocky outcrops, and Xbox technology allows you to take a virtual tour of the islands.

⊕ TOURS

MV Stardust   Boating
(☑07798 743858; www.skyeboat-trips.co.uk; Portree Harbour; adult/child £20/10) MV Stardust offers 1½-hour boat trips around Portree Bay, with the chance to see seals, porpoises and – if you're lucky – white-tailed sea eagles. There are longer two-hour cruises to the Sound of Raasay (£25/15). You can also arrange fishing trips, or to be dropped off for a hike on the Isle of Raasay and picked up again later.

⊜ SHOPPING

Skye Batiks   Gifts & Souvenirs
(www.skyebatiks.com; The Green; ⊙9am-6pm May-Sep, to 9pm Jul & Aug, to 5pm Mon-Sat Oct-Apr) Skye Batiks is a cut above your average gift shop, selling a range of interesting crafts such as carved wood, jewellery and batik fabrics with Celtic designs.

Isle of Skye Crafts@Over the Rainbow   Gifts & Souvenirs
(☑01478-612361; www.isleofskyecrafts.com; Quay Brae; ⊙9am-5pm Mon-Sat) Crammed with colourful knitwear and cross-stitch kits, lambswool and cashmere scarves, plus all kinds of interesting gifts.

Portree harbour

HOLGER LEUE / GETTY IMAGES ©

Isle of Skye Soap Co   Cosmetics

(☑01478-611350; www.skye-soap.co.uk; Somerled Sq; ☺10am-5pm Mon-Sat) A sweet-smelling gift shop that specialises in handmade soaps and cosmetics made using natural ingredients and aroma-therapy oils.

 EATING

Isle of Skye Baking Co   Cafe £

(www.isleofskyebakingco.co.uk; Old Woollen Mill, Dunvegan Rd; mains £4-9; ☺10am-5pm Mon-Sat; P ♿) ✔ Famous for its 'lunch bread' – a small loaf baked with a filling inside, like cheese and leek, or beef stew – and platters of Scottish cheese and charcuterie, this cafe is also an art gallery and craft shop.

Scorrybreac   Modern Scottish ££

(☑01478-612069; www.scorrybreac.com; 7 Bosville Tce; 3-course dinner £42; ☺5-9pm Wed-Sun year-round, noon-2pm mid-May–mid-Sep) ✔ Set in the front rooms of what was once a private house, and with just eight tables, Scorrybreac is snug and intimate, offering fine dining without the faff. Chef Calum Munro (son of Donnie Munro, of Gaelic rock band Runrig fame) sources as much produce as possible from Skye, including foraged herbs and mushrooms, and creates the most exquisite concoctions.

Sea Breezes   Seafood ££

(☑01478-612016; www.seabreezes-skye.co.uk; 2 Marine Bldgs, Quay St; mains £13-26; ☺noon-2pm & 5-9.30pm Apr-Oct) ✔ Sea Breezes is an informal, no-frills restaurant specialising in local fish and shellfish fresh from the boat – try the impressive seafood platter, a small mountain of langoustines, crab, oysters and lobster (£54 for two). Book early, as it's often hard to get a table.

Dulse & Brose   Modern Scottish ££

(☑01478-612846; www.bosvillehotel.co.uk; Bosville Hotel, 7 Bosville Tce; mains £17-23; ☺noon-3pm & 6-10pm May-Sep, 6-8.15pm Oct-Apr; ☺) ✔ This hotel restaurant sports a relaxed atmosphere, an award-winning chef and a menu that makes the most of Skye

 Talisker Distillery

Skye's oldest **distillery** (☑01478-614308; www.malts.com; tours from £10; ☺9am-5.30pm Mon-Sat, 10am-5.30pm Sun Apr-Oct, shorter hours Nov-Mar; P), established 1830, produces smooth, sweet and smoky Talisker single malt whisky. The guided tour includes a free dram.

TYLER W. STIPP / SHUTTERSTOCK ©

produce – including lamb, game, seafood, cheese, organic vegetables and berries – and adds a French twist to traditional dishes. The neighbouring Merchant Bar (food served noon to 5pm), also part of the Bosville Hotel, serves tapas-style bar snacks through the afternoon.

☺ DRINKING & NIGHTLIFE

Isles Inn   Pub

(☑01478-612129; Somerled Sq; ☺11am-11pm Mon-Thu, to midnight Fri & Sat, 12.30-11pm Sun; ☺) Portree's pubs are nothing special, but the Isles Inn is more atmospheric than most. The Jacobean bar, with its flagstone floor and open fires, pulls in a lively mix of young locals, backpackers and tourists.

L'Incontro   Cafe

(The Green; ☺5-11pm Tue-Sun) This adjunct to a popular pizza restaurant (upstairs beside the Royal Hotel) serves excellent Italian espresso, and also has an extensive range of Italian wines. The pizzas (£7 to £17) are damn fine, too.

The Duirinish Peninsula's Restaurants

There are quite a few places to eat in this corner of the islands, including some of the best restaurants and cafes on the island. Some are seasonal (closed in winter) and it's always best to book ahead.

Loch Bay (☑01470-592235; www.lochbay-restaurant.co.uk; Stein, Waternish; 3-course dinner £43.50; ☺12.15-1.45pm Wed-Sun, 6.15-9pm Tue-Sat Apr-early Oct; P) 𝄢 One of Skye's most romantic restaurants, awarded a Michelin star in 2018. The menu includes most things that swim in the sea or live in a shell, but there are non-seafood choices too. Book ahead.

Three Chimneys (☑01470-511258; www.threechimneys.co.uk; Colbost; 3-course lunch/dinner £40/68; ☺12.15-1.45pm Mon-Sat mid-Mar–Oct, plus Sun Easter-Sep, 6.30-9.15pm daily year-round; P🛜) 𝄢 Halfway between Dunvegan and Waterstein, this a superb romantic retreat combining a gourmet restaurant in a candlelit crofter's cottage. Book ahead.

Red Roof (☑01470-511766; www.redroofskye.co.uk; Glendale, Duirinish; 3-course dinner £35; ☺7-9pm Tue-Thu Apr-Oct; P🛜♿🧒) 𝄢 The dinner-only menu, served at 7.30pm, specialises in Skye seafood, game and cheeses served with salad leaves and edible flowers grown just along the road. Book ahead.

Stein Inn (☑01470-592362; www.stein-inn.co.uk; Stein, Waternish; mains £8-16; ☺kitchen noon-4pm & 6.30-9pm Easter-Oct, 12.30-2.30pm & 5.30-8pm Nov-Easter; P) Old country inn dating from 1790 with a lively little bar and a delightful beer garden beside the loch. The bar serves real ales from the Isle of Skye Brewery and excellent bar meals.

 INFORMATION

Portree Tourist Office (☑01478-612992; www.visitscotland.com; Bayfield Rd; ☺9am-6pm Mon-Sat, 10am-4pm Sun Jun-Aug, shorter hours Sep-May; 🛜) The only tourist office on the island; provides internet access (per 20 minutes £1) and currency exchange.

 GETTING AROUND

Much of the driving is on single-track roads – remember to use passing places to allow any traffic behind you to overtake. There are petrol stations at Broadford (open 24 hours), Armadale, Portree, Dunvegan and Uig.

Stagecoach (www.stagecoachbus.com) operates the main bus routes on the island, linking all the main villages and towns. Its Skye Dayrider/Megarider ticket gives unlimited bus travel for one/seven days for £9.20/34.60. For timetable info, call **Traveline** (☑0871 200 22 33; www.travelinescotland.com).

You can order a taxi or hire a car (arrange for the car to be waiting at Kyle of Lochalsh train station) from **Kyle Taxi Company** (☑01599-534323; www.skyecarhire.co.uk; car hire per day/week from around £40/240).

Contact **Island Cycles** (☑01478-613121; www.islandcycles-skye.co.uk; The Green; bike hire per 24hr £20; ☺9am-5pm Mon-Sat) for bike hire.

Trotternish

The Trotternish peninsula to the north of Portree has some of Skye's most beautiful scenery, including Quiraing (p269) and the Old Man of Storr (p268).

 SIGHTS

Skye Museum of Island Life
Museum

(☑01470-552206; www.skyemuseum.co.uk; Kilmuir; adult/child £2.50/50p; ☺9.30am-5pm Mon-Sat Easter-late Sep; P) The peat-reek of crofting life in the 18th and 19th centuries is preserved in the thatched cottages, croft houses, barns and farm implements of the Skye Museum of Island Life. Behind the museum is **Kilmuir Cemetery**, where a tall Celtic cross marks the grave of Flora MacDonald; the cross was erected in 1955 to replace the original monument, of which 'every fragment was removed by tourists'.

Duntulm Castle Castle

Near the tip of the Trotternish Peninsula is the ruined MacDonald fortress of Duntulm Castle, which was abandoned in 1739, reputedly because it was haunted. From the red telephone box 800m east of the castle, a faint path leads north for 1.5 miles to **Rubha Hunish coastguard lookout**, now restored as a tiny but cosy bothy overlooking the northernmost point of Skye.

Staffin Dinosaur Museum Museum

(www.staffindinosaurmuseum.com; 3 Ellishadder, Staffin; adult/child £2/1; ⊙9.30am-5pm; ᴾ) In an old stone barn by the roadside, this museum houses an interesting collection of dinosaur footprints, ammonites and other fossils discovered in the local Jurassic sandstones, which have become a focus for dinosaur research in recent years.

🍴 EATING

Single Track Cafe £

(www.facebook.com/singletrackskye; Kilmaluag; snacks £3-4; ⊙10.30am-5pm Sun-Thu mid-May–late Oct; ᴾ🛜) This turf-roofed, timber-clad art gallery and espresso bar will be familiar to fans of British TV's *Grand Designs* – it was featured on the Channel 4 series in 2012. The owners are serious about their coffee, and it's seriously good, as are the accompanying cakes and scones. Art by the owners and other Skye artists is on display, and for sale.

 Dunvegan Castle

Skye's most famous historic building, and one of its most popular tourist attractions, **Dunvegan Castle** (📞01470-521206; www.dunvegancastle.com; adult/child £14/9; ⊙10am-5.30pm Easter–mid-Oct; ᴾ) is the seat of the chief of Clan MacLeod. Among artefacts are the Fairy Flag, a diaphanous silk banner that dates from some time between the 4th and 7th centuries, and Bonnie Prince Charlie's waistcoat and a lock of his hair, donated by Flora MacDonald's granddaughter.

Stagecoach bus 56 runs from Portree to Dunvegan (£5.35, 50 minutes), four times on Saturday year-round, and also Monday to Friday from May to September.

ℹ GETTING THERE & AWAY

Two or three daily buses (four on Saturday) follow a circular route (in both directions) around the Trotternish peninsula, taking in Flodigarry (£4.60, 35 minutes), Kilmuir (£5.35, 45 minutes) and Uig (£4, 30 minutes).

Car ferries run from Uig to Tarbert (Harris; car/pedestrian £31/6.30, 1½ hours) and Lochmaddy (North Uist; car/pedestrian £31/6.30, 1¾ hours) in the Outer Hebrides, with one or two crossings a day.

Aerial view of London and Tower Bridge (p73)

In Focus

JAMES SLOAN / EYEEM / GETTY IMAGES ©

Great Britain Today

Britain is a nation poised on the brink of seismic change. For the first time in four decades, it will no longer be part of the EU (European Union), and despite two years of long and bitter negotiations, still no one has the faintest idea quite what the future holds. Hold on to your hats: it looks like Britain's in for a bumpy ride.

The Brexit Question

The fallout from Britain's decision to withdraw from the EU rumbles on across the UK. Decided by a narrow 52% to 48% vote in favour in the 2016 referendum, Britain's exit from the EU (colloquially known as Brexit) looms large wherever you care to look or listen: it's on every news bulletin, talk show and phone-in, and it's the prevailing topic of conversation in pubs, parks and workplaces up and down the land. With negotiations ongoing, so much remains up in the air: heavyweight questions over immigration, trade, investment and the hot-button topic of the Northern Irish border have yet, at the time of writing, to be decided. After the March 2019 deadline (when the UK ceases to be a voting member of the EU), a two-year transition period has been agreed to that will smooth the separation, at least for

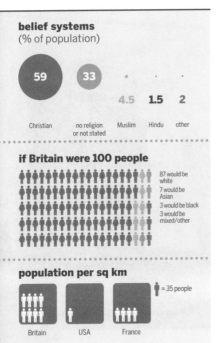

belief systems
(% of population)

59 Christian
33 no religion or not stated
4.5 Muslim
1.5 Hindu
2 other

if Britain were 100 people

87 would be white
7 would be Asian
3 would be black
3 would be mixed/other

population per sq km

≈ 35 people

Britain USA France

a while – but politicians can only dodge the really difficult questions for so long. In the meantime, supporters of Brexit (or Brexiteers, as they're dubbed by the press) maintain that the nation can look forward to a bright global future, while opponents point out a swath of negative economic forecasts. In truth, no one can really say with certainty how the long-term story will play out.

A Right Royal Affair

With HM Queen Elizabeth II in her 10th decade and Prince Harry's wedding to American actress Meghan Markle in 2018, thoughts are beginning to turn to the next generation of the British monarchy – particularly the question of succession. Officially, the next in line to the throne is the Queen's eldest son, Prince Charles, although some commentators believe that, thanks to his strong political views and controversial second marriage to Camilla Parker Bowles, he may perhaps pass over the throne in favour of his eldest son, Prince William. Despite the uncertainty, one thing seems clear – British support for the Royal Family remains high, with most opinion polls suggesting that more than three-quarters of Britons still support the idea of constitutional monarchy.

A Green & Pleasant Land?

Despite its reputation as a green and pleasant land, trouble is afoot in Britain's beloved countryside. Many wildlife species are in serious decline, affected by construction, habitat loss, pesticides and farming methods. A major report in 2016 stated that more than one in 10 of the UK's wildlife species are threatened with extinction, including much-loved icons such as the hedgehog. But it's not all doom and gloom: while many species are struggling, some – such as the badger and fox – are increasing in number, while others, such as the once-endangered otter, have staged unlikely comebacks. But with the prospect of climate change, major housebuilding programs and infrastructure projects on the horizon – including the controversial HS2 high-speed railway and a third Heathrow runway – the need to protect Britain's precious wildlife is now more urgent than ever.

Thankfully, the UK's network of 15 national parks and numerous AONBs (Areas of Outstanding Natural Beauty) have provided a much-needed safe haven for many threatened species. Plans are currently being considered to increase their number – not least because the Lake District became the first UK national park to be recognised as a Unesco World Heritage Site in 2017. But prestige and popularity bring their own pressures – just ask the Isle of Skye, which has pondered limiting visitor numbers in order to protect the island's natural environment.

Stonehenge (p101)

AROUNDWORLD / SHUTTERSTOCK ©

History

Britain is a small country on the edge of Europe, but it's rarely been on the sidelines. For thousands of years, invaders and immigrants have arrived, settled and made their mark. The result is Britain's fascinating mix of landscape, culture and language. That rich historic legacy – from Stonehenge to Culloden, via Hadrian's Wall and the Tower of London – is one of the country's most absorbing features.

4000 BC
Neolithic peoples migrate from continental Europe and establish residences and farms.

AD 43
Emperor Claudius leads the first proper Roman invasion of England. The Romans control most of southern England by AD 50.

c 410
After more than three centuries of relative peace and prosperity, Roman rule ends in Britain.

First Arrivals

Around 4000 BC a group of migrants arrived from Europe, but instead of hunting and moving on, they settled in one place and started farming. One of their most impressive legacies is the enigmatic stone circle at Stonehenge.

The Iron Age

During the Iron Age (from 800 BC to AD 100) the population expanded and began to divide into specific tribes. Forests were cleared as more land was used for farming. Territorial defence became an issue, so people built great earthwork 'castles' in southern England, stone forts in northern England and brochs (defensive towers) in Wales and Scotland.

850
Vikings, from today's Denmark, conquer east and northeast England. They establish their capital at Jorvik, today's city of York.

1066
The Battle of Hastings. Incumbent King Harold is defeated by the invading Normans. William the Conqueror is crowned.

1314
Robert the Bruce's army beats the English at Bannockburn; consolidated Scottish independence for 400 years.

Mounted Queen's Guard, London

VICTOR MOUSSA / SHUTTERSTOCK ©

Enter (& Exit) the Romans

Emperor Claudius led a ruthless campaign resulting in the Romans controlling pretty much everywhere in southern England by AD 50. Some locals fought back, including warrior-queen Boudica, who led an army as far as Londinium, the Roman port on the present site of London.

But by around AD 80 the new province of Britannia (much of today's England and Wales) was firmly under Roman rule – circumstances that lasted almost four centuries. The star of the Roman Empire eventually waned, however, and the Romans withdrew – the end of Roman power in Britain is generally dated at AD 410.

The Emergence of England

Britain's post-Roman power vacuum didn't go unnoticed and once again invaders arrived from the European mainland. Angles and Saxons (Teutonic tribes from the land we now call Germany) advanced across the former Roman turf.

The Waking of Wales & Scotland

While the Anglo-Saxons occupied eastern Britain, toward the end of the 5th century the Scotti (from today's Ireland) invaded what is today Wales and western Scotland. In response, by the 8th century the disparate tribes of Wales had started to band together and sow the seeds of nationhood. They called themselves *cymry* (fellow countrymen), and today Cymru is the Welsh word for Wales. The Picts were the dominant indigenous tribe in the north and east and named their kingdom Alba, which remains to this day the Gaelic word for Scotland.

The Viking Era

In the 9th century, Britain was yet again invaded by a bunch of pesky continentals. This time, it was the Vikings – Nordic people from today's Scandinavia. The English Anglo-Saxon

1459–71	1485	1509–47
The Wars of the Roses between the Houses of Lancaster and York. The Yorkists' King Edward IV eventually gains the throne.	Henry Tudor defeats Richard III at the Battle of Bosworth, becoming King Henry VII.	The reign of King Henry VIII sees the English Reformation – the founding of the Church of England.

armies led by Alfred the Great resisted. The battles that followed were seminal to the foundation of the nation-state of England; by 886 Alfred had gathered his strength and pushed the Vikings back to the north.

1066 & All That

The royal pendulum then swung between Saxon and Viking monarchs. By 1066, the crown had passed to Harold. But one of his relatives in Normandy (the northern part of today's France), called William, thought that he also had a right to the throne of England.

The result was the Battle of Hastings in 1066, the most memorable of dates for anyone who's studied English history. William sailed from Normandy with an army of Norman soldiers, the Saxons were defeated and Harold was killed (according to tradition, by an arrow in the eye).

Magna Carta

In 1215 the barons found the rule of King John erratic and forced him to sign a document called the Magna Carta (the Great Charter), limiting the monarch's power for the first time in British history. Although originally intended as a set of handy ground rules, the Magna Carta was a fledgling bill of human rights that eventually led to the creation of parliament – a body to rule the country, independent of the throne.

Henry VIII & the Break With Rome

In the mid-15th century, the Wars of the Roses raged between the House of Lancaster (emblem: a red rose) and the House of York (emblem: a white rose). By 1485, though, Henry VII (Henry Tudor) was in charge. But it's his son every school kid knows: Henry VIII. For him fathering a male heir was a problem, hence his famous six wives, but the pope's disapproval of divorce and remarriage led to a split with the Roman Catholic Church. Henry became the head of the Protestant Church of England.

The Elizabethan Age

Henry VIII's daughter, Elizabeth I, inherited a nasty mess of religious strife and divided loyalties, but after an uncertain start she gained confidence and turned the country around. Refusing marriage, she borrowed biblical imagery and became known as the Virgin Queen, making her perhaps the first British monarch to create a cult image.

It paid off. Her 45-year reign was a period of boundless optimism, characterised by the naval defeat of the Spanish Armada, the expansion of trade due to the global explorations of seafarers such as Walter Raleigh and Francis Drake, not to mention a cultural flourishing thanks to writers such as William Shakespeare and Christopher Marlowe.

1558–1603	**1603**	**1642–49**
Queen Elizabeth I reigns. Enter stage right playwright William Shakespeare. Exit Walter Raleigh and Francis Drake.	James VI of Scotland inherits the English throne, becoming James I of England, too.	English Civil War between the king's Cavaliers and Oliver Cromwell's Roundheads establishes the Commonwealth of England.

United & Disunited Britain

Elizabeth I died in 1603 without an heir, and was succeeded by her closest relative, James, the safely Protestant son of the executed Mary Queen of Scots. He became James I of England and James VI of Scotland, the first English monarch of the House of Stuart. Most importantly, James united England, Wales and Scotland into one kingdom for the first time in history – another step towards British unity.

But the divide between king and parliament continued to smoulder. The power struggle worsened during the reign of the next king, Charles I, and eventually degenerated into the Civil War of 1642–49. The antiroyalist (or 'Parliamentarian') forces were led by Oliver Cromwell, a Puritan who preached against the excesses of the monarchy and established Church. His army (known as the Roundheads) was pitched against the king's forces (the Cavaliers) in a conflict that tore England apart. It ended with victory for the Roundheads, with the king executed, England declared a republic and Cromwell hailed as 'Protector'.

The Return of the King

By 1653 Cromwell was finding parliament too restrictive and he assumed dictatorial powers, much to his supporters' dismay. On his death in 1658, he was followed half-heartedly by his son, but in 1660 parliament decided to re-establish the monarchy, as republican alternatives were proving far worse.

Charles II (the exiled son of Charles I) came to the throne, and his rule, known as 'the Restoration', saw scientific and cultural activity bursting forth. Exploration and expansion were also on the agenda. Backed by the army and navy (modernised, ironically, by Cromwell), British colonies stretched down the American coast, while the East India Company set up headquarters in Bombay (now Mumbai), laying foundations for what was to become the British Empire.

The next king, James II, had a harder time. Attempts to ease restrictive laws on Catholics ended with his defeat at the Battle of the Boyne by William III, the Protestant king of Holland, better known as William of Orange. William was married to James' own daughter Mary, but it didn't stop him having a bash at his father-in-law.

William and Mary came to the throne as King and Queen, each in their own right (Mary had more of a claim, but William would not agree to be a mere consort), and their joint accession in 1688 was known as the Glorious Revolution.

The Jacobite Rebellions

But in Scotland anti-English feeling refused to disappear. The Jacobite rebellions, most notably those of 1715 and 1745, were attempts to overthrow the Hanoverian monarchy and bring back the Stuarts. Although these are iconic events in Scottish history, in reality there was never much support for the Jacobite cause outside the Highlands: the people of the lowlands were mainly Protestant and feared a return to the Catholicism that the Stuarts represented.

1799–1815	1837–1901	1914
Emperor Napoleon threatens to invade; his ambitions are curtailed by Nelson and Wellington.	In the reign of Queen Victoria the British Empire expands through Canada, Africa, India, Australia and New Zealand.	Archduke Franz Ferdinand of Austria is assassinated in Sarajevo; the Great War (WWI) begins.

The Empire Strikes Out

In the mid-18th century the British Empire continued to grow in America, Canada and India. The first claims were made on Australia after Captain James Cook's epic voyage of exploration (1768–1771).

The Empire's first major reverse came when the American colonies won the War of Independence (1776–83). This setback forced Britain to withdraw from the world stage for a while, a gap not missed by French ruler Napoleon. He threatened to invade Britain and hinder the power of the British overseas, before his ambitions were curtailed by naval hero Admiral Nelson and military hero the Duke of Wellington at the famous battles of Trafalgar (1805) and Waterloo (1815).

The Perils of Kingship

Despite immense power and privilege, the position of monarch (or, perhaps worse, *potential* monarch) probably ranks as one of history's most dangerous occupations. English kings have been killed in battle (Harold), beheaded (Charles I), assassinated (William II), murdered by a wicked uncle (allegedly; Edward V) and bumped off by their queen and her lover (Edward II). Life was just as uncertain for the rulers of Wales and Scotland: some murdered by a wicked uncle (really; James I of Scotland), others killed in battle (Llewelyn the Last of Wales, and James IV of Scotland, last British monarch to die on the battlefield).

The Industrial Age

While the Empire expanded abroad, at home Britain became the crucible of the Industrial Revolution. Steam power (patented by James Watt in 1781) and steam trains (launched by George Stephenson in 1830) transformed methods of production and transport, and the towns of the English Midlands became the first industrial cities.

From about 1750, much of the Scottish Highlands were emptied of people, as landowners casually expelled entire farms and villages to make way for more profitable sheep, a seminal event in Scotland's history known as the Clearances. Although many of the dispossessed left for the New World, others headed to the burgeoning cotton mills of Lanarkshire and the shipyards of Glasgow.

Age of Empire

Despite the social turmoil of the early 19th century, by the time Queen Victoria took the throne in 1837 Britain's factories dominated world trade and British fleets ruled the oceans. The rest of the 19th century was seen as Britain's Golden Age, a period of confidence not enjoyed since the days of the last great queen, Elizabeth I.

World War I

But in continental Europe four restless military powers (Russia, Austria-Hungary, Turkey and Germany) were sabre-rattling in the Balkan states. The assassination of Archduke

1939–45	1948	1952
WWII rages in Europe, Africa and Asia. Britain and the Allies eventually defeat the armies of Germany, Japan and Italy.	Labour's Aneurin Bevan launches the National Health Service – the core of Britain as a 'welfare state'.	Princess Elizabeth becomes Queen Elizabeth II. Her coronation takes place in Westminster Abbey in June 1953.

Ferdinand at Sarajevo in 1914 finally sparked a clash that became the 'Great War' we now call WWI. Soldiers from Britain and Allied countries were drawn into a conflict of horrendous slaughter, most infamously on the killing fields of Flanders and the beaches of Gallipoli.

By the war's weary end in 1918, over a million Britons had died (plus millions more from many other countries) and there was hardly a street or village untouched by death, as the sobering lists of names on war memorials all over Britain still show.

Disillusion & Depression

For the soldiers that did return from WWI, the war had created disillusion and a questioning of the social order. Many supported the ideals of a new political force, the Labour Party, to represent the working class.

Meanwhile, the bitter Anglo-Irish War (1919–21) saw most of Ireland achieving full independence from Britain. Six counties in the north remained British, creating a new political entity called the United Kingdom of Great Britain and Northern Ireland. But the decision to partition the island of Ireland was to have long-term repercussions that still dominate political agendas in both the UK and the Republic of Ireland today.

The Labour Party won for the first time in the 1923 election, in coalition with the Liberals. James Ramsay MacDonald was the first Labour prime minister, but by the mid-1920s the Conservatives were back. The world economy was now in decline and in the 1930s the Great Depression meant another decade of misery and political upheaval.

World War II

In 1933 Adolf Hitler came to power in Germany and in 1939 Germany invaded Poland, once again drawing Britain into war. The German army swept through Europe and pushed back British forces to the beaches of Dunkirk (northern France) in June 1940. An extraordinary flotilla of rescue vessels turned total disaster into a brave defeat, and an event that is still remembered with pride and sadness every year in Britain.

Between September 1940 and May 1941, the German air force launched the Blitz, a series of (mainly night-time) bombing raids on London and other cities. Despite this, morale in Britain remained strong, thanks partly to Churchill's regular radio broadcasts. In late 1941 the USA entered the war, and the tide began to turn.

By 1944 Germany was in retreat. Russia pushed back from the east, and Britain, the USA and other Allies were again on the beaches of France. The Normandy landings (or D-Day, as they are better remembered) marked the start of the liberation of Europe's western side. By 1945 Hitler was dead and the war was finally over.

Swinging & Sliding

Despite victory in WWII, there was an unexpected swing on the political front in 1945. An electorate tired of war and hungry for change tumbled Churchill's Conservatives in favour of the Labour Party.

1960s	1979	1997
An era of African and Caribbean independence, including Nigeria (1960), Tanzania (1961), Jamaica (1962) and Kenya (1963).	A Conservative government led by Margaret Thatcher wins power, ushering in a decade of dramatic political and social change.	Tony Blair leads 'New' Labour to victory, with a record-breaking parliamentary majority, ending 18 years of Tory rule.

In 1952 George VI was succeeded by his daughter Elizabeth II and, following the trend set by earlier queens Elizabeth I and Victoria, she has remained on the throne for over six decades, overseeing a period of massive social and economic change.

By the late 1950s, recovery was strong enough for Prime Minister Harold Macmillan to famously remind the British people they had 'never had it so good'. By the time the 1960s had started, grey old Britain was suddenly more fun and lively than it had been for generations.

Although the 1960s were swinging, the 1970s saw an economic slide thanks to a grim combination of inflation, the oil crisis and international competition. The rest of the decade was marked by strikes, disputes and all-round gloom.

The British public had had enough, and in the elections of 1979 the Conservatives (Tories) won a landslide victory, led by a little-known politician named Margaret Thatcher.

The Thatcher Years

Soon everyone had heard of Margaret Thatcher. Love her or hate her, no one could argue that her methods weren't dramatic. Looking back from a 21st-century vantage point, most commentators agree that by economic measures the Thatcher government's policies were largely successful, but by social measures they were a failure and created a polarised Britain: on one side were the people who gained from the prosperous wave of opportunities in the 'new' industries, while on the other side were those left unemployed and dispossessed by the decline of the 'old' industries such as coal-mining and steel production.

Despite, or perhaps thanks to, policies that were frequently described as uncompromising, Margaret Thatcher was, by 1988, the longest-serving British prime minister of the 20th century.

New Labour, New Millennium, New Start

In 1997, however, 'New' Labour swept to power, with leader Tony Blair declared prime minister. The Labour Party enjoyed an extended honeymoon period, and the next election (in 2001) was another walkover. The Conservative Party continued to struggle, allowing Labour to win a historic third term in 2005, and a year later Tony Blair became the longest-serving Labour prime minister in British history.

In May 2010 Labour rule finally came to an end – to be replaced by a coalition government (the first in the UK since WWII) between the Conservatives and the Liberal Democrats.

By 2015 the Tories had won sole power, which in turn led to the EU referendum of 2016 where the people of the UK voted, by 52% to 48%, to leave the EU.

Prime Minister David Cameron resigned almost immediately after the referendum, succeeded by former home secretary Theresa May, whose premiership was marred by wrangling over the Brexit issue – as well as a misjudged decision to hold a snap general election in 2017, which resulted in her losing her majority in a hung parliament in the House of Commons.

2010	**2016**	**2018**
The minority Liberal Democrats align with the Conservatives to form the first British postwar coalition government.	In the EU Referendum, 52% vote to Leave, 48% vote to Remain.	Prince Harry weds American actress Meghan Markle, the first person identifying as biracial to marry into the Royal Family.

The Shard (p77), seen from Sky Garden (p88)

ANDREW SHIELS / SHUTTERSTOCK ©

Architecture

The history of British architecture spans some five millennia, from the mysterious stone circles of Stonehenge to the glittering skyscrapers of modern London. The country's built heritage includes Roman baths and parish churches, mighty castles and magnificent cathedrals, humble cottages and grand stately homes. Exploring it all is one of the great joys of a visit to Britain.

Early Foundations

The oldest surviving structures in Britain are the grass-covered mounds of earth called 'tumuli' or 'barrows', used as burial sites by the country's prehistoric residents. These mounds, measuring anything from a rough hemisphere just 2m high to oval domes around 5m high and 10m long, are dotted across the countryside and are especially common in areas of chalk downland such as Salisbury Plain in southern England.

Even more impressive than the giant tumuli are the most prominent legacy of the Neolithic era – such as the iconic stone circle at Stonehenge (p104) in Wiltshire. Again, its original purpose is a mystery, providing fertile ground for hypothesis and speculation. The most recent theories suggest that Stonehenge may have been a place of pilgrimage for the sick, like modern-day Lourdes, though it was also used as a burial ground and a place of ancestor worship.

The Roman Era

Remnants of the Roman Empire are found in many towns and cities (mostly in England and Wales, as the Romans didn't colonise Scotland). The bath house complex (p115) in the city of Bath is one of the most impressive sets of remains. But Britain's largest Roman relic is the 73-mile-long sweep of Hadrian's Wall, built in the 2nd century as a defensive line stretching from coast to coast across the island. Originally intended to defend the Empire's territories in the south from the marauding tribes further north, it became as much a symbol of Roman power as a fortification.

London's New Landmarks

At 306m the Shard (p77), in the centre of the capital, is one of Europe's tallest buildings, a giant, pointed glass skyscraper dominating the South Bank.

On the other side of the Thames, other giant new skyscrapers include **20 Fenchurch St** (nicknamed 'the Walkie-Talkie', thanks to its shape) and the slanting-walled **Leadenhall Building** (dubbed, inevitably, 'the Cheese Grater'). Reaching completion at press time, **1 Undershaft**, Bishopsgate (labelled 'the Trellis' for its external crosshatch bracing) will be the City of London's tallest building and the second tallest in Western Europe.

Medieval Masterpieces

In the centuries following the Norman Conquest of 1066, the perfection of the mason's art saw an explosion of architecture in stone, inspired by the two most pressing concerns of the day: religion and defence. Early structures of timber and rubble were replaced with churches, abbeys and monasteries built in dressed stone. The round arches, squat towers and chevron decoration of the Norman or Romanesque style (11th to 12th centuries) slowly evolved into the tall pointed arches, ribbed vaults and soaring spires of the Gothic (13th to 16th centuries), a history that can often be seen all in the one church – construction often took a couple of hundred years to complete. Many cathedrals remain modern landmarks, such as those at Salisbury (p108) and York (p176).

Stone was also put to good use in the building of elaborate defensive structures. Castles range from atmospheric ruins to stunning crag-top fortresses, such as Edinburgh Castle (p219). And then there's the most impressive of them all: the Tower of London (p43), guarding the capital for more than 900 years.

Stately Homes

The medieval period was tumultuous, but by the start of the 17th century life had become more settled and the nobility had less need for fortifications. While they were excellent for keeping out the riff-raff, castles were often too cold and draughty for comfortable aristocratic living.

Following the Civil War, the trend away from castles gathered pace, and throughout the 17th century the landed gentry developed a taste for fine 'country houses' designed by famous architects of the day. Many became the stately homes that are a major feature of the modern British landscape and a major attraction for visitors. Among the most extravagant are Castle Howard (p181) near York and Blenheim Palace (p137) near Oxford.

The great stately homes all display the proportion, symmetry and architectural harmony that was in vogue during the 17th and 18th centuries. These styles were later reflected

Windsor Castle (p56)

KANUMAN / SHUTTERSTOCK ©

★ **Best Castles & Stately Homes**

Edinburgh Castle (p219), Edinburgh

Blenheim Palace (p137), near Oxford

Tower of London (p43), London

Castle Howard (p181), near York

Windsor Castle (p56), near London

in the fashionable town houses of the Georgian era, most notably in the city of Bath, where the stunning Royal Crescent (p116) is the ultimate example of the genre.

Victoriana

The Victorian era was a time of great building activity. A style called Victorian Gothic developed, imitating the tall, narrow windows and ornamented spires featured in the original Gothic cathedrals. The most famous example is London's Houses of Parliament (the Palace of Westminster; p65) and Elizabeth Tower (home to Big Ben; p65), in London. Another Victorian Gothic highlight in England's capital is the Natural History Museum (p77).

Industrialisation

Through the late 19th and early 20th centuries, as Britain's cities grew in size and stature, the newly moneyed middle classes built smart townhouses in streets and squares. Elsewhere, the first town planners oversaw the construction of endless terraces of 'back-to-back' and 'two-up-two-down' houses to accommodate the massive influx of workers required for the country's factories. In many cases the terraced houses and basic tenements are not especially scenic, but they are perhaps the most enduring mark on the British architectural landscape.

The 21st Century

During the first decade of this century, many areas of Britain placed new importance on having progressive, popular architecture as part of a wider regeneration. Edinburgh's Scottish Parliament Building (p231) is a fine example.

Britain's largest and highest-profile architectural project of recent times was Olympic Park, the centrepiece of the 2012 Olympic Games. Situated in the London suburb of Stratford, it was renamed the Queen Elizabeth Olympic Park after the games. Alongside the main Olympic Stadium (p82), there's the much-admired Velodrome and Aquatics Centre, dramatic structures in their own right.

London continues to grow upwards and British architecture continues to push new boundaries of style and technology. The buildings may look a little different, but they're still iconic and impressive.

Crowd at a London music festival

Pop & Rock Music

Britain has been putting the world through its musical paces ever since a mop-haired four-piece from Liverpool tuned up their Rickenbackers and created The Beatles. And while some may claim that Elvis invented rock 'n' roll, it was the Fab Four who transformed it into a global phenomenon, backed by the other bands of the 1960s' 'British Invasion' – The Rolling Stones, The Who, Cream, The Kinks and soul man Tom Jones.

Glam to Punk

Glam rock swaggered onto the stage at the start of the 1970s, led by the likes of Marc Bolan and David Bowie in their tight-fitting jumpsuits and chameleon guises, and was succeeded by early boy-band Bay City Rollers, art-rockers Roxy Music, outrageously costumed Elton John and anthemic popsters Queen. In the same era, Led Zeppelin, Deep Purple and Black Sabbath laid down the blueprint for heavy metal, while the psychedelia of the previous decade morphed into the spacey noodlings of prog rock, epitomised by Pink Floyd, Genesis and Yes.

By the late '70s, glam and prog bands were looking out of touch in a Britain wracked by rampant unemployment and industrial unrest, and punk rock exploded onto the scene, summing up the air of doom with nihilistic lyrics and three-chord tunes. The Sex Pistols

Street art in Camden

★ **London Album-Cover Locations**

Abbey Rd: *Abbey Road*, The Beatles

Battersea Power Station: *Animals*, Pink Floyd

Berwick St: *(What's the Story) Morning Glory?* Oasis

Camden Market: *The Clash*, The Clash

remain the best-known band of the era, while other punk pioneers included The Clash, The Damned, The Buzzcocks and The Stranglers.

Punk begat New Wave, with acts such as The Jam and Elvis Costello blending spiky tunes and sharp lyrics into a more radio-friendly sound. A little later, along came bands like The Specials and baggy-trousered rude boys Madness, mixing punk, reggae and ska sounds. Meanwhile, another punk-and-reggae-influenced band called The Police – fronted by bassist Sting – became one of the biggest names of the decade.

Mode, Metal & Miserabilism

The conspicuous consumption of Britain in the early 1980s was reflected in the decade's pop scene. Big hair and shoulder pads became the uniform of New Romantics such as Spandau Ballet, Duran Duran and Culture Club, while the increased use of synthesisers led to the development of a new electronic sound in the music of Depeche Mode and The Human League. More hits and highlights were supplied by Texas, Eurythmics and Wham! – a boyish duo headed by a bright young fellow named George Michael.

Away from the glitz, fans enjoyed the doom-laden lyrics of The Cure, Bauhaus, and Siouxsie and the Banshees, while Britain's heavy-rock heritage inspired acts such as Iron Maiden. In a different tone entirely, the disaffection of mid-1980s Britain was summed up by the arch-priests of 'miserabilism', The Smiths, fronted by quiffed wordsmith Morrissey.

Raves, Indie & Britpop

The beats and bleeps of 1980s' electronica fuelled the burgeoning dance-music scene of the early '90s. An eruption of ecstasy-saturated rave culture, centred on famous clubs such as Manchester's Haçienda and London's Ministry of Sound, overflowed into the mainstream through chart-topping artists such as The Prodigy and Fatboy Slim. Manchester was also a focus for the burgeoning British 'indie' scene, driven by guitar-based bands such as The Charlatans, The Stone Roses, James and Happy Mondays.

Indie grew up in the mid- to late-1990s, and the term 'Britpop' was coined, with Oasis at the forefront, but covering a wide range of bands including Blur, Elastica, Suede, Supergrass, Ocean Colour Scene, The Verve, Pulp, Travis, Feeder, Super Furry Animals, Stereophonics, Catatonia and the Manic Street Preachers.

Pop Today, Gone Tomorrow

The new millennium saw no let-up in the British music scene's shape-shifting and reinvention. Jazz, soul, R&B and hip-hop have fused into an 'urban' sound epitomised by artists such as Dizzee Rascal, Tinie Tempah and Plan B.

In a totally different genre, British folk and roots music, and folk-influenced acoustic music, is enjoying its biggest revival since the 1960s, with major names including Eliza Carthy, Mumford & Sons and Welsh band Allan Yn Y Fan.

Meanwhile, the singer-songwriter, exemplified by Katie Melua, Ed Sheeran, the late Amy Winehouse, James Bay and the all-conquering Adele, has made a comeback, and the spirit of British punk and indie stays alive thanks to the likes of Florence & the Machine, Muse, Kasabian, Radiohead, The Horrors and breakthrough grunge-pop band Wolf Alice.

But the biggest commercial success of all has been boy-band One Direction, becoming the first artists ever to have each of their four albums debut at number one in the US charts, having the biggest grossing concert tour ever in 2014, and being named Billboard Artist of the Year in 2014, and winning many other prizes since.

A British Playlist

Get in the mood by loading up your music player with this Best of British play list featuring classic hits from the last 50 years of UK pop.

- 'God Save The Queen' by The Sex Pistols
- 'Teardrop' by Massive Attack
- 'Town Called Malice' by The Jam
- 'Sultans of Swing' by Dire Straits
- 'Waterloo Sunset' by The Kinks
- 'Patience of Angels' by Eddi Reader
- 'Ghost Town' by The Specials
- 'Bonkers' by Dizzee Rascal
- 'Hounds of Love' by Kate Bush
- 'A Design for Life' by Manic Street Preachers
- 'I Predict a Riot' by Kaiser Chiefs
- 'Common People' by Pulp
- 'Down By The Water' by PJ Harvey
- 'Shipbuilding' by Elvis Costello

Pop on Film

If you want to combine British pop music with British cinema, try some of these films:

Backbeat (1994) A look at the early days of The Beatles.

Sid and Nancy (1986) The demise of Sex Pistols bassist Sid Vicious and his American girlfriend.

Velvet Goldmine (1998) A tawdry glimpse of the 1970s' glam-rock scene.

24 Hour Party People (2002) A totally irreverent and suitably chaotic film about the 1990s Manchester music scene.

Gimme Shelter (1970) Classic rockumentary recording the final weeks of The Rolling Stones' US tour in 1969.

Control (2007) Biopic about Joy Division's lead singer Ian Curtis.

Nowhere Boy (2009) About John Lennon in his pre-Beatles days.

Amy (2015) Much praised documentary on the short life of singer Amy Winehouse.

Performers at Shakespeare's Globe (p50)

Writers & Artists

Britain's artistic heritage is astoundingly rich and globally renowned. Literary roots stretch from Early English epics such as Beowulf through Chaucer, Shakespeare, Burns, Austen and Tolkien to today's best seller: JK Rowling. Artistic notables include Turner, Constable, Henry Moore and Damien Hirst. These literary and artistic legacies are strong, and links and artworks can be found in countless cities, museums and galleries.

Authors & Poets

Chaucer

The first big name in Britain's literary history is Geoffrey Chaucer, best known for *The Canterbury Tales*. This mammoth collection of fables, stories and morality tales, using travelling pilgrims (the Knight, the Wife of Bath, the Nun's Priest and so on) as a narrative hook, is considered an essential of the English-language canon.

A stained-glass portrait of Charles Dickens

Shakespeare

For most visitors to Britain (and for many locals) drama means just one name: Shake-speare. Born in 1564 in the Midlands town of Stratford-upon-Avon, William Shakespeare made his name in London, where most of his plays were performed at the Globe Theatre.

He started writing plays around 1585, and his early theatrical works are grouped together as 'comedies' and 'histories', many of which are household names today – such as *All's Well that Ends Well*, *The Taming of the Shrew*, *A Midsummer Night's Dream*, *Richard III* and *Henry V*. Later in his career Shakespeare wrote the plays known collectively as the 'tragedies', including *Romeo and Juliet*, *Macbeth*, *Julius Caesar*, *Hamlet* and *King Lear*. His brilliant plots and spectacular use of language, plus the sheer size of his body of work, have turned him into a national – and international – icon.

Today, over 400 years after he shuffled off his mortal coil, the Bard's plays still pull in big crowds, and can be enjoyed at the rebuilt Globe on London's South Bank and at the Royal Shakespeare Company's own theatre in his original hometown of Stratford-upon-Avon.

Burns

Familiar to pretty much everyone in Britain are the words of 'Auld Lang Syne', penned by Scotland's national poet Robert Burns, and traditionally sung at New Year. His more unusual 'Address to a Haggis' is also still recited annually on Burns Night, a Scottish celebration held on 25 January (the poet's birthday).

★ **Literary Locations & Their Writers**

Stratford-upon-Avon: Shakespeare

Lake District: Wordsworth

Edinburgh: Burns, Scott, Stevenson, JK Rowling

Oxford: Tolkien, Lewis Carroll, CS Lewis

Bath: Jane Austen

Half-timbered houses in Stratford-upon-Avon

Wordsworth & the Romantics

As industrialisation began to take hold in Britain during the late 18th and early 19th century, a new generation of writers, including William Blake, John Keats, Percy Bysshe Shelley, Lord Byron and Samuel Taylor Coleridge, drew inspiration from human imagination and the natural world (in some cases aided by a healthy dose of laudanum). Known as the 'Romantics', the best known of all was William Wordsworth; his famous line from the poem commonly known as 'Daffodils' – 'I wandered lonely as a cloud' – was inspired by a walk along the shores of Ullswater in the Lake District.

Dickens, Eliot, Hardy & Scott

During the reign of Queen Victoria (1837–1901), key novels of the time explored social themes. Charles Dickens' *Oliver Twist* is a tale of child pickpockets surviving in the London slums, while *Hard Times* is a critique of the excesses of capitalism.

At around the same time, but in a rural setting, George Eliot (the pen name of Mary Anne Evans) wrote *The Mill on the Floss*, whose central character, Maggie Tulliver, searches for true love and struggles against society's expectations.

Thomas Hardy's classic *Tess of the D'Urbervilles* deals with the peasantry's decline, and *The Trumpet Major* paints a picture of idyllic English country life interrupted by war and encroaching modernity.

Waverley, by Scotland's greatest historical novelist, Sir Walter Scott, was written in the early 19th century and set in the mountains and glens of Scotland during the time of the Jacobite rebellion. It is usually regarded as the first historical novel in the English language.

Modern Authors

Britain – and its literature – changed forever following WWI and the social disruption of the period. This fed into the modernist movement, with DH Lawrence perhaps its finest exponent. *Sons and Lovers* follows the lives and loves of generations in the English Midlands as the country changes from rural idyll to industrial landscape, while his controversial exploration of sexuality in *Lady Chatterley's Lover* was banned until 1960 because of its 'obscenity'.

Other highlights of this period included Daphne du Maurier's romantic suspense novel *Rebecca;* Evelyn Waugh's *Brideshead Revisited,* an exploration of moral and social disintegration among the English aristocracy in the 1920s and '30s; and Richard Llewellyn's Welsh classic *How Green Was My Valley*. After WWII, Compton Mackenzie lifted postwar spirits with *Whisky Galore,* a comic novel about a cargo of booze shipwrecked on a Scottish island. In the 1950s, the poet Dylan Thomas found fame with the radio play *Under Milk Wood* (1954), exposing the social tensions of small-town Wales.

Post-1970s writers of note include Martin Amis (*London Fields*); Ian McEwan (*Atonement* and *On Chesil Beach*); Kate Roberts (*Feet in Chains*); Bruce Chatwin (*On the Black Hill*) and Irvine Welsh (*Trainspotting*).

British Art

Portraits & Landscapes

In the 19th century, leading painters favoured the landscape. John Constable's best-known works include *Salisbury Cathedral* and *The Hay Wain,* depicting a mill in Suffolk (and now on show in the National Gallery, London), while JMW Turner was fascinated by the effects of light and colour, with his works becoming almost entirely abstract by the 1840s – vilified at the time but prefiguring the Impressionist movement that was to follow 50 years later.

Children's Literary Favourites

Britain's greatest literary phenomenon of the 21st century is JK Rowling's *Harry Potter* series, a set of otherworldly adventures that have entertained millions of children (and many grown-ups, too) from the publication of the first book in 1996 to the stage play, *Harry Potter and the Cursed Child,* in 2016. The magical tales, brought vividly to life in the Harry Potter movies, are the latest in a long line of British children's classics that are also enjoyed by adults. The pedigree stretches back to the works of Lewis Carroll (*Alice's Adventures in Wonderland*), E Nesbit (*The Railway Children*), AA Milne (*Winnie-the-Pooh*), CS Lewis (*The Chronicles of Narnia*) and Roald Dahl (*Charlie and the Chocolate Factory*).

Victorian Art

In the mid- to late-19th century, the Pre-Raphaelite movement harked back to the figurative style of classical Italian and Flemish art, tying in with the prevailing Victorian taste for fables, myths and fairy tales. An iconic work is Sir John Everett Millais' *Ophelia,* showing the damsel picturesquely drowned in a river, which can be seen at the Tate Britain.

William Morris saw late-19th-century furniture and interior design as increasingly vulgar, and with Dante Gabriel Rossetti and Edward Burne-Jones founded the Arts and Crafts movement to encourage the revival of a decorative approach to features such as wallpaper, tapestries and windows.

North of the border, Charles Rennie Mackintosh, fresh from the Glasgow School of Art, fast became a renowned artist, designer and architect. He is still Scotland's greatest art nouveau exponent.

Pop Art & Brit Art

The mid-1950s and early '60s saw an explosion of British artists plundering TV, music, advertising and popular culture for inspiration. Leaders of this new 'pop art' movement included David Hockney, who used bold colours and simple lines to depict his dachshunds and swimming pools, and Peter Blake, who designed the collage cover for The Beatles' landmark *Sgt. Pepper's Lonely Hearts Club Band* album.

A new wave of British artists came to the fore in the 1990s. Dubbed 'Britart', its leading members included Damien Hirst, initially famous (or infamous) for works involving pickled sharks, semidissected human figures and a diamond-encrusted skull entitled *For the Love of God*.

The Turner Prize (named after JMW Turner) is a high-profile (and frequently controversial) annual award for British visual artists. As well as Hirst, other winners and their works have included Martin Creed (a room with lights going on and off), Mark Wallinger (a collection of antiwar objects), Simon Starling (a shed converted to a boat and back again), Rachel Whiteread (a plaster cast of a house) and Antony Gormley (best known for his gigantic *Angel of the North*).

English footballer Harry Kane

Sport

If you want a short cut into the heart of British culture, then watch the British at play. They're passionate about their sport – as participants and spectators. Every weekend thousands of people turn out to cheer their favourite teams, and sporting highlights such as Wimbledon keep the entire nation enthralled.

Playing (and Watching) the Game

The British invented many of the world's favourite team sports, or at least codified their modern rules, including cricket, tennis, rugby, golf and football (soccer). Although the men's national teams aren't always that successful internationally, the women's national teams have a better record of success, with the England women's football team taking third place in the 2015 FIFA Women's World Cup, and the England women's cricket team winning the 2009 World Cup.

But whether the British 'home teams' are winning or losing – be they the individual teams of England, Wales and Scotland, or national teams representing Great Britain or the whole of the UK – nothing dulls the enthusiasm of the fans.

Football (Soccer)

The English Premier League has some of the finest teams in the world, dominated recently by Arsenal, Liverpool, Chelsea, Manchester United and Manchester City. But their wealth wasn't enough in 2016, when unfancied Leicester City stunned pundits and delighted neutrals by winning the league (only for Chelsea and Manchester City to return to form by winning titles in 2017 and 2018).

Seventy-two other teams play in the English divisions called the Championship, League One and League Two. In Scotland the game has long been dominated by Glasgow teams Celtic and Rangers, while in Wales football is less popular (rugby is the national sport) and the main Welsh sides – such as Swansea, Cardiff and Wrexham – play in the English leagues.

The football season runs from August to May. Tickets for Premier League matches are like gold dust; you're better off trying for lower-division games. You can often buy these tickets on the spot at stadiums. Otherwise go to club websites or online agencies such as www.ticketmaster.co.uk and www.myticketmarket.com.

Football or Soccer?

The word 'soccer', often used outside Britain, derives from the sport's official name Association Football (as opposed to rugby football), or possibly from 'sock' – a leather foot-cover worn in medieval times, ideal for kicking a pig's bladder around the park on a Saturday afternoon.

Rugby

A wit once said that football was a gentlemen's game played by hooligans, while rugby was a hooligans' game played by gentlemen. Whatever the truth, it's worth catching a game; tickets generally cost between £15 and £50.

There are two versions of the British game: Rugby Union (www.englandrugby.com) is played more in southern England, Wales and Scotland, and is traditionally the game of the middle and upper classes. Rugby League (www.rugby-league.com) is played predominantly in northern England, traditionally by the working classes.

Both codes trace their roots back to a football match in 1823 at Rugby School, in Warwickshire. A player called William Webb Ellis, frustrated at the limitations of mere kicking, reputedly picked up the ball and ran with it towards the opponents' goal – and a whole new sport was born. The Rugby Football Union was formally inaugurated in 1871, while the Rugby World Cup is named the Webb Ellis trophy after this enterprising tearaway.

The highlight of Rugby Union's international calendar is the Six Nations Championship (www.rbs6nations.com), between England, Wales, Scotland, Ireland, France and Italy.

Cricket

Although it is also played in Wales and Scotland, cricket is a quintessentially English sport. Dating from the 18th century – although its roots are much older – the sport spread throughout the Commonwealth during Britain's colonial era. Australia, the Caribbean and the Indian subcontinent took to the game with gusto, and today the former colonies delight in giving the old country a good spanking on the cricket pitch.

While many English people follow cricket like a religion, to the uninitiated it can be an impenetrable spectacle. Spread over one-day games or five-day test matches, progress seems slow and is dominated by arcane terminology such as innings, over, googly, outswinger, leg-bye and silly mid-off. Nonetheless, at least one cricket match should feature in your travels. If you're patient and learn the intricacies, you could find cricket as absorbing and enriching as all the fans who remain glued to their radio or computer all summer, 'just to see how England are getting on'.

One-day games and internationals are played at grounds including Lord's in London, Edgbaston in Birmingham and Headingley in Leeds. Tickets range from £30 to more than £200. The County Championship features teams from around the country; tickets cost from £5 to £25. See the English Cricket Board website (www.ecb.co.uk) for more information.

Tennis

Tennis is widely played in Britain, but the best-known tennis tournament for spectators is the All England Championships – known to everyone as Wimbledon – when tennis fever sweeps through Britain in the last week of June and first week of July. Imagine British (and Scottish) delight in 2013 when Scotsman Andy Murray became the first British men's singles champion since 1936, winning again in 2016.

Demand for seats always outstrips supply, but about 6000 tickets are sold each day (excluding the final four days). You'll need to rise early: dedicated fans start queuing before dawn. For more information, see www.wimbledon.com.

Golf

Millions take to the golf fairways in Britain each week. The main tournament is the Open Championship ('The Open' or 'British Open'). The oldest of professional golf's major championships, it dates back to 1860 and is the only one held outside the USA. It's held in different locations each year, usually over the third weekend in July; see www.theopen.com.

There are around 2000 private and public golf courses in Britain. Most private clubs welcome visitors; public courses are open to anyone. A round costs around £10 to £30 on public courses, and up to £200 on famous championship courses.

Horse Racing

The tradition of horse racing in Britain stretches back centuries, and there's a 'race meeting' somewhere pretty much every day. Buy tickets from the British Horse Racing Authority's website (www.greatbritishracing.com).

The top event is Royal Ascot at Ascot Racecourse in mid-June, where the rich and famous come to see and be seen. Other highlights include the Grand National steeplechase at Aintree in early April and the Derby at Epsom on the first Saturday in June.

Full English breakfast

SLAWOMIR FAJER / SHUTTERSTOCK ©

Food & Drink

British cuisine was once a bit of a joke. But a culinary landmark came in 2005, when food bible Gourmet magazine singled out London as having the best restaurants in the world. Since then the choice for food lovers – whatever their budget – has continued to improve. With organic, seasonal and sustainable dishes gracing many menus, London is now a global gastronomic capital, and great food can be found Britain-wide.

The Full British Breakfast

Many people in Britain make do with toast or a bowl of cereal before dashing to work, but visitors staying in hotels and B&Bs will undoubtedly encounter a phenomenon called the 'full English breakfast' – or one of its regional equivalents. This usually consists of bacon, sausages, eggs, tomatoes, mushrooms, baked beans and fried bread. In Scotland the 'full Scottish breakfast' might include *tattie* scones (potato bread) instead of fried bread. In Wales you may be offered laver bread, which is not a bread at all, but seaweed – a tasty speciality often served with oatmeal and bacon on toast. In northern England you may get black pudding. And just in case you thought this insufficient, it's all still preceded by cereal, and followed by toast and marmalade.

Chicken tikka masala

★ Britain's Most Popular Restaurant Dish

Britain's most popular restaurant dish is chicken tikka masala, an 'Indian' curry dish created specifically for the British palate and unheard of in India itself.

Lunch

One lunchtime classic is the ploughman's lunch. Basically bread and cheese, these days the meal usually includes butter, salad, and pickled onion. Variations include a farmer's lunch (bread and chicken), stockman's lunch (bread and ham), Frenchman's lunch (brie and baguette) and fisherman's lunch (yes – with fish).

Or try Welsh rarebit – a sophisticated variation of cheese on toast, seasoned and flavoured with butter, milk and sometimes a little beer. For a takeaway lunch in Scotland, look out for Forfar bridies (pastry turnovers filled with minced beef and onion).

Dinner

For generations, a typical British dinner has been 'meat and two veg'. The meat is pork, beef or lamb, one of the vegetables is potatoes and the other inevitably carrots, cabbage or cauliflower.

Roast beef is synonymous with Britain; perhaps the most famous beef comes from Scotland's Aberdeen Angus cattle, while the best-known meat from Wales is lamb. Venison – usually from red deer – is readily available in Scotland, and in parts of Wales and England. Yorkshire pudding is another speciality. It's simply roast batter, but very tasty when cooked well. Perhaps the best-known British meal is fish and chips, often bought from the 'chippie' wrapped in paper to carry home.

Puddings & Desserts

A classic British pudding (ie dessert) is rhubarb crumble: the juicy stem of a large-leafed garden plant, stewed and sweetened, then topped with a crunchy mix of flour, butter and more sugar, and served with custard or ice cream.

Scotland's classic pudding is 'clootie dumpling' (a rich fruit pudding that is wrapped in a cotton cloth and steamed). Another sweet temptation is cranachan, whipped cream flavoured with whisky and mixed with toasted oatmeal and raspberries.

Tea & Coffee

Britain's best-known beverage is tea, usually made with dark tea leaves to produce a strong, brown drink. More bitter in taste than tea served in some other Western countries, it's usually served with a dash of milk.

But Brits also consume 165 million cups of coffee a day. When you're ordering and the server says 'white or black', it just means 'Do you want milk in it?'

Beer & Cider

British beer typically ranges from dark brown to amber in colour, and is often served at room temperature. Technically it's called ale and is more commonly called 'bitter' (or 'heavy' in Scotland). This is to distinguish it from lager – the drink that most of the rest of the word calls 'beer', which is generally yellow and served cold. Bitter that's brewed and served traditionally is called 'real ale' to distinguish it from mass-produced brands, and there are many regional varieties.

The increasing popularity of real ales and a backlash against the conformity of multinational brewing conglomerates has seen a huge rise in the number of artisan brewers and microbreweries springing up all over Britain – by 2016 there were around 1500, with around 75 in London alone. They take pride in using only natural ingredients, and many try to revive ancient recipes, such as heather- and seaweed-flavoured ales.

Another must-try is cider – available in sweet and dry varieties and, increasingly, as craft cider, often with various fruit or herbal flavours added.

Nose-to-Tail Cuisine

One of many trends in modern British cuisine is the revival of 'nose-to-tail' cooking – making use of the entire animal, not just the more obvious cuts. So as well as dishes involving liver, heart and chitterlings (intestines), traditional delights such as bone marrow on toast, or tripe (cow's stomach lining) with onions are once again gracing fashionable tables. The movement has been spearheaded by chef Fergus Henderson at his St John restaurant in London, and through his influential book, *Nose to Tail Eating: A Kind of British Cooking* (1999).

Whisky

The spirit most visitors associate with Britain – and especially Scotland – is whisky. There's a big difference between single malt whisky, made purely from malted barley in a single distillery, and blended whisky, made from a mix of cheaper grain whisky and malt whiskies from several distilleries.

A single malt, like a fine wine, somehow captures the terroir or essence of the place where it was made and matured – a combination of the water, the barley, the peat smoke, the oak barrels in which it was aged and (in the case of certain coastal distilleries) the sea air and salt spray. Each distillation varies from the one before, like different vintages from the same vineyard.

Bars & Pubs

In Britain the difference between a bar and a pub is sometimes vague, but generally bars are smarter, larger and louder than pubs, possibly with a younger crowd. Drinks are more expensive, too, unless there's a drink promotion (there often is).

As well as beer, cider and wine, pubs and bars offer the usual choice of spirits, often with a 'mixer', producing British favourites such as gin and tonic, rum and coke, and vodka and lime. These drinks are served in measures called 'singles' and 'doubles'. A single can be either 25mL or 35mL (depending on the bar) – just over one US fluid ounce. A double is, of course, 50mL or 70mL.

Remember that drinks in British pubs are ordered and paid for at the bar, and that it's not usual to tip pub and bar staff. If you're ordering a large round, however, or the service has been good, you can say to the person behind the bar '...and one for yourself'. They may not have a drink, but they'll add the monetary equivalent to the total and keep it as a tip.

London bus in front of Big Ben (p65)

SAMOT / SHUTTERSTOCK ©

Survival Guide

Directory A–Z

Accessible Travel

All new buildings have wheelchair access, and even hotels in grand old country houses often have lifts, ramps and other facilities. Hotels and B&Bs in historic buildings are often harder to adapt, so you'll have less choice here.

Modern city buses and trams have low floors for easy access, but few have conductors who can lend a hand when you're getting on or off. Many taxis take wheelchairs, or just have more room in the back.

For long-distance travel, coaches may present problems but the main operator, National Express (www.nationalexpress.com) has wheelchair-friendly coaches on many routes. For details, see the website or ring the Disabled Passenger Travel Helpline (0371 781 8181).

On most intercity trains there's more room and better facilities, compared with travel by coach, and usually station staff around; just have a word and they'll be happy to help. A Disabled Person's Railcard (www.disabledpersons-railcard.co.uk) costs £20 and gets you 33% off most train fares.

Useful organisations:

- Disability Rights UK (www.disabilityrightsuk.org) Published titles include a holiday guide. Other services include

a key for 7000 public disabled toilets across the UK.

- Good Access Guide (www.goodaccessguide.co.uk)
- Tourism for All (www.tourismforall.org.uk)

Accessible Travel Online Resources

Download Lonely Planet's free Accessible Travel guides from http://lptravel.to/AccessibleTravel.

Accommodation

Booking your accommodation in advance is recommended, especially in popular holiday areas and on islands (where options are often limited). Summer and school holidays (including half-terms) are particularly busy. Book at least two months ahead for July and August.

B&Bs

The B&B (bed and breakfast) is a great British institution. At smaller places it's pretty much a room in somebody's house; larger places may be called a 'guesthouse' (halfway between a B&B and a full hotel). Prices start from around £40 per person for a simple bedroom and shared bathroom; for around £45 to £55 per person you get a private bathroom, either down the hall or en suite.

Prices Usually quoted per person, based on two people sharing a room. Single rooms for solo travellers are harder to find, and attract a 20% to 50% premium.

Booking Advance reservations are preferred at B&Bs and are

essential during popular periods. You can book many B&Bs via online agencies, but rates may be cheaper if you book directly. Many B&Bs require a minimum two-night stay at weekends. Some places reduce rates for longer stays (two or three nights) mid-week.

Food Most B&Bs serve enormous breakfasts; some offer packed lunches (around £6) and evening meals (around £15 to £20).

Bed & Breakfast Nationwide (www.bedandbreakfast nationwide.com)

Hostels & Camping

There are two types of hostel in Britain: those run by the **Youth Hostels Association** (www.yha.org.uk) and **Scottish Youth Hostels Association** (www.syha.org.uk); and independent hostels, most listed in the **Independent Hostel Guide** (www.independenthostel guide.co.uk).

Campsites range from farmers' fields with a tap and basic toilet, costing from £5 per person per night, to smarter affairs with hot showers and many other facilities, charging up to £15, sometimes more.

Book Your Stay Online

For more accommodation reviews by Lonely Planet authors, check out http://hotels.lonelyplanet.com/great-britain. You'll find independent reviews, as well as recommendations on the best places to stay. Best of all, you can book online.

Hotels

There's a massive choice of hotels in Britain, from small town houses to grand country mansions, from no-frills locations to boutique hideaways. At the bargain end, single/double rooms cost from £45/60. Move up the scale and you'll pay £100/150 or beyond.

There's no such thing as a 'standard' hotel rate in Britain. Many hotels, especially larger places or chains, vary prices according to demand – or have different rates for online, phone or walk-in bookings – just like airlines and train operators. So if you book early for a night when the hotel is likely to be quiet, rates are cheap. If you book late, or aim for a public holiday weekend, you'll pay a lot. But wait until the very last minute, and you can sometimes get a bargain as rates drop again.

Chain hotels can be a good, affordable and functional option, though most are lacking in ambience. Some options:

Ibis Hotels (www.ibis.com)

Premier Inn (www.premierinn.com)

Travelodge (www.travelodge.co.uk)

Pubs & Inns

As well as selling drinks, many pubs and inns offer lodging, particularly in country areas. For bed and breakfast, you'll pay around £35 per person for a basic room, around £45 to £50 per person for something better.

Rental Accommodation

If you want to stay in one place, renting for a week can be ideal. Choose from neat apartments in cities or quaint old houses (always called 'cottages', whatever the size) in country areas. Cottages for four people cost between £275 and £700 in high season. Rates fall at quieter times and you may be able to rent for a long weekend. Some handy websites include the following:

Cottages & Castles (www.cottages-and-castles.co.uk)

Cottages4you (www.cottages4you.co.uk)

Hoseasons (www.hoseasons.co.uk)

National Trust (www.nationaltrust.org.uk/holidays)

Stilwell's (www.stilwell.co.uk)

Climate

London

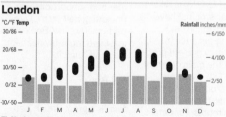

Edinburgh

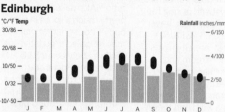

Cardiff

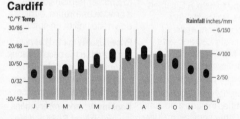

Customs Regulations

Travellers arriving in the UK from EU countries don't have to pay tax or duty on goods for personal use, and can bring in as much EU duty-paid alcohol and tobacco as they like. However, if you bring in more than the following, you'll probably be asked some questions:

- 800 cigarettes
- 1kg of tobacco
- 10L of spirits
- 90L of wine
- 110L of beer

Travellers from outside the EU can bring in, duty-free:

- 200 cigarettes *or* 100 cigarillos *or* 50 cigars *or* 250g of tobacco
- 16L of beer
- 4L of non-sparkling wine
- 1L of spirits *or* 2L of fortified wine or sparkling wine
- £390 worth of all other goods, including perfume, gifts and souvenirs

Anything over this limit must be declared to customs officers on arrival. For further details, and for information on reclaiming VAT on items purchased in the UK by non-EU residents, go to www.gov.uk and search for 'Bringing goods into the UK'.

Discount Cards

There's no specific discount card for visitors to Britain, although travel cards (eg rail cards) are discounted for younger and older people.

Electricity

**Type G
230V/50Hz**

Food

The following price ranges refer to a main dish.

Category	London	Elsewhere
£	less than £12	less than £10
££	£12–25	£10–20
£££	more than £25	more than £20

Health

- If you're an EU citizen, a European Health Insurance Card (EHIC) – available from health centres or, in the UK, post offices – covers you for most medical care. An EHIC will not cover you for non-urgent cases, or emergency repatriation. This arrangement could change once Britain exits the EU; check the latest situation with your own national health service before travelling.
- Citizens from non-EU countries should find out if there is a reciprocal arrangement for free medical care between their country and the UK.
- If you do need health insurance, make sure you get a policy that covers you for the worst possible scenarios, including emergency flights home.
- For medical advice that is not an emergency you can call the NHS 111 service (phone 111).

Insurance

Although everyone receives free emergency treatment, regardless of nationality, travel insurance is still highly recommended in Britain. It will usually cover medical and dental consultation and treatment at private clinics, which can be quicker than NHS places – as well as the cost of any emergency flights – plus all the usual stuff like loss of baggage.

Worldwide travel insurance is available at www.lonelyplanet.com/travel-insurance. You can buy, extend and claim online anytime – even if you're already on the road.

Internet Access

- 3G and 4G mobile broadband coverage is good in large population centres, but limited or sometimes nonexistent in rural areas.
- EU citizens can now use their own mobile/cellphone data roaming allowance in the UK for no charge, but travellers from non-EU countries will usually incur high charges – check with your provider before travelling.
- Most hotels, B&Bs, hostels, stations and coffee shops (even some trains and buses) have wi-fi access, charging anything from nothing to £6 per hour.
- Internet cafes are surprisingly rare in Britain, especially away from big cities and tourist spots. Most charge from £1 per hour, but

out in the sticks you can pay £5 per hour.

○ Public libraries often have computers with free internet access, but only for 30-minute slots, and demand is high. All the usual warnings apply about keystroke-capturing software and other security risks.

Legal Matters

○ Police have the power to detain, for up to six hours, anyone suspected of having committed an offence punishable by imprisonment (including drugs offences). Police have the right to search anyone they suspect of possessing drugs.

○ You must be over 18 to buy alcohol and cigarettes. You usually have to be 18 to enter a pub or bar, although rules are different for under-18s if eating. Some bars and clubs are over-21 only.

○ Illegal drugs are widely available, especially in clubs. Cannabis possession is a criminal offence; punishment for carrying a small amount may be a warning, a fine or imprisonment. Dealers face stiffer penalties, as do people caught with other drugs.

○ On buses and trains (including the London Underground), people without a valid ticket are fined on the spot (£80, reduced to £40 if you pay within 21 days).

LGBTIQ+ Travellers

Britain is a generally tolerant place for gays and lesbians. London, Manchester and Brighton have flourishing gay scenes, and in other sizeable cities (even some small towns), you'll find communities not entirely in the closet. That said, you'll still find pockets of homophobic hostility in some areas. Resources include the following:

Diva (www.divamag.co.uk)

Gay Times (www.gaytimes.co.uk)

Switchboard LGBT+ Helpline (www.switchboard.lgbt; 0300 330 0630)

Money

Currency

The currency of Britain is the pound sterling (£). Paper money ('notes') comes in £5, £10, £20 and £50 denominations. Some shops don't accept £50 notes because fakes circulate. Other currencies are rarely accepted, except at some gift shops in London, which may take euros, US dollars, yen and other major currencies.

Scottish banks issue their own sterling bank notes. They are interchangeable with Bank of England notes, but you'll sometimes run into problems outside Scotland – shops in the south of England may refuse to accept them. They are also harder to exchange once you get outside the UK, though British banks will always exchange them.

ATMs

ATMs (usually called 'cash machines' in Britain) are common in cities and even small towns. Cash withdraw-

als from some ATMs may be subject to a small charge, but most are free. If you're not from the UK, your home bank will likely charge you for withdrawing money overseas.

Credit & Debit Cards

Visa and Mastercard credit and debit cards are widely accepted in Britain. Other credit cards, including Amex, are not so widely accepted. Most businesses will assume your card is 'Chip and PIN' enabled (using a PIN instead of signing). If it isn't, you should be able to sign instead, but some places may not accept your card. Some smaller country B&Bs don't take cards, so you'll need to pay with cash.

Moneychangers

Cities and larger towns have banks and exchange bureaux for changing your money into pounds. Check rates first; some bureaux offer poor rates or levy outrageous commissions. You can also change money at some post offices – very handy in country areas, and exchange rates are fair.

Tipping

Restaurants Around 10% in restaurants and teashops with table service. Nearer 15% at smarter restaurants. Tips may be added to your bill as a 'service charge'. Paying a tip or a service charge is not obligatory.

Pubs & Bars Not expected unless table service for your meal and drinks is provided, then 10% is usual.

Taxis Around 10%, or rounded up to the nearest pound, especially in London.

Opening Hours

Opening hours may vary throughout the year, especially in rural areas where many places have shorter hours or close completely from October or November to March or April.

Banks 9.30am–4pm/5pm Monday to Friday; some open 9.30am–1pm Saturday

Pubs & Bars Noon–11pm Monday to Saturday (many till midnight or 1am Friday and Saturday, especially in Scotland), 12.30–11pm Sunday

Shops 9am–5.30pm (or to 6pm in cities) Monday to Saturday, and often 11am–5pm Sunday; big-city convenience stores open 24/7

Restaurants Lunch noon–3pm, dinner 6–9pm/10pm (or later in cities)

Public Holidays

If a public holiday falls on a weekend, the nearest Monday is usually taken instead. Virtually everything – attractions, shops, banks, offices – closes on Christmas Day, although pubs are open at lunchtime. There's usually no public transport on Christmas Day, and a very minimal service on Boxing Day.

New Year's Day 1 January (plus 2 January in Scotland)

Easter March/April (Good Friday to Easter Monday inclusive)

May Day First Monday in May

Practicalities

Newspapers Tabloids include the *Sun* and *Mirror,* and *Daily Record* (in Scotland); quality 'broadsheets' include (from right to left, politically) the *Telegraph, Times, Independent* and *Guardian*.

TV All TV in the UK is digital. Leading broadcasters include BBC, ITV and Channel 4. Satellite and cable TV providers include Sky and Virgin Media.

Radio The main BBC stations and wavelengths are Radio 1 (98–99.6MHz FM), Radio 2 (88–92MHz FM), Radio 3 (90–92.2 MHz FM), Radio 4 (92–94.4MHz FM) and Radio 5 Live (909 or 693 AM). National commercial stations include Virgin Radio (1215Hz MW) and non-highbrow classical specialist Classic FM (100–102MHz FM). All are available digitally.

DVD PAL format (incompatible with NTSC and Secam).

Weights & Measures Britain uses a mix of metric and imperial measures (eg petrol is sold by the litre but beer by the pint; mountain heights are in metres but road distances are in miles).

Spring Bank Holiday Last Monday in May

Summer Bank Holiday Last Monday in August

Christmas Day 25 December

Boxing Day 26 December

Safe Travel

Britain is a remarkably safe country, but crime is not unknown – especially in London and other cities.

○ Watch out for pickpockets and hustlers in crowded areas popular with tourists, such as around Westminster Bridge in London.

○ When travelling by tube, tram or urban train services at night, choose a carriage containing other people.

○ Many town centres can be rowdy on Friday and Satur-

day nights when the pubs and clubs are emptying.

○ Unlicensed minicabs – a driver with a car earning money on the side – operate in large cities, and are worth avoiding unless you know what you're doing.

Telephone

The UK uses the GSM 900/1800 network, which covers the rest of Europe, Australia and New Zealand, but isn't compatible with the North American GSM 1900. Most modern mobiles can function on both networks, but check before you leave home.

Roaming charges within the EU were removed from June 2017, meaning that EU citizens can use their home call, SMS and data allowances for no extra cost.

Roaming charges for non-EU citizens can be prohibitively high, however, and you'll probably find it cheaper to get a UK number. This is easily done by buying a SIM card (from £5 including calling credit) and sticking it in your phone. Your phone may be locked to your home network, however, so you'll have to either get it unlocked, or buy a cheap pay-as-you-go phone along with your SIM card (from £10 including calling credit).

Pay-as-you-go phones can be recharged by buying vouchers from any post office or at supermarkets and convenience stores where you see the green 'top-up' sign.

Phone Codes

Dialling into the UK Dial your country's international access code then 44 (the UK country code), then the area code (dropping the first 0) followed by the telephone number.

Dialling out of the UK The international access code is 00; dial this, then add the code of the country you wish to dial.

Making a reverse-charge (collect) international call Dial 155 for the operator. It's an expensive option, but not for the caller.

Area codes in the UK Codes do not have a standard format or

length, eg Edinburgh 0131, London 020, Ambleside 015394. Omit the code if you're inside that area.

Directory Assistance A host of agencies offer this service – numbers include 118 118, 118 500 and 118 811 – but fees are extortionate (around £6 for a 45-second call); search online for free at www.thephonebook. bt.com.

Mobile phones Codes usually begin with 07.

Free calls Numbers starting with 0800 or 0808 are free.

National operator 100

International operator 155

Time

Britain is on GMT. The clocks go forward one hour for 'summer time' at the end of March, and go back at the end of October.

Tourist Information

Most British cities and towns, and some villages, have a tourist information centre or visitor information centre – for ease of reference Lonely Planet refers to all these places as 'tourist offices'. Some

can assist with booking accommodation.

Before leaving home, check the comprehensive website of Britain's official tourist board, Visit Britain (www.visitbritain.com).

Visas

Further Information

○ Due to the uncertainty surrounding the Brexit negotiations, this information is particularly prone to change, so it's worth double-checking the latest rules before you travel.

○ If you're a citizen of the EEA (European Economic Area) nations or Switzerland, you don't need a visa to enter or work in Britain – you can enter using your national identity card.

○ Currently, if you're a citizen of Australia, Canada, New Zealand, Japan, Israel, the USA and several other countries, you can stay for up to six months (no visa required), but are not allowed to work.

○ Nationals of many countries, including South Africa, will need to obtain a visa: for more info, see www.gov.uk/ check-uk-visa.

○ British immigration authorities have always been tough; dress neatly and carry proof that you have sufficient funds with which to support yourself. A credit card and/or an onward ticket will help.

Emergency & Important Numbers

Britain (& UK) country code	44
International access code	00
Emergency (police, fire, ambulance, mountain rescue, coastguard)	112 or 999

Transport

Getting There & Away

Air

Visitors to the UK arriving by air generally do so at one of London's two largest airports, Heathrow and Gatwick, which have a huge range of international flights to pretty much all corners of the globe. International flights also serve the capital's three other airports (Stansted, Luton and London City) and regional hubs such as Manchester, Bristol and Edinburgh.

London Airports

The national carrier is **British Airways** (www. britishairways.com).
 The main airports:

Heathrow (www.heathrowairport.com) Britain's main airport for international flights; often chaotic and crowded. About 15 miles west of central London.

Gatwick (www.gatwickairport. com) Britain's number-two airport, mainly for international flights, 30 miles south of central London.

Stansted (www.stanstedairport. com) About 35 miles northeast of central London, mainly handling charter and budget European flights.

Luton (www.london-luton. co.uk) Some 35 miles north of central London, well known as a holiday-flight airport.

London City (www.londoncity airport.com) A few miles east of central London, specialising in flights to/from European and other UK airports.

Regional Airports

Some planes on European and long-haul routes use major regional airports including Manchester and Glasgow. Smaller regional airports, including Bristol, are served by flights to and from continental Europe and Ireland.

Edinburgh Airport (EDI; www. edinburghairport.com) Eight miles west of the city, it has numerous flights to other parts of Scotland and the UK, Ireland, mainland Europe and further afield.

Heritage Organisations

A highlight of a journey through Britain is visiting the numerous castles and historic sites that pepper the country. Membership of a heritage organisation gets you free admission (usually a good saving) as well as information handbooks and so on.

National Trust (NT; www.nationaltrust.org.uk) A charity protecting historic buildings and land with scenic importance across England and Wales. Annual membership is £69 (discounts for under-26s and families). A Touring Pass allows free entry to NT properties for one/two weeks (one person £31/36, two people £55/66, family £61/77). The **National Trust for Scotland** (www.nts.org.uk) is a similar organisation in Scotland; annual membership is £57.

English Heritage (EH; www.english-heritage.org.uk) A state-funded organisation responsible for numerous historic sites. Annual membership is £56 (couples and seniors get discounts). An Overseas Visitors Pass allows free entry to most sites for nine/16 days for £33/39 (couples £57/67, families £62/72). In Wales and Scotland the equivalent organisations are **Cadw** (www.cadw. wales.gov.uk) and **Historic Environment Scotland** (www.historicenvironment.scot). You can join at the first location you visit. If you join an English heritage organisation, it covers you for Wales and Scotland, and vice versa.

Ferry

The main ferry routes between Great Britain and other European countries include the following:

- Dover–Calais (France)
- Dover–Boulogne (France)
- Newhaven–Dieppe (France)
- Liverpool–Dublin (Ireland)
- Holyhead–Dublin (Ireland)
- Fishguard–Rosslare (Ireland)
- Pembroke Dock–Rosslare (Ireland)
- Newcastle–Amsterdam (Netherlands)
- Harwich–Hook of Holland (Netherlands)
- Hull–Rotterdam (Netherlands)
- Hull–Zeebrugge (Belgium)
- Cairnryan–Larne (Northern Ireland)

- Portsmouth–Santander (Spain)
- Portsmouth–Bilbao (Spain)

Ferry Fares

Most ferry operators offer flexible fares, meaning great bargains at quiet times of day or year. For example, short cross-channel routes such as Dover to Calais or Boulogne can be as low as £45 for a car plus two passengers, although around £75 to £105 is more likely. If you're a foot passenger, or cycling, there's less need to book ahead; fares on short crossings cost about £30 to £50 each way.

Ferry Bookings

Book direct with one of the operators listed following, or use the very handy www.directferries.co.uk – a single site covering all sea-ferry routes, plus **Eurotunnel** (www.eurotunnel.com).

Brittany Ferries (www.brittany-ferries.com)

DFDS Seaways (www.dfds seaways.co.uk)

Irish Ferries (www.irishferries.com)

P&O Ferries (www.poferries.com)

Stena Line (www.stenaline.com)

Bus & Coach

You can easily get between Britain and other European countries via long-distance bus or coach. The international network **Eurolines** (www.eurolines.com) connects a huge number of destinations; you can buy tickets online via one of the national operators.

Services to/from Britain are operated by **National Express** (www.nationalexpress.com). Sample journeys and times to/from London include Amsterdam (12 hours); Barcelona (24 hours); Dublin (12 hours); and Paris (eight hours).

Train

Channel Tunnel Passenger Service

High-speed **Eurostar** (www.eurostar.com) passenger services shuttle at least 10 times daily between London and Paris (2½ hours) or Brussels (two hours). Buy tickets from travel agencies,

major train stations or the Eurostar website.

The normal one-way fare between London and Paris/Brussels costs around £154; advance booking and off-peak travel gets cheaper fares, as low as £29 one way.

Channel Tunnel Car Service

Drivers use **Eurotunnel** (www.eurotunnel.com). At Folkestone in England or Calais in France, you drive onto a train, get carried through the tunnel and drive off at the other end.

Trains run about four times an hour from 6am to 10pm, then hourly through the night. Loading and unloading takes an hour; the journey lasts 35 minutes.

Book in advance online or pay on the spot. The standard one-way fare for a car and up to nine passengers is between £75 and £100 depending on the time of day; promotional fares often bring it down to £59 or less.

Train & Ferry Connections

As well as Eurostar, many 'normal' trains run between Britain and mainland Europe. You buy one ticket, but get off the train at the port, walk onto a ferry, then get another train on the other side. Routes include Amsterdam–London (via Hook of Holland and Harwich). Travelling between Ireland and Britain, the main train-ferry-train route is Dublin–London, via Dún Laoghaire and Holyhead. Ferries also run between Rosslare and Fishguard or Pembroke (Wales), with train connections on either side.

Climate Change & Travel

Every form of transport that relies on carbon-based fuel generates CO_2, the main cause of human-induced climate change. Modern travel is dependent on aeroplanes, which might use less fuel per kilometre per person than most cars but travel much greater distances. The altitude at which aircraft emit gases (including CO_2) and particles also contributes to their climate change impact. Many websites offer 'carbon calculators' that allow people to estimate the carbon emissions generated by their journey and, for those who wish to do so, to offset the impact of the greenhouse gases emitted with contributions to portfolios of climate-friendly initiatives throughout the world. Lonely Planet offsets the carbon footprint of all staff and author travel.

Getting Around

Air

If you're really pushed for time, flights on longer routes across Britain (eg Exeter or Southampton to Newcastle, Edinburgh or Inverness), or to the Scottish islands, are handy, although you miss the glorious scenery in between. On some shorter routes (eg London to Newcastle, or Manchester to Newquay) trains compare favourably on time, once airport downtime is factored in. On costs, you might get a bargain airfare, but trains can be cheaper if you buy tickets in advance. Some of Britain's domestic airline companies:

British Airways (www.british airways.com)

easyJet (www.easyjet.com)

FlyBe (www.flybe.com)

Loganair (www.loganair.co.uk)

Ryanair (www.ryanair.com)

Bicycle

Britain is a compact region, and hiring a bike – for an hour or two, or a week or longer – is a great way to really see the country if you've got time to spare.

Rental in London

London is famous for its **Santander Cycles** (⏍0343 222 6666; www.tfl.gov.uk/modes/cycling/santander-cycles), known as 'Boris bikes' after the mayor that introduced them to the city. Bikes can be hired on the spot from automatic docking stations. For more information visit the website. Other

rental options in the capital are listed at www.lcc.org.uk (under Advice/Bike Shops).

Rental Elsewhere

The nextbike (www.next bike.co.uk) bike-sharing scheme has stations in Exeter, Oxford, Coventry, Glasgow, Stirling and Bath as at the time of research, while tourist towns such as York and Cambridge have plentiful bike-rental options.

Bikes on Trains

Bicycles can be taken free of charge on most local urban trains (although they may not be allowed at peak times when the trains are crowded with commuters) and on shorter trips in rural areas, on a first-come, first-served basis – though there may be space limits.

Bikes can be carried on long-distance train journeys free of charge, but advance booking is required for most conventional bikes. (Folding bikes can be carried on pretty much any train at any time.)

The PlusBike scheme provides all the information you need for travelling by train with a bike. Leaflets are available at major stations, or downloadable from www.nationalrail.co.uk/118390.aspx.

Boat

There are around 90 inhabited islands off the western and northern coasts of Scotland, which are linked to the mainland by a network of car and passenger ferries. There are two main ferry operators:

Caledonian MacBrayne (CalMac; ⏍0800 066 5000; www.calmac.co.uk) Operates car ferry services to the Inner

and Outer Hebrides and the islands in the Firth of Clyde.

Northlink Ferries (⏍0845 600 0449; www.northlinkferries.co.uk) Operates car ferry services from Aberdeen and Scrabster to the Orkney and Shetland Islands.

Bus

If you're on a tight budget, long-distance buses (called coaches in Britain) are nearly always the cheapest way to get around, although they're also the slowest – sometimes by a considerable margin.

Long-Distance Buses

National Express (www.nationalexpress.com) is the main coach operator, with a wide network and frequent services between main centres.

Scottish Citylink (www.citylink.co.uk), Scotland's leading coach company. Services link with National Express.

Megabus (www.megabus.com) operates a budget coach service between about 30 destinations around the country.

Passes & Discounts

National Express offers discount passes to full-time students and under-26s, called Young Persons Coachcards. They cost £12.50 and give you 30% off standard adult fares. Also available are coachcards for people over 60, families and travellers with disabilities.

For those who aren't UK citizens, National Express offers Skimmer passes, allowing unlimited travel for seven/14/28 days (£69/119/199). You don't need to book journeys in advance: if the coach has a spare seat, you can take it.

Car & Motorcycle

Travelling by car or motorbike around Britain means you can be independent and flexible, and reach remote places. Downsides for drivers include traffic jams, the high price of fuel and high parking costs in cities.

Most rental cars have manual gears (stick shift).

Car Rental

Compared with many countries (especially the USA), hire rates are expensive in Britain; the smallest cars start from about £130 per week, and it's around £190 and upwards per week for a medium car. All rates include insurance and unlimited mileage, and can rise at busy times (or drop at quiet times).

Some main players:

Avis (www.avis.co.uk)

Budget (www.budget.co.uk)

Europcar (www.europcar.co.uk)

Sixt (www.sixt.co.uk)

Thrifty (www.thrifty.co.uk)

Another option is to look online for small local car-hire companies in Britain that can undercut the international franchises. Generally those in cities are cheaper than in rural areas. Using a rental-broker or comparison site such as **UK Car Hire** (www.ukcarhire.net) or **Kayak** (www.kayak.com) can also help find bargains.

Motorhome Rental

Hiring a motorhome or campervan (£650 to £1200 a week) is more expensive than hiring a car, but saves on accommodation costs and gives almost unlimited freedom. Sites to check include:

Just Go (www.justgo.uk.com)

Wicked Campers (www.wickedcampers.co.uk)

Wild Horizon (www.wildhorizon.co.uk)

Motoring Organisations

Motoring organisations in Britain include the **Automobile Association** (www.theaa.com) and the **RAC** (www.rac.co.uk). For both, annual membership starts at around £40, including 24-hour roadside breakdown assistance.

Britannia (www.lv.com/breakdown-cover) offers better value at £30 a year, while a greener alternative is the **Environmental Transport Association** (www.eta.co.uk); it provides breakdown assistance but doesn't campaign for more roads.

Insurance

It's illegal to drive a car or motorbike in Britain without (at least) third-party insurance. This will be included with all rental cars. If you're bringing a car from Europe, you'll need to arrange it.

Parking

Many cities have short-stay and long-stay car parks; the latter are cheaper though may be less convenient. 'Park & Ride' systems allow you to park on the edge of the city then ride to the centre on frequent nonstop buses for an all-in-one price.

Yellow lines (single or double) along the edge of the road indicate parking restrictions. Nearby signs will spell out when you can and can't park. In London and other big cities, traffic wardens operate with efficiency; if you park on the yellow lines at the wrong time, your car will be clamped or towed away, and it'll cost you £130 or more to get driving again. In some cities there are also red lines, which mean no stopping at any time.

Also beware of other areas that may be restricted in some other way (eg for local residents or pass-holders only).

Roads

Motorways and main A-roads deliver you quickly from one end of the country to another. Lesser A-roads, B-roads and minor roads are much more scenic – ideal for car or motorcycle touring. You can't travel fast, but you won't care.

Speed limits are usually 30mph (48km/h) in built-up areas, 60mph (96km/h) on main roads and 70mph (112km/h) on motorways and most (but not all) dual carriageways.

Road Rules

A foreign driving licence is valid in Britain for up to 12 months.

Drink-driving is taken very seriously; you're allowed a maximum blood-alcohol level of 80mg/100mL (0.08%) in England and Wales, and 50mg/100mL (0.05%) in Scotland.

Some other important rules:

o drive on the left (!)

o wear fitted seatbelts in cars

o wear helmets on motorcycles

o give way to your right at junctions and roundabouts

o always use the left lane on motorways and dual carriageways unless overtaking (although so many people ignore this rule, you'd think it didn't exist)

○ don't use a mobile phone while driving unless it's fully hands-free (another rule frequently flouted)

Local Transport

Local Buses

There are good local bus networks year-round in cities and towns. Buses also run in some rural areas year-round, although timetables are designed to serve schools and businesses, so there aren't many midday and weekend services (and they may stop running during school holidays), or buses may link local villages to a market town on only one day each week.

Local Bus Passes

If you're taking a few local bus rides in one area, day passes (with names like Day Rover, Wayfarer or Explorer) are cheaper than buying several single tickets. Often they can be bought on your first bus, and may include local rail services. It's always worth asking ticket clerks or bus drivers about your options.

Taxi

There are two sorts of taxi in Britain: those with meters that can be hailed in the street; and minicabs, which are cheaper but can only be called by phone. Unlicensed minicabs operate in some cities.

In London, most taxis are the famous 'black cabs' (some with advertising livery in other colours), which charge by distance and time. Depending on the time of day, a 1-mile journey takes five to 10 minutes and costs £6 to £9. Longer journeys are proportionally cheaper.

Black cabs also operate in some other large cities around Britain, with rates usually lower than in London.

In London, taxis are best flagged down in the street; a 'for hire' light on the roof indicates availability. In other cities, you can flag down a cab if you see one, but it's usually easier to go to a taxi rank.

Apps such as **Uber** (www. uber.com) and **Kabbee** (www.kabbee.com) allow you to book a minicab in double-quick time.

In rural areas, taxis need to be called by phone; the best place to find the local taxi's phone number is the local pub. Fares are £3 to £5 per mile.

Traintaxi (www.traintaxi. co.uk) is a portal site for journeys between the train station and your hotel or other final destination.

Train

For long-distance travel around Britain, trains are generally faster and more comfortable than coaches but can be more expensive, although with discount tickets they're competitive – and often take you through beautiful countryside. The British like to moan about their trains, but around 85% run on time. The other 15% that get delayed or cancelled mostly impact commuter services rather than long-distance journeys.

Information

Your first stop should be **National Rail Enquiries** (www.nationalrail.co.uk), the nationwide timetable and fare information service. Its website advertises special

offers and has real-time links to station departure boards and downloadable maps of the rail network.

Operators

About 20 different companies operate train services in Britain, while Network Rail operates track and stations. For some passengers this system can be confusing at first, but information and ticket-buying services are mostly centralised. If you have to change trains, or use two or more train operators, you still buy one ticket – valid for the whole journey. The main railcards and passes are also accepted by all train operators.

Where more than one train operator services the same route, eg York to Edinburgh, a ticket purchased from one company may not be valid on trains run by another. So if you miss the train you originally booked, it's worth checking which later services your ticket will be valid for.

Tickets & Reservations

Once you've found the journey you need on the National Rail Enquiries website, links take you to the relevant train operator to buy the ticket. This can be mailed to you (UK addresses only) or collected at the station on the day of travel from automatic machines. There's usually no booking fee on top of the ticket price.

You can also use a centralised ticketing service to buy your train ticket. These cover all train services in a single site, but they will charge a booking fee on top of every ticket price. The main players include:

QJump (www.qjump.co.uk)
Rail Easy (www.raileasy.co.uk)
Train Line (www.thetrainline.com)

To use operator or centralised ticketing websites, you always have to state a preferred time and day of travel, even if you don't mind when you go, but you can change it as you go through the process, and with a little delving around you can find some real bargains.

You can also buy train tickets on the spot at stations, which is fine for short journeys (under about 50 miles), but discount tickets for longer trips are usually not available and must be bought in advance by phone or online.

Costs

For longer journeys, on-the-spot fares are always available, but tickets are much cheaper if bought in advance. The earlier you book, the cheaper it gets. You can also save if you travel off-peak. Advance purchase usually gets a reserved seat, too.

Whichever operator you travel with and wherever you buy tickets, these are the three main fare types:

Anytime Buy anytime, travel anytime – usually the most expensive option.

Off-peak Buy ticket any time, travel off-peak (what is off-peak depends on the journey).

Advance Buy ticket in advance, travel only on specific trains – usually the cheapest option.

For an idea of the (substantial) price differences, an Anytime single ticket

from London to York will cost £127 or more, an Off-peak around £109, with an Advance around £44 to £55. The cheapest fares are usually nonrefundable, so if you miss your train you'll have to buy a new ticket.

Mobile train tickets are gradually becoming more common across the network, but it's a slow process – for now printed tickets are still the norm.

Onward Travel

If the train doesn't get you all the way to your destination, you can add a **PlusBus** (www.plusbus.info) supplement when making your reservation to validate your train ticket for onward travel by bus. This is more convenient, and usually cheaper, than buying a separate bus ticket.

Train Classes

There are two classes of rail travel: first and standard. First class costs around 50% more than standard fare (up to double at busy periods) and gets you bigger seats, more leg-room, and usually a more peaceful business-like atmosphere, plus extras such as complimentary drinks and newspapers. At weekends some train operators offer 'upgrades' to first class for an extra £5 to £25 on top of your standard class fare, payable on the spot.

Train Passes

Discount Passes

If you're staying in Britain for a while, passes known as Railcards (www.railcard.co.uk) are worth considering:

16-25 Railcard For those aged 16 to 25, or full-time UK students.

Two Together Railcard For two specified people travelling together.

Senior Railcard For anyone over 60.

Family & Friends Railcard Covers up to four adults and four children travelling together.

Railcards cost £30 (valid for one year, available from major stations or online) and give a 33% discount on most train fares, except those already heavily discounted. With the Family card, adults get 33% and children get 60% discounts, so the fee is easily recouped in a couple of journeys.

Local & Regional Passes

Local train passes usually cover rail networks around a city (many include bus travel too). If you're concentrating your travels on southeast England (eg London to Dover, Weymouth, Cambridge or Oxford), a **Network Railcard** (per year £30) covers up to four adults and up to four children travelling together outside peak times.

National Passes

For country-wide travel, **BritRail** (www.britrail.net) passes are available for visitors from overseas. They must be bought in your country of origin (not in Britain) from a specialist travel agency. They're available in seven different versions (eg England only; Scotland only; all of Britain; UK and Ireland) for periods from four to 30 days.

Behind the Scenes

Acknowledgements

Climate map data adapted from Peel MC, Finlayson BL & McMahon TA (2007) 'Updated World Map of the Köppen-Geiger Climate Classification', Hydrology and Earth System Sciences, 11, 1633-44.

Illustrations pp44-5, pp200-1, pp226-7, pp232-3 by Javier Zarracina.

This Book

This 2nd edition of Lonely Planet's *Best of Great Britain* guidebook was curated by Damian Harper, and written and researched by Damian, Oliver Berry, Fionn Davenport, Marc Di Duca, Belinda Dixon, Catherine Le Nevez, Sophie McGrath, Hugh McNaughtan, Lorna Parkes, Andy Symington, Greg Ward and Neil Wilson. The previous edition was written by Oliver Berry, Belinda Dixon, Peter Dragicevich, Damian Harper, Catherine Le Nevez, Hugh McNaughtan, Isabella Noble, Andy Symington and Neil Wilson. This guidebook was produced by the following:

Destination Editor James Smart, Clifton Wilkinson

Senior Product Editor Genna Patterson

Product Editor Will Allen

Regional Senior Cartographer Mark Griffiths

Book Designer Wibowo Rusli

Assisting Editors Sarah Bailey, Andrew Bain, Judith Bamber, Michelle Bennett, Nigel Chin, Katie Connolly, Lucy Cowie, Jacqueline Danam, Andrea Dobbin, Victoria Harrison, Kellie Langdon, Jodie Martire, Lou McGregor, Kristin Odijk, Monique Perrin

Cartographer Hunor Csutoros

Assisting Book Designer Aomi Ito

Cover Researcher Naomi Parker

Thanks to Anne Mason, Kathryn Rowan

Send Us Your Feedback

We love to hear from travellers – your comments keep us on our toes and help make our books better. Our well-travelled team reads every word on what you loved or loathed about this book. Although we cannot reply individually to postal submissions, we always guarantee that your feedback goes straight to the appropriate authors, in time for the next edition. Each person who sends us information is thanked in the next edition, the most useful submissions are rewarded with a selection of digital PDF chapters.

Visit lonelyplanet.com/contact to submit your updates and suggestions or to ask for help. Our award-winning website also features inspirational travel stories, news and discussions.

Note: We may edit, reproduce and incorporate your comments in Lonely Planet products such as guidebooks, websites and digital products, so let us know if you don't want your comments reproduced or your name acknowledged. For a copy of our privacy policy visit lonelyplanet.com/privacy.

Index

Symbols & Map Key

Look for these symbols to quickly identify listings:

◉ Sights
❸ Activities
❺ Courses
❻ Tours
❹ Festivals & Events
❽ Eating
❾ Drinking
❿ Entertainment
🔒 Shopping
ℹ️ Information & Transport

These symbols and abbreviations give vital information for each listing:

🌿 Sustainable or green recommendation
FREE No payment required

☎ Telephone number
🕐 Opening hours
Ⓟ Parking
⊘ Nonsmoking
❄ Air-conditioning
@ Internet access
📶 Wi-fi access
🏊 Swimming pool
🚌 Bus
⛴ Ferry
🚊 Tram
🚆 Train
📋 English-language menu
🥗 Vegetarian selection
👪 Family-friendly

Find your best experiences with these Great For... icons.

 Art & Culture
 History
 Beaches
 Local Life
 Budget
 Nature & Wildlife
 Cafe/Coffee
 Photo Op
 Cycling
 Scenery
Detour
Shopping
Drinking
Short Trip
Entertainment
Sport
Events
Walking
Family Travel
Winter Travel
Food & Drink

Sights

Beach
Bird Sanctuary
Buddhist
Castle/Palace
Christian
Confucian
Hindu
Islamic
Jain
Jewish
Monument
Museum/Gallery/ Historic Building
Ruin
Shinto
Sikh
Taoist
Winery/Vineyard
Zoo/Wildlife Sanctuary
Other Sight

Points of Interest

Bodysurfing
Camping
Cafe
Canoeing/Kayaking
Course/Tour
Diving
Drinking & Nightlife
Eating
Entertainment
Sento Hot Baths/ Onsen
Shopping
Skiing
Sleeping
Snorkelling
Surfing
Swimming/Pool
Walking
Windsurfing
Other Activity

Information

Bank
Embassy/Consulate
Hospital/Medical
Internet
Police
Post Office
Telephone
Toilet
Tourist Information
Other Information

Geographic

Beach
Gate
Hut/Shelter
Lighthouse
Lookout
Mountain/Volcano
Oasis
Park
Pass
Picnic Area
Waterfall

Transport

Airport
BART station
Border crossing
Boston T station
Bus
Cable car/Funicular
Cycling
Ferry
Metro/MRT station
Monorail
Parking
Petrol station
Subway/S-Bahn/ Skytrain station
Taxi
Train station/Railway
Tram
Tube Station
Underground/ U-Bahn station
Other Transport

Marc Di Duca

A travel author for over a decade, Marc has worked for Lonely Planet in Siberia, Slovakia, Bavaria, England, Ukraine, Austria, Poland, Croatia, Portugal, Madeira and on the Trans-Siberian Railway, as well as writing and updating tens of other guides for other publishers. When not on the road, Marc lives near Mariánské Lázně in the Czech Republic with his wife and two sons.

Belinda Dixon

Only happy when her feet are suitably sandy, Belinda has been (gleefully) travelling, research-ing and writing for Lonely Planet since 2006. It's seen her navigating mountain passes and soaking in hot-pots in Iceland's Westfjords, marvelling at Stonehenge at sunrise, scrambling up Italian mountain paths, horse riding across Donegal's golden sands, gazing at Verona's frescoes and fossil hunting on Dorset's Jurassic Coast. Belinda is also a podcaster and adventure writer and helps lead wilderness expeditions. See her blog posts at https://belindadixon.com.

Catherine Le Nevez

Catherine's wanderlust kicked in when she road-tripped across Europe from her Parisian base aged four, and she's been hitting the road at every opportunity since, travelling to around 60 coun-tries and completing her Doctorate of Creative Arts in Writing, Masters in Professional Writing, and postgraduate qualifications in Editing and Publishing along the way. Over the past dozen-plus years she's written scores of Lonely Planet guides and articles covering Paris, France, Europe and far beyond. Her work has also appeared in numerous online and print publications. Topping Catherine's list of travel tips is to travel without any expectations.

Sophie McGrath

Sophie McGrath is a London-based travel writer who has written for many UK publications. For-merly on staff at *Lonely Planet Traveller* magazine, she was named 2017 AITO Young Travel Writer of the Year. Her most memorable adventures include chasing the Northern Lights in Norway, getting stranded on a mountain in China and falling head over heels for Addis Ababa, Ethiopia.

Hugh McNaughtan

A former English lecturer, Hugh swapped grant ap-plications for visa applications and turned his love of travel intro a full-time thing. Having done a bit of restaurant-reviewing in his home town (Melbourne) he's now eaten his way across four continents. He's never happier than when on the road with his two daughters. Except perhaps on the cricket field.

Lorna Parkes

Londoner by birth, Melburnian by palate and ex-Lonely Planet staffer in both cities, Lorna has contributed to numerous Lonely Planet books and magazines. She's discovered she writes best on planes, and is most content when researching food and booze. Wineries and the tropics (not at the same time!) are her go-to happy places, but Yorkshire will always be special to her. Follow her @Lorna_Explorer.

Andy Symington

Andy has written or worked on over a hundred books and other updates for Lonely Planet (es-pecially in Europe and Latin America) and other publishing companies, and has published articles on numerous subjects for a variety of newspapers, magazines, and websites. He part-owns and oper-ates a rock bar, has written a novel and is currently working on several fiction and non-fiction writing projects. Andy, from Australia, moved to Northern Spain many years ago. When he's not off with a backpack in some far-flung corner of the world, he can probably be found watching the tragically poor local football side or tasting local wines after a long walk in the nearby mountains.

Greg Ward

Since whetting his appetite for travel by following the hippy trail to India, and later living in northern Spain, Greg has written guides to destinations all over the world. As well as covering the USA from the Southwest to Hawaii, he has ranged on recent assignments from Corsica to the Cotswolds, and Japan to Corfu. See www.gregward.info, for his favourite photos and memories.

Neil Wilson

Neil was born in Scotland and has lived there most of his life. Based in Perthshire, he has been a full-time writer since 1988, working on more than 80 guidebooks for various publishers, including the Lonely Planet guides to Scotland, England, Ireland and Prague. An outdoors enthusiast since child-hood, Neil is an active hill-walker, mountain-biker, sailor, snowboarder, fly-fisher and rock-climber, and has climbed and tramped in four continents, including ascents of Jebel Toubkal in Morocco, Mount Kinabalu in Borneo, the Old Man of Hoy in Scotland's Orkney Islands and the Northwest Face of Half Dome in California's Yosemite Valley.

Our Story

A beat-up old car, a few dollars in the pocket and a sense of adventure. In 1972 that's all Tony and Maureen Wheeler needed for the trip of a lifetime – across Europe and Asia overland to Australia. It took several months, and at the end – broke but inspired – they sat at their kitchen table writing and stapling together their first travel guide, *Across Asia on the Cheap*. Within a week they'd sold 1500 copies. Lonely Planet was born.

Today, Lonely Planet has offices in Franklin, London, Melbourne, Oakland, Dublin, Beijing, and Delhi, with more than 600 staff and writers. We share Tony's belief that 'a great guidebook should do three things: inform, educate and amuse'.

Our Writers

Damian Harper

With two degrees (one in modern and classical Chinese from SOAS), Damian has been writing for Lonely Planet for over two decades, covering China, Beijing, Shanghai, Vietnam, Thailand, Ireland, London, Mallorca, Malaysia, Singapore & Brunei, Hong Kong, southwest China and the UK. A seasoned guidebook writer, Damian has penned articles for numerous newspapers and magazines, including *The Guardian* and *The Daily Telegraph,* and currently makes Surrey, England, his home. A self-taught trumpet novice, his other hobbies include collecting modern first editions, photography and Taekwondo. Follow Damian on Instagram @damian.harper.

Oliver Berry

Oliver is a writer and photographer from Cornwall. He has worked for Lonely Planet for more than a decade, covering destinations from Cornwall to the Cook Islands, and has worked on more than thirty guidebooks. He is also a regular contributor to many newspapers and magazines, including *Lonely Planet Traveller.* His writing has won several awards, including The Guardian Young Travel Writer of the Year and the TNT Magazine People's Choice Award. His latest work is published at www.oliverberry.com.

Fionn Davenport

Irish by birth and conviction, Fionn has spent the last two decades focusing on the country of his birth and his nearest neighbour, England, which he has written about extensively for Lonely Planet. In between writing gigs he's lived in Paris and New York, where he was an editor, actor, bartender and whatever else paid the rent. For the last 15 years or so he's also presented a series of radio programs on Irish radio, most recently as host of *Inside Culture* on RTE Radio 1. A couple of years ago he moved to the northwest of England where he lives (and commutes from) with his partner Laura and their car Trevor.

More Writers

STAY IN TOUCH LONELYPLANET.COM/CONTACT

AUSTRALIA The Malt Store, Level 3, 551 Swanston St, Carlton, Victoria 3053 📞03 8379 8000, fax 03 8379 8111

IRELAND Digital Depot, Roe Lane (off Thomas St), Digital Hub, Dublin 8, D08 TCV4

USA 124 Linden Street, Oakland, CA 94607 📞510 250 6400, toll free 800 275 8555, fax 510 893 8572

UK 240 Blackfriars Road, London SE1 8NW 📞020 3771 5100, fax 020 3771 5101

 twitter.com/ lonelyplanet

 facebook.com/ lonelyplanet

 instagram.com/ lonelyplanet

 youtube.com/ lonelyplanet

 lonelyplanet.com/ newsletter